CULT
EPICS

THE FILMS OF TINTO BRASS

FROM THE AVANT-GARDE TO EROTICA

EDITED BY **Nico B**

Cover photo by
Marisa Rastellini

Copyright © 2024

The Films of Tinto Brass: From the Avant-Garde to Erotica

ISBN: 978-0-9998627-7-3

10 9 8 7 6 5 4 3 2 1

Edited by **Nico B**

Designed by **Mark Berry**

Proofread by **Laura Smith**

Published by **Cult Epics**

cultepics.com

Printed by Prolong Press Limited
Manufactured in China
Fabriqué en Chine

Cover photo by Marisa Rastellini
Licensed from Mondadori Portfolio / Bridgeman Images

Distributed by SCB Distributors

Contents

Editor's Foreword

THE PHOTO ON THE COVER OF THIS BOOK shows Tinto Brass at home, shot in 1979 in the country house where he resides to this day, by the photographer Marisa Rastellini. It was the year when *Caligula* was released, the film that made him famous, or should we say infamous, as the film was re-edited without his permission into a Triple X feature. Unknown to many, he was known previously as an avant-garde filmmaker, pushing boundaries, when he was hailed as a genius—and afterwards became the maestro of erotic cinema. Tinto Brass is an intellectual, art and film connoisseur, artist and anarchist, who was not afraid to create controversy.

I had the pleasure of meeting Tinto in 2001 (and later collaborated with him in 2008 when I produced *Kick the Cock*) when I interviewed him for the first time on the island Torcello, where his family has a famous hotel-restaurant, where Ernest Hemingway resided in the past, and which the British royal family visited. In the interview he expressed his feelings on many subjects, which were used in parts of this book as his voice. The book originally was written in 2005 but put on a back burner by a UK publisher, and then rewritten by myself and others in 2023 now to be published by Cult Epics. As an editor I have combined both versions of the text to tell the story about the making of the films he directed. An additional biography was written in 2023 to make it historically significant as a book. We hope you enjoy reading, and viewing the promotional images we have gathered from our archives as a film distributor among others. I would like to thank Tinto Brass, Ranjit Sandhu, and Rayo Casablanca for their contributions.

Sincerely, **Nico B**

Left and Right: Behind the scenes of ***Kick the Cock*** *(2008), with director Tinto Brass, actress Angelita Franco, and producer Nico B*

*On location with Tinto Brass directing **The Howl**, 1968*

Introduction

DESCRIBING THE CAREER OF TINTO BRASS, *Variety* once used the word *hallucinatory*. That was perfectly appropriate for this eccentric and unusual Italian filmmaker. Over the first two decades of his career, Tinto made a series of remarkable and unpredictable works, no two of which were alike. His first two feature films were a good start, they were divisive, and they were largely suppressed. He then briefly became a director for hire, but, even when given the flimsiest of stories, he inserted enough of his own ideas to make for engaging entertainment, and the results were striking. His ideal was to stir people out of their complacency, and to cause them to rethink all their ideas, as well as ideas about authority and about society. He did so not by employing didacticism, but rather by absurdism and comedy.

Apart from *Caligula*, Tinto Brass' name is not widely known in the United States, though a few Americans are familiar with his later erotic works. The minority who have dug a bit deeper have discovered a rich body of work that breaks all the rules, a filmography of tremendous range, from nearly incomprehensible avant-garde to comic satire to pop-art to educational to theatre of the absurd to social rebellion.

Not only were Tinto's early films entertaining, they were also thought-provoking and brilliantly made—most of them with minimal budgets. He had a strong sense of cinema and some of his films were extremely demanding. However challenging some of his films are, they are nonetheless playful, filled with visual jokes and preposterous humor. Tinto also had a propensity to experiment with mimicking thought processes, offering a barrage of flashing images and sounds that should be discordant, but which are actually soothing, as they mesh so well with our thought patterns. He would admix naturalism with absurdism, stir both together with comedy, and add lyricism with a frothing of insouciance, to create movies unlike anything else. Especially amusing was his habit of placing actors in actual crowds and shooting with hidden cameras—or, sometimes, with cameras that were not hidden. The interaction of documentary and make-believe is irresistible. The bedrock upon which his stories were founded, though, was something different, something usually unnoticeable until one studies several of his films: his cherishing of kindness, consideration, caring, and genuine selfless affection (which he sometimes defines as true "culture"), and his disdain for their opposites (which he sometimes defines as "civilization").

Publicity photo: **P.O. Box Tinto Brass**, *1995*

There was another ingredient, as well: These films were evidently made by a person who had no love of the *status quo* and who had entirely different ideas about who is sane and who is not. Those who had caring hearts, those who had poetic sensibilities, were those at the bottom of the social ladder; they were "the losers," as Tinto affectionately called them. Those who lacked these qualities were the bureaucrats at the top. The stories sympathized with "the losers," even those "losers" who were so emotionally retarded as to be cruel. In Tinto's view, they deserve sympathy as well, for however horrid they may be, they still have the simplicity of infants. This idea is not explicitly hammered home in any of his movies. It is a subtle undercurrent, barely perceptible, almost subliminal. These movies were made by someone who had no use for social customs and genuflection to authority figures in a world forever going to war. "Civilization," he explained, "has not learned to live in a cultured way. It has always avoided looking at certain aspects of human nature, not cultivated dignity as a solid basic passion." His political views also imbued all his films. Initially sympathetic toward Communism, Tinto soon enough came to abhor all political structures, whether of the Left or of the Right, which maintain and increase their power only through violence. As a lifelong admirer of Wilhelm Reich, he made his films critical of all authorities and all -isms. His overriding theme, evident in nearly everything he has ever done, is personal and individual freedom above all else.

What is Tinto Brass known for? Softcore! It is ironic that his fame came from his creation of sex-filled features. Yet he is not really a pornographer, for his softcore works are too lively, wry, good-natured, and innocent to be categorized as exploitation. As one of his assistant directors described them, they are "Rabelaisian Commedia dell'arte."[1]

Therein lies the irony. How can a master avant-garde filmmaker be known only for softcore films? Part of the answer is that Tinto is openly an exemplar of great intellect and the highest culture as well as of the basest culture, equally, proudly, shamelessly. When a serious and scholarly person interviews him, his answers are serious and scholarly. When a gossip columnist interviews him for *outré* sensationalism, he obliges, enthusiastically. Another part of the answer is mere accident of fate, an accident that provided him a handsome income, respect, and great personal joy.

Source Notes:

1 Alan Sekers: email, 2 November 2020

Before the Beginning

THOUGH TINTO BRASS is extremely outgoing, his personal life and his genealogy have been hidden from view. Tinto says that part of his family was Austro-Hungarian,[2] which is true, but it is impossible to follow that thread. We know vaguely of a family, possibly from Dalmatia[3] or from neighboring Croatia,[4] whose name could properly be spelled Brasević or Brasović. Dalmatia had once been controlled by Hungary, but came under the Republic of Venice in 1420. We know that a part of this Brasović family abridged the surname and settled in Venetian-controlled Friuli. In 1797, Napoléon conquered Venice, which left Austria free to capture Friuli. After a mere few years, Friuli came under control of the Italic kingdom. That was in 1805, but with the Bourbon Restoration a decade later, Austria again acquired a piece of Friuli, namely the County of Gorizia and Gradisca.

Tinto's great-grandfather, Michele Brass, was a wine merchant in Gorizia, and part of his ancestry was German. Despite his Teutonic/Slavic family tree, he identified only as Italian, and the Austrian police consequently filed a report on him: "innkeeper and wine shopkeeper in Gorizia... An unrepentant drinker, still in permanent relationships with Favetti."[5] Carlo Favetti, to make clear, was a Friulian poet as well as the founder of the Italian irredentist movement in the County of Gorizia and Gradisca.[6]

There is an amusing story about Michele Brass that is worth recounting, since Tinto Brass' own devious behavior a century later was tellingly similar. We may quote from Cossár's *Gorizia d' altri tempi*,[7] which mentioned a hand-cranked street organ with a cylinder that played Johann Strauss' *Radetzky March*:

Among the peculiarities of old Gorizia it is worth mentioning Saint Silvestro's day (New Year's Eve).

On the eves of important festivals, a hand organ sounded through the streets and squares of the city. The blind Schilo and his one-armed companion came down from the Via della Cappella, where they lived in a shack, and carried with them a hand organ that burst the eardrums of peaceful citizens. While Schilo turned the crank of the old device, his unfortunate companion, with his cap in his hand, went to the shops to gather pennies, with his perennial refrain: "I beg alms for a poor blind man and for a poor one-armed man."

Among the musical repertoire of that instrument there was a military march, which the people of Gorizia nicknamed "I Shall Kick, I Shall Kick, I Shall Kick Your Ass!" In 1866, the Austrian government had rounded up those who harbored passionate feelings of Italianness and imprisoned them in Temesvàr in Hungary. Thus, the hand organ's march wreaked havoc on the nerves of patriots.

We wish to speak about Michele Brass, who kept a wine warehouse in Piazza del Corno. When the one-armed man came to beg for alms, Brass offered him not only money, but also a glass of wine. Schilo noticed that whenever his companion returned to empty his large sack after begging in the square, his breath smelled of wine. Hearing the reason why, he wished to accompany his companion, together with the hand organ, to the entrance of the shopkeeper's bar. Brass welcomed them in, and, taking advantage of their greed, played a trick on them, which certainly would not have been expected. After getting them drunk, he offered them a bucketful of wine to drink at home. The two beggars then, in the unconsciousness produced by intoxication, poured the contents into the barrel of the hand organ and wobbled home to sleep it off. When the effects of the wine wore down, they were stupefied to discover that the organ would no longer play... The wine had ruined the sound cylinder of the Radetzky march, thanks to the cunning used by the old irredentist. Thus was the repertoire of this instrument forever ended, without Brass having to suffer any consequences from the ever-vigilant Austrian police.

Michele Brass risked trouble by participating in demonstrations in the hopes that his Gorizia would be united with Italy. It is interesting to note that, among those advocating for union with Italy, were people bearing

Slavic and Germanic names. Michele Brass' wife, Maria, for instance, had a Germanic name, Happacher, and that is probably another source of Tinto's claim of Austro-Hungarian heritage. The Happacher family has since changed its name to Appiani.[8]

Michele and Maria had six children, and with the second child, born on 14 December 1870, Michele made his wishes known even more publicly, for he bestowed upon the infant an unmistakably meaningful name: Italico. Though Michele had hoped that Italico would follow him into the wine business, he recognized his son's prodigious talent at painting, and freely allowed him to pursue his own destiny.[9] Italico was Tinto's beloved grandfather.

At age 17, Italico Brass studied in Monaco, but soon switched to the Academy of Fine Arts in Munich, where he studied under Karl Raupp for just over a year. From there he traveled to Paris to the school of Jean-Paul Laurens and William-Adolphe Bouguereau. Italico mastered several different styles: realism, Academic, and post-impressionism, though he quickly jettisoned Academic.[10]

It was in Paris that Italico met Lina Rebecca "Nina" Vigdoff, an émigré from Odessa, whose father had worked as an engineer on the building of the Trans-Siberian railway.[11] Explained Tinto, "She was an extraordinary woman and, for her time, incredibly emancipated and modern. It was certainly uncommon, of course, at the end of the nineteenth century, for a Russian girl to leave her country to study medicine at the Sorbonne."[12] On 6 June 1895, she and Italico married, and later that year they settled in Venice,[13] in the neighborhood of San Trovaso. Italico fell in love with his new home and identified as a Venetian painter. Venice and its people became the primary subjects of his canvases. Nonetheless, Gorizia considered him a native son and renamed the street where he had been born: Via Italico Brass.[14]

Though little remembered today, Italico Brass was artistic royalty and quite the globetrotter.[15] At age 22, he won bronze medals at the Exposition Universelle in Paris and at the Salon de Paris.[16] He would go on to win prizes at the Panama-Pacific International Exposition in San Francisco, California, in 1915, and at the Jubiläum Ausstellung des Künstlerhaus in Vienna in 1936.[17] His works appeared in numerous museums around the Western world, from Athens to Santiago to Sydney to Pittsburgh.[18] In 1920, he purchased the Scuola Vecchia dell'Abbazia di Santa Maria della Misericordia, which had been damaged in the war. He restored it and re-opened it as an art gallery.[19] In 1942, he was commissioned to work on the set design of a Venetian feature film called *Canal Grande*.

The one child we know about, probably the only child, was Alessandro, born on 20 January 1898. As a youngster, he proved to have an exceptional gift for drawing, though he never pursued the avocation.[20] He did, though, become a noted art collector and art dealer.[21] He volunteered for the First World War and emerged mutilated,[22] to become the president of the Venetian Section of the National Association of Those Mutilated and Disabled in War.[23] He participated in the March on Rome[24] (1922) and became a staunch fascist.[25] His disability did not stop his ambitions as a sportsman, for, in 1925, he was the race director for the first Fascist Regatta on the Venetian Grand Canal,[26] and in 1926 he won a rowing championship.[27] He began his legal career in the office of Francesco Carnelutti[28] and soon became a prominent criminal lawyer.[29] In 1928, he became the manager of the Ente Sportivo Fascista,[30] and with the political support of his fellow sportsmen,[31] he was appointed deputy mayor (Vize-Podestà) of Venice in February 1938, upon which he helped engineer the ouster of the mayor, Mario Alverà, to have him replaced by the fascist party's choice, Giovanni Marcello, on 5 September 1938.[32] In March 1939, he was named to the Chamber of Fasces and Corporations as member of the pension and credit corporation.[33] There are some nuances here, and we should pay attention. When we turn to R.J.B. Bosworth's *Italian Venice*, we discover a little of what fascism meant to Alessandro:

> **Alessandro Brass... lamented that, presently, ordinary children in Venice could not enjoy a single proper playground (or swimming pool), while popular housing stock too often consisted of putrid "hovels" rather than what might be expected under Fascism.**[34]

In about 1929, Alessandro married Carla Curletti,[35] born in 1909 or 1910 in Milan,[36] and the couple had four children, all boys: Italico, Giovanni (not yet called Tinto), Maurizio, and Andrea. All were of an artistic bent. The eldest of the four brothers, Italico, became an art collector. Maurizio, or Malo as he was called, was an architect and sometime movie actor. The youngest, Andrea, was a poet.[37] The second child, Giovanni (born 26 March 1933), was unusual, impetuous, transgressive, and guilty of gross misconduct—and he is quite open about it. "[My parents had] once forbidden me to go out. Out of anger, I went to the balcony and peed on the passers-by."[38] He attended grammar school at the Cavanis Fathers' Gymnasium,[39] where he proved himself an uninterested student, but, with his unusually good memory, he received top marks and managed to skip a year.[40] After four years of schooling by the priests, he emerged "serenely atheist."[41]

Giovanni was much more at home with his grandparents, Italico and Nina, and spent more time with them than with his immediate family. He was impressed that they were open-minded enough to live happily apart, each on a separate floor of their house.[42] While staying with his grandparents, Giovanni was, he said, bombarded by images not only of his grandfather's paintings, but of all the countless sixteenth- through eighteenth-century paintings in his collection.[43] The child began to draw and paint, enthusiastically, constantly, on every piece of paper he could find. Italico said of his favorite grandson,[44] "We have a little Tintoretto in the house,"[45] and the nickname stuck. Little Tinto, though a terror at his own home, was the perfect child when with his grandparents.

Grandmother Nina was young Tinto's rôle model: "From her, I learned languages and the taste of freedom."[46] Indeed, she taught him fluent French as well as enough German, Russian, and English to get by. It was she, more than anyone else, who raised Tinto, and the boy simply adored her.[47] In his later years, he admitted to a theme that pervaded his works and his life, and his statement would probably come as a surprise to most people who are familiar with him: "All political power should be put into the hands of women. Men are finished; they should just give it up. The future will bring us a matriarchy."[48] It is a little bit difficult to reconcile that sentiment with his other statements, but we shall cover that complication by and by.

Despite the family's personal connection with those in power, Tinto was only vaguely aware that there was a war. He recalls the "beautiful time" when he and his family stayed in Asolo.[49] Edward Cecil Guinness, the First Earl of Iveagh, head of Guinness beer, the richest man in Ireland, owned what had been Eleanora Duse's villa. He died in 1927, but his family then established a business in Asolo called SCARPA. In 1938, ownership of the Duse property seems to have been vested in the company, which arranged for the Brass family to take up residence there. Little Tinto had the run of the place, except for the library, which was locked and strictly off-limits. The interdict was too much of a tease, and he managed to sneak in.[50] That is where he discovered the "forbidden" books, such as *Lady Chatterley's Lover*, which he read in English[51] (to another interviewer,[52] he said he read the French translation).

The youngster was also becoming aware of movies, and attended the local cinemas habitually. One of his earliest movie memories was seeing the posters for *San Giovanni decollato* (Saint John Beheaded) posted on a bridge that led to the famous Teatro Malibran. He would have been seven at that time. He soon became intrigued by the various movie posters pasted onto announcement boards.[53] The film that particularly struck him was the 1931 version of *Dr. Jekyll and Mr. Hyde*, which he saw at a little cinema in Asolo. When Miriam Hopkins performed a striptease, Tinto unexpectedly discovered that he had ruined his kneepants.[54]

Tinto was enamored of the cinema, and spent hours each day discussing movies with friends his age as well as with adults.[55] As soon as he began attending movies, he determined that he wanted to make his own.[56]

At age 12, he had his first sexual adventure:

I had my first ancillary loves in Asolo, where we had been displaced for the war. I was 12 years old. I don't remember if it was the ass of Emilietta or another of the three maids, all beautiful. I put my hand in her underwear as she was cleaning my shoes. "But no, sir, what are you doing?" "Oh, shush; just keep on polishing."[57]

Tinto further elaborated upon his predilection, in his typically abstruse way: "We had three beautiful maids at home that my mother was forced to replace constantly because of the strange episodes that happened in which I was the protagonist."[58]

His parents decided not to have him continue studying under the priests, and so enrolled him at the nearby secular Marco Polo high school, just after the war.[59] By the time he was 13, Tinto was seriously interested in cinema, passionate about it, and was regularly attending the Cineforum Veneziano and the Circolo del Cinema Francesco Pasinetti,[60] seeing two or three films each day.[61] He and his friends heard the whispered rumors of hardcore stag films, and, with some determination, they managed to find and view some of those oddities.[62] Since Alessandro, the eminent lawyer, was constantly traveling, Tinto discovered that other cities and towns also had their cinema clubs, and he attended.[63] It may have been at about this time that Tinto acquired an 8mm movie camera and began exhibiting his abstract silent films at a local cineclub. He was in love with that device and became intrigued by the mechanics of it.[64] He also, at age 12 or 13, gained his first admittance to a brothel.[65] The story here gets even more vague:

During my adolescence, my relationship with [my father] became increasingly tense and intransigent, until it completely broke apart. Over the years, I understood that the exacerbation of the frictions between us took place in conjunction with my discovery of sex. When you realize that you can do the same things your parent does, you automatically question his absolute authority, and your relationship to him becomes less deferential and more equal, bringing about an upheaval in family balances. When I discovered sex, my dreams, my ideals, and my aspirations became irreconcilable with his figure, and my most intimate reality began to clash violently with his principles.

As we hear so often from Tinto, this is a summary devoid of any detail. This episode might tie in with the time when Alessandro had his 14-year-old son committed to the San Clemente lunatic asylum,[66] though we do not know specifically what led to that drastic decision.

Unfortunately, we know nothing about Tinto's mother, Carla Curletti. Tinto once made a terse comment that she was a harpy who was convinced he was mentally malformed.[67] Considering what little we know of Tinto's childhood behavior, it would be difficult to fault Carla for her conclusion.

Tinto recalls that by age 16 he was a regular at all the cinemas and brothels in Venice. Tinto explains that brothels then were not what they are now:

> **...I was a very keen brothel customer. When I grew up in Venice, I would go to three brothels every day, because there were 30 brothels in Venice, in the '40s and '50s, and 30 cinemas. So, it was almost automatic: You went into a movie house and then you went into the vagina of a woman, and *vice versa*. It was really very natural, a very straight connection. And I had these memories, that the situation was not as it has always been shown in other films, a dramatic situation of exploitation. Yes, there was that also, but there was a kind of very nice atmosphere, a nice relationship; you used to go there to lose time, not only to make sex. You used to go there to pass time, to talk, to make jokes, things that are absolutely impossible nowadays, for instance. They speak of opening the brothels again, etc., but it is impossible, because the mentality has changed. I saw this Eros centre in Holland, or in Germany, Amsterdam, Hamburg. It is strange; you cannot pass time. The whole concept is to make it very quick, straight. You go and look in the book, that girl, that room, without meeting anybody else. In the brothel, the most typical situation was the common room, the salon, where you met everybody—a professor, even some priests sometimes. And there it was very warm, very natural; sexuality became something very natural, very nice. And then there was a lot of culture in the prostitutes—I mean the culture, the erotic culture that has been lost with the closing of the brothels. I think that the closing of the brothels is something similar, on the erotic point of view, as the burning of the library of Alexandria in Egypt. There you lost a lot, a treasure of history, culture, and documents. Here, with the closing of the brothels, you lost a treasure of erotic civilization.**[68]

Since the brothels were meeting grounds for intellectuals, that is where the youngster first heard the exciting conversations about politics. It was in 1948 that he first heard Communist leader Palmiro Togliatti's rallies. Altogether, this was a revelation. He had never encountered such ideas before. "I liked the Left because it meant transgression, even on the sexual level."[69] In his mind, sex and politics were about the same thing: liberation and the overthrow of values:

> **With sex, I discovered politics. I mean that for me they were two things that went together. I'll explain. I went to those brothel houses and heard the discussions about Togliatti. I don't know how, but surely sincerely, though in a coarse manner, it seemed to me that it was a little bit a question of the same thing; that is, subverting the values and teachings that politics preached and taught was the same as the subversion of values and teachings that I was practicing with my youthful experiences. Because I went against my family, which was a bourgeois, rich, fascist family—or at least my father was—and to go against my family was also to put oneself in conflict with society. Oh, how I liked those discussions about Togliatti...**[70]

He was enamored of Communism, though he would soon give it up. His guiding principle was liberation, and to liberate society, the minds of individuals first needed to be liberated from imposed values.[71] It would be reasonable to suppose that it was at about this same time that he was introduced to the works of Wilhelm Reich, whose anti-authoritarian stance meshed perfectly with his own. Tinto was soon addicted to this world of ideas, which did not bode well for life at a home in San Trovaso[72] that was ruled over by a fascist father who wanted no values overthrown. His father, Alessandro, was such a diehard and inflexible fascist that he had even turned down a request made to him in 1943 by Mussolini, in person, to join the Italian Social Republic (the Republic of Salò, colloquially), a German puppet state.[73] Not even at Mussolini's request would he compromise his ideals—or, perhaps, was there a somewhat different reason? Did Alessandro realize that the Allies would win, and that fascism was a lost cause? Was it time to prepare for a different future, and to make himself acceptable to the victors?

Lest we suspect that home life was the epitome of chaos, we should point out that there was mutual respect. In later years, Tinto recalled that, though there was no physical affection, no kisses, no hugs, no warmth, there was admiration:

> **My father had such an overwhelming sensuality that one breathed it in the family. He was certainly in love with my mother and he felt a great passion for her: He always kept his hands on her legs and I often saw that he touched her under her skirts. I was never shocked. Indeed, thanks to his behavior, without false and stupid modesty, I was able to approach sex in a serene way.**

Dad was a Sean Connery type, male, virile, good-looking, what is said to be a handsome man. By profession he was a lawyer; he had a gift with words and he was a brilliant conversationalist. As an adult, I appreciate these qualities. In childhood and adolescence, I felt persecuted by this mania about good speech, to the point that, fearing that I could not properly express myself, I avoided talking to him. There were precise rules that he tried to inculcate in me: "The thought," he said, "must be fully expressed and well-articulated."[74]

Tinto's fear of not being able to express himself adequately has never left him. Though he can create marvelously intricate stories and brilliant, even heart-rending dialogues for his movies, he is incapable of speaking expansively. He is not a raconteur, and his descriptions of his life are terse at best. That is what makes recording his biography well-nigh impossible. Dates are vague and contradictory, and details are lacking.

Tinto commented further on his father's deep, resonant speaking voice, perfectly suited to his profession. "Sometimes I secretly went to court to listen to his pleadings. It was nice to hear his voice, set and solemn, to catch the nuances of his courtly, refined oratorical style."[75] Though "it wasn't a great relationship," Tinto now admits that the fault "was more because of me than because of him." He confesses, "Today, I must say that he was almost always right."[76]

In the U.S. *Federal Register* of 23 November 1950, we discover a curious entry from the Office of Alien Property, concerning a certain Alessandro Brass and Lina Widgopf [*sic*] Brass.[77] We can piece a little bit together. Italico died on 16 August 1943, bequeathing his art collection to Nina and Alessandro. Three weeks later, with the Armistice of Cassibile, Italy surrendered to the Allies. Alessandro Brass surely realized that Germany would lose the war, and he hurriedly got the art collection safely over the border to Switzerland and thence to the U.S., to protect it from German looting. It seems that Alessandro had trouble finding work for several years, given his political affiliation. To make ends meet, he sold a number of paintings by the old masters. Since the paintings were already in the U.S., he sold them to Americans. We know that he sold Giovanni Battista Pittoni's *Martirio de San Bartolomeo* (1735) to the Nelson-Atkins Museum of Art in Kansas City, Missouri, in 1947,[78] and that he sold Giovanni Battista Tiepolo's *Una giovane donna in un tricorno* (circa 1755/1760) to the Samuel H. Kress Foundation in 1948.[79] He sold Alessandro Magnasco's *Interno di una sinagoga* (1725–1735) to the Chicago Art Institute in 1949,[80] and, in 1950, he sold Giuseppe Bazzani's *La pietà con la Maddalena* to Severance A. Milliken of Cleveland.[81] Perhaps there were other sales as well. It was probably these transactions that alerted the authorities, who discovered that Nina's and Alessandro's possessions had been stored in the United States since 1943 or 1944, while Italy remained an enemy state until 10 February 1947, with the signing of the Paris Peace Treaty. Ironically, by virtue of the legal requirement that enemy property be returned, Alessandro got his collection back!

By about 1950, at about age 17, Tinto had enrolled at Università a Padova, a mere 20 miles from home, and, since he still could not work up the courage to contradict his father's wishes, he majored in jurisprudence. As a reward for a high mark on an exam, he received a spring-wound Paillard-Bolex 16mm silent camera, presumably from his parents.[82]

There was another escapade at age 17, which, we can only guess, was during a vacation break during the university year:

One episode that angered my father was finding some of his books at a junk dealer. I was the one who sold them, to get money so that I could go to the brothel, and dad recognized them, since he was in the habit of signing his name to them. He was not so outraged at the way I had spent the money—he was broad-minded—but he could not understand why I had stripped him of his library. "Why didn't you ask me for the money?" he kept repeating. "I would have given it to you."[83]

Tinto found himself grounded, but, since he had an appointment, he left the house anyway. When he returned, his key no longer fit in the lock and his clothes were outside, together with a message never to cross the threshold again.[84] Tinto understood that this was just his father's way of getting a point across, but that it was not truly an eviction.[85] Alessandro simply thought that Tinto was setting a bad example for his younger brothers,[86] and so he felt he had to take some sort of action. An apology from the lad would have gained him re-entry. Nonetheless, Tinto took this as an affront and decided it was a good time to make the break. He rented a room in Giudecca (an island in the Venetian lagoon) and continued working as a freelance photographer. Since the income was not enough to live on, his mother began sending him money, probably with the tacit approval of his father,[87] but only on condition of his earning good grades.[88] Apparently, his mother truly did care about him. Tinto understood that full well and he was grateful for her kindness. With that stream of income, Tinto would be able to continue his university studies.

Tinto visited Harry's Bar to vent, but the time and the circumstances are impossible to pin down. Tinto's recollection is that this was in 1950, just after he had been locked out, and that he had already begun flirting with the owner's daughter, Carla Cipriani[89] (three years his senior), whom he had first met at the Locanda Cipriani on the island of Torcello, where he was enjoying his hobby of *valesana* rowing (rowing a gondola with crossed oars). He noticed her behind the counter, made up with *oci sboròni* (eyeliner).[90] Carla's recollection is quite different. Asked how she first met Tinto, she replied:

> **At Harry's Bar, owned by my father. I already knew Tinto's brother [Italico], a boy of my age. In 1953, it must have been January, Tinto came to pick up a Negroni. He had a red beard. When I saw him again, without a beard, in Campo Santo Stefano, with that big face, he made an impression!**[91]

Soon enough, she asked him out on a date. Though Carla had no interest in movies, she regularly attended the Malibran and Rossini cinemas, not to watch the screen but simply to nest in a box and make out. This time, though, she chose the Cinema San Marco, where Chaplin's *Monsieur Verdoux* was being presented. Tinto and Carla were both so enraptured by the film that they forgot to cuddle. All feature films in Italy had intermissions every hour or so, and, when the lights came up halfway into the movie, they tried to make up for lost time, but they were still both so captivated by what they had just seen that they could hardly speak.[92] For most couples, that would be the end, but for Tinto and Carla, it was the beginning. They realized they were right for each other, and Carla was well on her way toward falling in love with the movies.

We can presume that Tinto's military service was from 1951 through 1953, and it was during that time that he began to shoot film on his Paillard-Bolex.[93] After military service, Tinto continued his university studies. Since he socialized with painters, he got to know Albino Lucatello, whose wife Giselda was the daughter of a Mrs. Flavia Paulon, a screenwriter who ran a movie magazine called *Sequenze* and who also dealt with cineclubs. Mrs. Paulon arranged to get Tinto a job shooting photographs for Camera Foto, the Venetian news agency.[94] Tinto also found himself working as a reporter for Swiss television[95] (presumably submitting rolls of 16mm film by mail), but whether Mrs. Paulon was responsible for that gig, we do not know. We do know that Mrs. Paulon arranged to get him hired at the Venice Film Festival's press office, probably in 1954. One of his duties was to take photos of starlets on the terrace atop the Palazzo del Cinema.[96] Carla had a different take on that duty: "He went to the Lido, and, with the pretext of working at the film festival, he got blown by all the starlets."[97] It seems that he worked for the festival in 1955 and 1956 as well.[98] His office job by the filing cabinet was instrumental in introducing him to various people in the movie business. Indeed, that was the office that arranged the VIP lunches and the gala dinners. It was while working in that office that he met Lotte Eisner, who was an old friend of Mrs. Paulon as well as a prominent film scholar and archivist who had co-founded the Cinémathèque Française.

Tinto admired Eisner's ardent passion for the cinema, and he was irritated that she was never invited to the lunches and dinners. Tinto understood why: She was in her late fifties and she did not look like a starlet. He decided to do something about the situation. When he was placing invitations to these events, he made sure to misdirect some to her in-box. She was more than grateful, and gave him a standing invitation to visit her at the Cinémathèque.[99]

Tinto transferred from the Università a Padova to the Università degli Studi di Ferrara (about 70 miles from Venice) to complete his law degree. He tells an amusing story, which may or may not be true. He says he left Padova when the local brothels were closed, and transferred to Ferrara, where the brothels were still open.[100] Perhaps that story is correct, but Italian brothels did not begin to close nationally until 20 February 1958, which was half a year after he graduated. The closure was courtesy of law number 75, the *Legge Merlin*.[101]

He frequently skipped class, and often ignored his textbooks, but he received top marks. One can only assume that it was his having been steeped in law at home that allowed him these easy grades. Tinto told an anecdote to Mario Gagliardotto:

> **Once, for example, I shamelessly lied to Giuseppe Bettiol, professor of criminal law, an eminent jurist—so much so that his legal arguments were being studied at the time—as well as an illustrious honorable member of the Christian Democrats. The day I showed up to take the criminal-law examination, he gave me a good 30. [*Comment: 30 is the top mark in Italian schools.*] But then he asked me if I was also ready for the criminal-procedure examination. I was absolutely unprepared, so I hesitated for a moment and then, with a sublimely impudent face, I answered yes. So, I received a 28 even in procedure without ever having opened a book.**[102]

It was probably at about this time that Tinto painted a self-portrait, the only painting of his ever to have been published.[103] It is rather accomplished for an amateur work, but it is difficult to interpret.

In it, we see a Tinto far more serious than he has ever appeared in a photograph, far more wary, with gigantic jaundiced Mediterranean eyes looking suspiciously askance, rather than his own small Slavic eyes that are ever friendly and humorous, if sometimes weary.

Tinto graduated from Ferrara in the summer of 1957, and then, on that very day, returned to Venice to pack an absurdly oversized trunk to make a pilgrimage to Paris,[104] or so he has said. He did not go straight to Paris. To film scholar Lorenzo Codelli, he filled in a gap:

Before going to Paris, I moved to Rome for a short time. I had just graduated and I wanted to make movies at all costs. Arriving in the city, my first impression was certainly not positive. I was unable to have a good relationship with the reality of the city. Now I appreciate it much more. Rome has always been a city of pleasure, but at the time I was quivering with intellectual and æsthetic curiosities and could not find any such fervor there.[105]

Tinto confessed that he had entered Rome with "provincialism and years of illusions," but that the reality of the film business and its endless regulations was more than disappointing.[106] To find intellectual fervor and aesthetic curiosity, he took Lotte Eisner up on her invitation. For Tinto, this was a delicious transgression:

The Cineforum didn't allow [transgression]. It censored kissing in films. One of the reasons why I went to Paris was undoubtedly related to that fact. Paris was sparkling. Everything that was said about women became more fascinating when it was said in French; it became full of sin and transgression.[107]

Carla did not approve of the travel plan, and, after an argument, she refused to accompany him.[108] On the train to Paris, Tinto shared a compartment with a family—a mother, her son, and a daughter who was about Tinto's age. The family's name was Langlois, a name that, at the time, meant nothing to Tinto. He and the young lady had a brief rendezvous in a dark corridor, and the mother never found out.[109]

When Tinto arrived at the Gare de Lyon train station in Paris, he deposited his enormous trunk and headed straight for the Cinémathèque. As he reminisced to Mario Gagliardotto:[110]

When I arrived at the Cinémathèque, Eisner had just returned from an interview with Akira Kurosawa. I remember the scene as if it were yesterday. "Lotte, c'est moi, Tinto!" I began. "Oui, bonjour! Tu savait que Akira Kurosawa tourne avec trois cameras?" she replied. She had found out that Kurosawa shot with three cameras at the same time, and she was so excited by this that she didn't care if I was there or not. So, as she continued talking about Kurosawa, she went to the restroom, pulled up her skirt, sat down on the toilet, and pissed, leaving the door wide open. She was truly "possessed" by cinema and didn't care about anything else!

As Tinto began his new career, a gentleman approached him, held out his hand, and introduced himself as the director of the Cinémathèque. "I'm Langlois. Pleased to meet you." Tinto was floored, and thought that this was the father of the lady in the train. Alas, there was no relation at all.[111] It was just a bizarre coincidence, and with such bizarre coincidences was Tinto's life filled.

Since Tinto was an intern, the Cinémathèque paid for his lodgings at the rue Danielle Casanova, but not for anything else. Life devoid of income led to adventures, but Tinto was over the moon to be in Paris, which breathed the fervor and aesthetic curiosity that he craved, and which had been nowhere in evidence in Rome:

It was a very vital reality... In Paris the situation was distinctly different. I immediately found myself at the center of the *Nouvelle Vague* that belonged to the Cinémathèque. The screenings in the film library, Henri Langlois' activities, were fundamental for the directors who belonged to the *Nouvelle Vague*.[112]

The Cinémathèque, Tinto said, was the mythical land of Bengodi, the Land of Plenty, with 50,000 films on deposit. He decided that he wished to spend the remainder of his life with people such as those at the Cinémathèque, people who put cinema ahead of any other consideration.[113]

In this wonderful land of opportunities, Tinto spent his summer evenings with his new acquaintances at the brasseries of Saint Germain and Montmarte. They could never eat twice at the same restaurant, for, not having any money, they dashed away without ever paying the bills.[114] Tinto spent some nights working with Langlois on his "delusional memoirs,"[115] and he was the projectionist for 16mm screenings at schools. He would see, on average, three films every morning and another three in the afternoon. He also had charge of the screenplay library and the stills library.[116]

He arrived at the Cinémathèque just a decade after the movie business had been entirely altered by a legal case, *United States v. Paramount Pictures, Inc.*, 334 U.S. 131 (1948). Prior to that case, Hollywood executives ruled the movie industry in the Western world. Actors, directors, writers, and technicians had been on long-term contracts, and the major studios, which owned their own cinema chains, controlled the booking. In a single day, that system fell to pieces. Actors, directors, writers, and technicians were now freelancers and independent contractors. The studios were required to divest themselves of the cinema chains, and so lost control of booking their own products. This created a power vacuum, which compelled directors to set up their own small corporations to produce films. Studios, distributors, and cinema chains would invest in those small corporations in return for licenses. Further, new lightweight equipment and faster film stocks with finer grain allowed indigent amateurs to create films that looked as professional as studio productions. Tinto's timing could hardly have been better. In this new *milieu*, he had an opportunity to enter the business and to write and create what pleased him, rather than merely take dictation from a board of directors.

An interviewer asked who his friends were at the time:

At that time, the Cinémathèque Française was frequented by many of those who went on to found France's *Nouvelle Vague*. Then there was Joris Ivens, Alberto Cavalcanti, Roberto Rossellini, Sjöström, and Chagall. I frequented all of them. They all had a great love of cinema in common. Then, of course, there was Langlois, who founded the Cinémathèque. During the German occupation, he actually buried all the films to save them from destruction.[117]

His first job was to assist Joris Ivens, who was editing Langlois' documentary on Marc Chagall. That was when he learned the craft of editing, the syntax of film, and that became his first love. Sadly, *Chagall* was never released. As Tinto explained, Langlois had decided, privately, to withhold the film until Chagall died, thinking it would be worth more that way.[118] (The film then vanished. A diligent search through the Cinémathèque after Langlois' death turned up only a few minutes of blurry outtakes. There is an indication that Chagall may have confiscated Langlois' film in 1963, in order to clear the way for Lauro Venturi's short documentary.)

About two months after Tinto arrived in Paris, Carla decided to follow him. They married on Saturday, 12 October 1957, which was coincidentally Columbus Day, and from then on Carla was known to one and all as Tinta. Her adoration of Tinto was visible, and to the end of her days she doted on him. The feeling was mutual. How did she feel about his endless stream of momentary flings? Was she jealous? "Always! But I am always present, in the sense that I am always aware of what he's doing; I am always on the alert."[119]

Having learned of Tinto's skill with *Chagall*,[120] Roberto Rossellini hired him to edit a documentary called *L'India vista da Rossellini* (India Seen by Rossellini), which consisted of random 16mm color footage taken in India. Tinto was thrilled. He had seen all of Rossellini's films and held them in the highest regard. Rossellini had a 16mm Moviola installed in Tinto's flat on rue Danielle Casanova, gave him notes about ideas for sequences, and then let the youngster go at it.[121]

This job led to new friendships. Rossellini "was part of the group of artists who circulated around the Cinémathèque: Chabrol, Truffaut, Godard."[122] Those were three of the several young critics who became film directors, and who came to be known as the "Nouvelle Vague," or New Wave. Deeply inspired by Hollywood's extinct golden years, these young men ironically also rebelled against it. They rejected the Hollywood type of assembly-line filmmaking. They wanted to make films that were more personal, with stories that were from the heart, in which a single person would be in charge of the script, the design, the music score, the location scouting, the casting, the editing. Asked which of the *Nouvelle Vague* filmmakers he admired most, Tinto had a ready answer: "Jean-Luc Godard more than anyone else. It was generally his way of making movies that interested me. However, I had a whole visual culture behind me regarding French cinema, starting with Jean Vigo."[123] Indeed, many of Tinto's films would have a distinctly Godardian ring, and would even borrow Godard's ideas and techniques directly.

To back up a year or so, Rossellini had received an official invitation to make some movies in India, but, as always, he created turmoil wherever he went. He was at the time married to Ingrid Bergman, a marriage that had already caused a scandal and was even debated in the U.S. Congress, since both he and Bergman were married to others when she bore him a child. In India, since Rossellini steadfastly refused to put pen to paper, he hired a screenwriter named Sonali Sen Roy Das Gupta, who seemed happily married. That did not stop an affair that resulted in a pregnancy. There was the requisite outrage, a pair of divorces, a sudden termination of contracts by the scandalized government of India, and a deportation. Das Gupta, noticeably pregnant, followed Rossellini to France, and the couple sought refuge from the hordes of gossip columnists. Rossellini hid in one location while Das Gupta hid at Henri Cartier-Bresson's photo studio (19 rue Danielle Casanova).[124] Tinto served as their go-between, delivering messages back and forth, all the while trying to keep the paparazzi from learning anything about the couple's whereabouts.[125] This trustworthiness led to a friendship. Said Tinto of Rossellini, "A relationship of true friendship had been established between us. Rossellini was a master of life."[126] Elsewhere he stated: "I had an infinite admiration for Rossellini. Rossellini as a man had a Socratic understanding. Rossellini was a teacher of life."[127] One lesson that Rossellini taught Tinto was to abandon Communism and to be wary of any dogma.[128] Tinto took heed. His parlor, until then filled with images of Lenin and Mao, was now filled with posters of nudes.[129]

Rossellini cared nothing for editing, which is why he turned the footage over to Tinto, who spent his nights at his small flat on the rue Danielle Casanova piecing the footage into some sort of coherence. Tinto related the story to Mario Gagliardotto:

...while he was having a good time at night with the Indian lover he had brought with him from the trip, I was editing ["mounting"] the film on the Moviola. Then, in the morning, he came to check how my work was going. Most of the time, he was really satisfied: "Wonderful, perfect!" he said. But when he had not had a good time at night: "This shit is no good; you have to do it all over again!" he barked. The truth is that he didn't give a damn; the important thing was that he could devote himself in peace to the other "mounting," that of the Indian. I must admit, however, that I found myself working very well with him; he never imposed anything on me and always gave me ample freedom. He watched with me those kilometers of film that he had shot in India, and then he limited himself only to giving me some suggestions.[130]

Tinto reminisced, more succinctly: "There was a joke I would say in Italian: While he was *montando* the Indian girl, I was *montando* the Indian program. *Montando* means 'editing,' but also 'making love.' If his *montando* went well, my work was also very nice; in the morning I was a genius. If his night went wrong, I was a shit; I had to do everything again."[131]

L'India vista da Rossellini, in ten parts, was broadcast, in black-and-white, on Italian television beginning in January 1958. A year later, from January through August 1959, it was shown on French television, again in black-and-white, under the title *J'ai fait un beau voyage* (I Had a Nice Trip). (Color television would not be introduced to France until 1967 or to Italy until 1972. *L'India vista da Rossellini* has never been shown to the public in its original color version.)

We also discover that Tinto's name (or, actually, Giovanni Brass' name) is listed as an assistant on Rossellini's other film shot at the same time in 35mm, which has been released under a multitude of titles, but which is usually now referred to as *India: Matri Bhumi*. Precisely what Tinto's rôle was, we do not know, though he was probably an assistant editor. One of the principal actors in *India: Matri Bhumi* was Raimù, the performing monkey. While working on this film, Tinto was also babysitting Rossellini's young children, who were staying at a hotel, and he gave them a present: a pet monkey! The children appropriately named it Raimù. Roberto Rossellini was enchanted. The hotel staff were less than enchanted.[132]

India: Matri Bhumi was an exceptionally fine film that, sadly, got almost no play. It was briefly available in the U.S. only in poor 16mm black-and-white copies. Most copies of the film currently available are incomplete and of inferior quality.

Nicholas Schöffer wished for a filmic record of his new "Cybernetic Art" creation, a motorized kinetic sculpture that he named CYSP 1, a machine of moving parts that reacted in somewhat unpredictable ways to light and color. The Cinémathèque Française received the commission to produce this film, and Tinto was given the assignment. One might be right to guess that Tinto's five-minute film, *Spatiodynamisme*, bears some similarity to his 8mm abstract works shown at the Venetian cineclub, but absolute knowledge is impossible, since nobody has seen those 8mm films since the 1950s. *Spatiodynamisme* was silent, without music, and it was surely shot with the spring-wound Paillard-Bolex that Tinto had received as a gift some years earlier. The film consists of impressionistic close-ups of whirling color wheels and twirling antennae, all quite beautiful and mesmerizing, but utterly incomprehensible until the final few seconds, when the camera finally retreats to allow us to see the machine in its entirety. *Spatiodynamisme* has rarely been seen, but the Schöffer Foundation has been trying for years to raise funds to get this and other related films issued on home video.

Tinto's next assignment took him back to Venice. He would this time be an assistant director to a Brazilian filmmaker, Alberto Cavalcanti, who had made a name for himself with *avant-garde* films in the 1920s and 1930s. Tinto admired his works tremendously:

Cavalcanti was another documentary maker, another life teacher. Politically, he had had a very troubled life. I was fascinated by the aspect of Cavalcanti's work that was more closely linked to the *avant-garde* period of the 1920s and 1930s. I was struck by the opportunity to experiment with cinema. Given my formal, visual obsession, his cinema greatly intrigued me. Cavalcanti was living in Paris while I was attending the Cinémathèque.[133]

Alas, Cavalcanti was in no position to make an avant-garde film in 1959. He instead accepted a commission from a wealthy admirer to direct *Venetian Honeymoon*, a comical farce. Tinto and Tinta returned to Venice to work on this film. While Tinto was disappointed that this was a mere commercial project, Tinta was happy to be involved. Asked when Tinto had aroused her passion for cinema, Tinta replied, "From the first film!" That first film, of course, was *Venetian Honeymoon* (known in France as *Les noces vénitiennes* and in Italy as *La prima notte*). She continued:

Everything Tinto does is very interesting. If he had been a doctor, maybe it would not have been the same thing, but if he had been a pimp, maybe yes! The first set I worked on in Venice with Tinto was that of Alberto

Cavalcanti's film, *La prima notte*, in which I was in charge of public relations. I went to meet all the actors at the station because I spoke English and French. I accompanied them on the set, and so I stole the production secretary's job.[134]

Tinto's (or Giovanni's) next assignment was to return yet again to Italy to assist Rossellini on a new film called *Il generale Della Rovere*, loosely based on a true story of a scoundrel who was imprisoned by the Nazis and strangely became a hero of the resistance when he was shot by a firing squad. The story is strong, the script was written in all sincerity, but it did not originate from Rossellini's own ideas. It was producer Moris Ergas who hired Rossellini to make the film. What Rossellini thought about the project is open to debate, since he told conflicting stories. As for Tinto, he was not impressed with the screenplay:

...to all intents and purposes, *Il general Della Rovere* was a commission, strongly desired by producer Moris Ergas, but for which Rossellini never showed any rapture, not even during the shooting. On the other hand, I think that his lack of enthusiasm is clear from the film, which in fact, despite winning the Golden Lion, is a bit rhetorical and conventional, a reshaping of his previous works. Personally, I was very bored on set and I was happy when I had to go to Paris to look for repertory material to include in the film. I found the sequences I needed, including that of the bombing of Milan, in the Pathé archives, to which Truffaut introduced me.[135]

He added other details in a different interview:

With Rossellini I did *Il generale Della Rovere*, as assistant director on the set at Cinecittà. I must honestly say that I was very bored during the work. Rossellini brought the whole family, children and grandchildren, to the set. I then decided to deal only with the archival inserts. When I was in Paris for this job, I had help from Truffaut. The search took me to the various archives, to Pathé, etc.[136]

Searching the various archives for war footage led to his first feature film, and we shall get to that story in the next chapter.

Tinto's début appearance in a gossip column was probably on 8 September 1959, and to explain it, we need to know that Tinta was not only employed by her brother Arrigo Cipriani, the manager of Harry's Bar in Venice, she and Arrigo were the children of Giuseppe and Giulia (*née* Andolfi) Cipriani, who had opened Harry's Bar in 1931 as well as the Locanda Cipriani on the island of Torcello in 1934. The Locanda was a six-suite inn and restaurant, patronized by the likes of Charlie Chaplin, Winston Churchill, Ernest Hemingway, and various other celebrities as well as royalty. We discover something from an item entitled "Hollywood Today," syndicated by the North American Newspaper Alliance. The piece was by gossip columnist Sheilah Graham, who published a juicy little tidbit:

Roberto Rossellini and his beauty from India are staying at the Hotel Cipriani at Torcello as the guests of Tinto Brass, third assistant director of Roberto's acclaimed festival entry, "Il generale Della Rovere," which might take the grand prize in spite of the excellence of Otto Preminger's "Anatomy of a Murder."[137]

Next, Tinto was hired as an assistant director to Joris Ivens, who had been commissioned by Enrico Mattei to make a three-part television documentary entitled *L'Italia non è un Paese povero* (Italy Is Not a Poor Country). Ivens admired Mattei. Tinto, on the other hand, was not so sanguine, but that did not matter. He was an assistant, and he would assist, gladly. We may quote from Carlos Böker's thesis, *Joris Ivens, Film-Maker: Facing Reality*:

...Ivens was approached by Enrico Mattei, head of ENI, the Italian State Natural Gas Monopoly. Mattei, who died mysteriously in an air crash in 1962, and was the subject of a later film by Francesco Rosi (*Il caso Mattei*, The Mattei Affair, 1972), had been put in charge of ENI on the understanding that he would wind it up. However, he expanded its activities and investment programme against much internal political opposition and external opposition from the U.S.-controlled multinational oil firms. Ivens's films, collectively entitled *Italia non è un Paese povero*, were to be shown on television... By the time the film was finished, Mattei was in a weak political position, and RAI-TV refused to show the films as they were... From being three programmes each 45 minutes long, the film was cut down [by 25 minutes] and was shown, at Ivens's insistence, under the general description "Fragments of a film by Joris Ivens." He left the country secretly taking a complete copy with him, and this original version had its first showing at an Ivens retrospective in Modena in 1979.[138]

Böker was wrong. Ivens had left Italy before he realized what was happening to his film. Tinto was more blunt in describing the censorship:

In 1959 Enrico Mattei, then president of ENI, asked Ivens to make this documentary to convince Italians that raw materials were a reality in our country and to denounce the American influence in the field of hydrocarbon extraction and refining in Italy... The RAI officials, who, like any self-respecting television officials,

were afraid of everything and were real ass-kissers. They thought the film offered a slice of Italy that was too raw. Faithful to the adage that dirty laundry must be washed at home, they refused to air it in full. What bothered RAI's top management the most were certain passages that denounced the extreme poverty of the South, such as that of Ferrandina in Lucania, where the survival of as many as seven families depends on a single olive tree, or even individual images, such as that of a child's face full of flies. Nor did they like the argument against the "Seven Sisters," the major oil companies, and the whole philosophy behind the film, which was the same philosophy as Mattei's, according to which Italy "was not a poor country" and did not need American aid. Politicians and television, on the contrary, wanted to paint the nation as a country servile to the United States. That's why the documentary was cut in a brutal manner and was broadcast as "Fragments of a film by Joris Ivens."

The heavy censorship intervention sent Ivens into a rage. He asked me to steal the original copy of the film, the one he had edited and mixed himself. I obviously had access to the Moviola, so one night I stole it and took it to Paris. Now that more than forty years have passed and the statute of limitations has expired, I can proudly say that I stole a copy of *Italy Is Not a Poor Country*.[139]

Not a word about the theft was leaked until a screening of the full film at Cannes in 2000, which Tinto introduced in person.

With those experiences under his belt, Tinto had completed his apprenticeship. It was time to make his own kinds of movies, and that led to some of the strangest adventures in cinema history.

Source Notes:

2 Lorenzo Codelli, *Nerosubrass* (Udina and Rome: Dino Audino Editore, 1996), p. 22

3 Stefano Lorenzetto, "Siete peggio voi giornalisti che vendete il cervello," *Corriere della Sera*, circa March 2009, p. 106

4 John Charles, "Ted Rusoff, il mostro della Fono-Roma," *Video Watchdog*, #159, November/December 2010, p. 33

5 Stefano Cosma, "I Brass, l'arte raffinata di Italico e il cinema tutto sesso di Tinto," *Il Piccolo*, 5 January 2011

6 "Carlo Favetti," *Wikipedia.org*

7 Ranieri Mario Cossár, *Gorizia d' altri tempi* (Gorizia: Amministrazione Provinciale, 1934), pp. 248–249

8 Cosma, *Il Piccolo*

9 Alessandra Brass, "Biografia," in Maria Masau Dan, ed., *Italico Brass* (Gorizia: Electa, 6 July 1991), p. 128

10 Giuseppe M. Pilo, "Italico Brass, pittore europeo di Venezia," in Maria Masau Dan, ed., *Italico Brass*

11 (Gorizia: Electa, 6 July 1991), pp. 13–14 Lorenzetto, *Corriere della Sera*, p. 106

12 Mario Gagliardotto, *Obiettivo Brass* (Modena: Edizioni Il Fiorino, January 2005), p. 7

13 Alessandra Brass, *Italico Brass*, p. 128

14 Codelli, *Nerosubrass*, p. 22

15 Ibid.

16 Pilo, *Italico Brass*, p. 14

17 Ugo Nebbia, *Italico Brass: Commemorazione* (Castello di Gorizia, 3–17 August 1947), p. 1

18 Alessandra Brass, *Italico Brass*, p. 130

19 "Italico Brass," *Wikipedia.org*

20 Tinto Brass, "La serratura," in Gianfranco Micali, ed., *Di papa ce n'è uno solo* (Milano: Rusconi Libri, February 1994), p. 219

21 A letter he wrote to art historian Rodolfo Pallucchini on 2 December 1946 can be seen at "Lettera di Alessandro Brass a Rodolfo Pallucchini," *Università degli Studi di Udine, teche.uniud.it*

22 "Alessandro fu vicepodestà di Venezia," *Il Piccolo*, 5 January 2011

23 Sezione di Venezia dell'Associazione Nazionale fra Mutilati ed Invalidi di Guerra. Marco Donadon, *Per una dimensione imperial: Ca' Foscari e Venezia di fronte al colonialismo e imperialismo italiano (1848–1943)*, "Studia di Storia" 10 (Venice: Università Ca' Foscari Venezia, 2019), p. 119

24 Gagliardotto, *Obiettivo Brass*, p. 9

25 *Bolletino Associazione* "Primo Lanzoni? fra gli Antichi Studenti della R. Scuola Superiore di Commercio in Venezia, anno VI", June 1928, p. 33, *fc.cab.unipd.it*. Interestingly, Italico was friends with the American poet Ezra Pound, another fascist.

26 "Anno 1925," *Regatta storica Venezia del XIII sec. regatastoricavenezia.it*

27 "La nostra storia," *Bucintoro*, "Ivo Redolfi Tezzat annuncia il suo addio al remo. Lui e Giampaolo D'Este non vogheranno," *Il Gazzettino*, Thursday, 10 September 2015

28 Lorenzetto, *Corriere della Sera*, p. 104

29 At least one of his defenses still survives at the Archivio dell'Ateneo Veneto.

30 Marco Tiozzo Fasiolo, *Consensus for Mussolini? Popular Opinion in the Province of Venice (1922–1943)* (University of Birmingham Research Archive: 2017), p. 143

31 Renato Camurri, "L'ottocento e il novecento 2 – La societa veneziana: La classe politica Naztionalfascista," *Storia di Venezia* (Treccani, 2002), *treccani.it*

32 "Giovanni Marcello," *Wikipedia.org*

33 "Consiglieri nazionali della Camera dei fasci e delle corporazioni, Regno d'Italia XXX legislatura," *WikiZe*

34 R.J.B. Bosworth, *Italian Venice: A History*, (New Haven and London: Yale University Press, 2014), p. 151

35 Andrea Priante, "Venezia, Tinto Brass ei suoi fratelli: sentenza mette fine alla faida," *Corriere della Sera*, 29 November 2018

36 "Carla Épouse Brass," *Ancestry.com*

37 Codelli, *Nerosubrass*, p. 26

38 Brass, "La serratura," p. 218

39 Codelli, *Nerosubrass*, p. 23

40 Gagliardotto, *Obiettivo Brass*, p. 9

41 Lorenzetto, *Corriere della Sera*, p. 106

42 Brass, "La serratura," p. 218

43 Codelli, *Nerosubrass*, p. 21

44 Giulia Massari, "Playboy intervista: Tinto Brass: candida conversazione con il 'regista maledetto' del cinema italiano, dal sesso nazista di 'Salon Kitty' a quello storico di 'Caligola.' Ogni film una polemica," *Playboy* (Italian edition), Vol. 6, #3, p. 19

45 Gagliardotto, *Obiettivo Brass*, p. 7

46 Lorenzetto, *Corriere della Sera*, p. 106

47 Gagliardotto, *Obiettivo Brass*, p. 7

48 Brass: interviewed by Ranjit Sandhu, 3 April 2004, unpublished

49 Codelli, *Nerosubrass*, p. 23

50 Gagliardotto, *Obiettivo Brass*, p. 8

51 Codelli, *Nerosubrass*, p. 23

52 Gagliardotto, *Obiettivo Brass*, p. 8

53 Codelli, *Nerosubrass*, p. 23

54 Gagliardotto, *Obiettivo Brass*, p. 8

55 Massari, *Playboy* (Italian edition), p. 19

56 Codelli, *Nerosubrass*, p. 26

57 Lorenzetto, *Corriere della Sera*, p. 104

58 Codelli, *Nerosubrass*, p. 25

59 Gagliardotto, *Obiettivo Brass*, p. 7

60 Codelli, *Nerosubrass*, p. 23

61 Massari, *Playboy* (Italian edition), p. 19

62 Ibid.

63 Ibid.

64 Brass: 3 April 2004

65 Massari, *Playboy* (Italian edition), p. 20

66 Raffaele Panizza, "Sesso, sesso, sesso: tutto il resto è noia," *Panorama*, 28 August 2013

67 Ibid.

68 Nico B, "Tinto Brass: Maestro of Erotic Cinema," interview conducted 3 November 2001, Torcello (Los Angeles: Cult Epics, 2014)

69 Codelli, *Nerosubrass*, p. 32

70 Massari, *Playboy* (Italian edition), p. 20

71 Ibid.

72 Lorenzetto, *Corriere della Sera*, p. 104

73 Gagliardotto, *Obiettivo Brass*, p. 9

74 Brass, "La serratura," p. 217

75 Gagliardotto, *Obiettivo Brass*, p. 9

76 Brass, "La serratura," p. 217

77 *Federal Register*, Vol. 15, Part XI, Thursday, November 23, 1950, p. 8067

78 "Martyrdom of Saint Bartholomew," The Nelson-Atkins Museum of Art

79 "Young Lady in a Tricorn Hat," National Gallery of Art

80 "The Synagogue," Art Institute Chicago, *www.artic.edu*

81 "Lot 304: Giuseppe Bazzani," *Invaluable.com*; Paolo Bertelli, "La pala dello 'Schivenoglia' di Barbasso e alcune note sul collezionismo bazzaniano" (Università di Verona), p. 82, *iris.univr.it*

82 Codelli, *Nerosubrass*, p. 26

83 Brass, "La serratura," p. 219

84 Massari, *Playboy* (Italian edition), p. 22

85 Brass, "La serratura," p. 220

86 Gagliardotto, *Obiettivo Brass*, p. 9

87 Brass, "La serratura," p. 220

88 Codelli, *Nerosubrass*, pp. 25–26

89 Massari, *Playboy* (Italian edition), p. 22

90 Lorenzetto, *Corriere della Sera*, p. 104

91 Lorenzo Codelli, "Monellando," in Tinto Brass and Lorenzo Codelli, *Monella: la storia di un'iniziazione amorosa in un libro che raccoglie sceneggiatura e appunti di lavorazione del nuovo film di un maestro dell'eros* (Venice: Marsilio Editori, 1998), p. 31

92 Massari, *Playboy* (Italian edition), p. 22; Lorenzetto, *Corriere della Sera*, p. 104; Codelli, "Monellando," p. 29

93 Codelli, *Nerosubrass*, pp. 21, 26 Tinto thinks the year he started shooting 16mm might have been 1954.

94 Codelli, *Nerosubrass*, p. 27

95 Lina Coletti, "Il sesso parlante," *L'Europeo*, Vol. 32, #29, 16 July 1976, p. 57

96 Codelli, *Nerosubrass*, p. 27

97 Codelli, "Monellando," p. 31

98 98 Ligato, "Un'orgia (di cinema) a Parigi," *Oggi*, circa January 2002, p. 83

99 Ibid.

100 Codelli, *Nerosubrass*, p. 23

101 "Legge Merlin," *Wikipedia*

102 Gagliardotto, *Obiettivo Brass*, pp. 7–8

103 Codelli, *Nerosubrass*, back cover

104 Ligato, *Oggi*, p. 83

105 Codelli, *Nerosubrass*, p. 30

106 Coletti, *L'Europeo*, p. 57

107 Codelli, *Nerosubrass*, p. 30

108 Ligato, *Oggi*, p. 83

109 Ibid., p. 84

110 Gagliardotto, *Obiettivo Brass*, p. 10

111 Ligato, *Oggi*, p. 84

112 Codelli, *Nerosubrass*, p. 30.

113 Ligato, *Oggi*, p. 84

114 Ibid., p. 86; Chiara Nano, "Ma vie en rose... Tinto Brass/director," *TamTam Cinema*, 2 January 2002

115 Codelli, *Nerosubrass*, p. 27

116 Gagliardotto, *Obiettivo Brass*, p. 10

117 Nano, "Ma vie en rose... Tinto Brass/director," *TamTam Cinema*, 2 January 2002

118 Codelli, *Nerosubrass*, p. 28

119 Codelli, "Monellando," p. 30

120 Codelli, *Nerosubrass*, p. 28

121 Ligato, *Oggi*, p. 86

122 Ibid., p. 84

123 Codelli, *Nerosubrass*, p. 32

124 Dileep Padgaonkar tells the full story in *Under Her Spell: Roberto Rossellini in India* (New Delhi: Penguin Viking, 2008).

125 Ligato, *Oggi*, pp. 84, 86

126 Codelli, *Nerosubrass*, p. 28

127 Coletti, *L'Europeo*, p. 57

128 Brass: interviewed in Massimiliano Zanin, *Istintobrass* (2012)

129 "Introducing Tinto Brass," *Cinéma 66*, #103, February 1968, p. 10

130 Gagliardotto, *Obiettivo Brass*, p. 11

131 Nico B, "Tinto Brass: Maestro of Erotic Cinema," interview conducted 3 November 2001, Torcello (Los Angeles: Cult Epics, 2014).

132 Padgaonkar, *Under Her Spell*, p. 246

133 Codelli, *Nerosubrass*, p. 29

134 Codelli, "Monellando," p. 29

135 Gagliardotto, *Obiettivo Brass*, p. 12

136 Codelli, *Nerosubrass*, pp. 28–29

137 Sheilah Graham, "Hollywood Today" (wire story from the North American Newspaper Alliance), as published in the *Rockford* (Illinois) *Register-Republic*, Tuesday, 8 September 1959, p. 8

138 Carlos Böker, Joris Ivens, "Studies in Photography and Cinematography, No. 1," *Film-Maker: Facing Reality* (UMI Research Press, 1978)

139 Gagliardotto, *Obiettivo Brass*, p. 12

Instruction manual for the Paillard-Bolex H16 Reflex – Tinto's first 16mm film camera

LOSE
LOOSE

Tinto Brass shooting
Yankee, *1966*

THE FILMS OF TINTO BRASS

PART ONE

THE AVANT-GARDE

Publicity photo:
Sady Rebbot and
Pascale Audret, 1963

I

Who Works is Lost

(*Chi lavora è perduto* AKA *In capo al mondo*)

TINTO BRASS' FIRST FEATURE FILM was easily one of his finest and most enjoyable works, probably his cheapest work, and it was made almost by accident.

There was an unpreventable delay on a different film. Someone on the crew suggested, "Why not make another movie in the meantime?" Tinto broached the idea to his producer, the Greek-Italian Moris Ergas, who agreed to fund two weeks of shooting. If he liked what he saw, he would pay for the rest. That was almost unbelievably casual, but in 1963 some Italian producers were apparently rather casual. Tinto reminisced, "The film... originates from long nights spent chatting with my closest friends, including Kim [Arcalli]. Gianni Scarabello was my classmate and, although he does not appear in the opening credits of the film, he was a true collaborator."

One might be forgiven for guessing that a new filmmaker would have dreamt of becoming the next John Ford or the next Howard Hawks. Tinto Brass had no such ambitions. He took inspiration instead from Roland Barthes' *Mythologies*, from avant-garde films of years past, from the recent underground films emanating from the United States, and, above all, from the brand-new works of the *Nouvelle Vague* filmmakers he had befriended at the Cinémathèque Française. His favorite of those *Nouvelle Vague* filmmakers was Jean-Luc Godard, and Tinto's first feature film would borrow more than a little bit from Godard's latest film, *Vivre sa vie*. He borrowed its lead actor, Sady Rebbot, its billboard, and even some of its footage. The result was a film that nobody predicted, a film that some critics praised effusively, going so far as to call it the standout of the 1963 Venice Film Festival. Other critics, though, were not enthusiastic.

While in Yugoslavia on business, Tinto quickly dashed off a first-draft scenario and phoned his friend, Franco "Kim" Arcalli, to come on over to Yugoslavia to assist. Arcalli fleshed out the story and polished it. Back in Venice, they shot for two weeks. Ergas liked what he saw and told them to continue.

The resulting film was ingenious, refreshing, vibrant, confusing, and troubling. It was also painfully cheap, about IT£45,000,000,[140] the equivalent of about US$72,500 at the time. Such a minimal budget would not allow for known stars, nor would it allow for sets. The film had to be made on natural locations and it needed to employ unknowns and nonprofessionals. Tinto thrived under those restrictions and he continued to adopt them, even when he did not need to, for the next two decades.

How to save on money? How to save on extras? The answer was remarkably simple: Shoot it with hidden cameras, with the actors placed in actual crowds. Another cost-saving strategy was not to bother with the acting. Much of the film would be told in voice-overs as characters merely walked hither and thither through Venice. The voice-overs would be penned afterwards.

Also to save money, Piero Piccioni was not hired to score the completed film. Instead, he wrote a dozen tunes that he thought would fit the mood of the various scenes, and handed them to Tinto to do as he wished with them.

Cheery, bouncy music accompanies aerial shots of Venice, and we get the idea that we are in for an upbeat light comedy. We are not prepared for what is to come. Once the story proper gets going, we see that it can be expressed in a single sentence: A 27-year-old of mediocre skill does not want to accept a job offer. That's it. That's the whole story. The movie is not about the story. The movie is layer upon layer of reflection, for we see that the characters in the story all have variations on the same flaw. As we watch, we can hardly help but ponder: What does a young child feel about a family's dogmatic adherence to fascism? What does a nonconformist feel about military indoctrination? What does a creative person feel about corporate bureaucracy? What does a cosmopolitan feel about Italian nationalism? The questions continue, for the protagonist of the story, initially appealing, wins our sympathy, but then little by little he reveals himself to be a wastrel. By the time we witness his infantile tantrums and his horrid treatment of his enchanting girlfriend, we lose our ability to judge him. How are we to judge any character in the film? How are we to judge anyone at all? It is those questions that the film refuses to answer, except to suggest that there are no set answers.

Bonifacio B. runs along a seemingly endless canal walkway on his way to a job interview at a firm called AG, Assicurazioni Generali. The job interview is not what we would now consider a job interview. Instead, it is a psychiatric evaluation. It is not what we would now consider a psychiatric evaluation. It is what we now would consider harassment. The unseen psychoanalyst, who does not deserve his license, shoots off his rapid-fire questions at double-speed (an idea borrowed from a 1947 Dadaist film called *Dreams That Money Can Buy*). Before Bonifacio has time to open his mouth to answer one question, he is already being assaulted by the next and then the next. "Did you come for the interview? You're Bonifacio B. Draftsman? Please have a seat. Tell me, are you ever afraid of failing? Are you ever embarrassed because others are watching you? Do you mind being disturbed while working? Will you end up in hell? Do you ever have red marks all over your body? Is the sex act disgusting? Do you like women who have strong personalities? Do you ever hear strange voices? Tell me if you agree or disagree with the following statements. Prostitution ought to be controlled by the state. Modern art ought not to be allowed in churches. Women are more to blame for extramarital affairs than men. Foreigners are filthier than Italians. It's hard to sing the national anthem properly. Tell me immediately, what rhymes with progress? Now, what rhymes with money? Which newspapers do you read? Do you have friends? From what social circle? Do you fit in with your parents? Are you married? Did you serve in the military? Do you have debts? Do you like to drink?"

No self-respecting person would respond to such impertinent questions. No self-respecting person would agree to work for a firm that required such an interrogation. The impression that the film gives us is that all office jobs in the Italy of 1963 required such an examination of all applicants, and that all Italians have submitted themselves to such humiliating exercises. The interview is demoralizing, and one can understand instantly why Bonifacio is such a defeatist.

The problem is that Bonifacio would be a defeatist anyway. There is clearly something wrong with him. He is frequently insouciant, which is a plus. He has a sense of irony, which is good. He seems intelligent. He is witty, certainly. He has a habit of coming up with amusing rhymes. Yet he is also depressive and he has no idea how to deal with others, he has no understanding of other people's emotions, and he certainly does not know how to deal with the females of the species.

We watch Bonifacio over the course of a single day, morning to afternoon, as he wanders about, lost in his thoughts. (To give him the proper accent, Venetian actor Tonino Micheluzzi dubbed his lines.) His thoughts, though, span his entire 27-year life so far, and, impressionistically, in a momentary recollection, a momentary fantasy, a momentary reminder, we are given all the ingredients of his biography. His father, more than old enough to be his grandfather, was forever threatening, but little Bonifacio could only be amused by the antics. Daddy is a proud fascist, as are all his family. Bonifacio thinks of his relatives as no better than dead. There was his unfortunate stint as a young altar boy, endlessly groped by a desperate father confessor. There is the group of would-be revolutionaries with whom he hangs around for no particular reason. They speak only nonsense and achieve nothing. Their purposeless conversation reminds him of his days in the military, with clearly deranged superiors whom he comically imagines as inept soldiers of the Roman empire. The first rule his platoon is taught is that they are no longer men, that they must destroy their identities in order to become soldiers. Laughter is forbidden.

Back from his reveries, he visits a gallery to see what the latest artists are up to, and that reminds him of what he has been taught by the authorities, namely, that only Italians create true art. Yet he sees instead that the Abstract Expressionist works on display are designed to move nobody's emotions. One particularly ugly glob of metal catches his attention, and a pretty young woman starts talking to him. She posed, she says, as the model for that shapeless mass, and her sister posed for the one next to it.

In a mere few moments of flashbacks, the story of his romance with Gabriella is told succinctly. Before they knew what had happened, she was pregnant, and neither is emotionally prepared. They agree to visit an abortionist in Geneva, but the doctors have all vanished. As their funds shrink almost to zero, they discover that Gabriella needs to be examined by a psychiatrist before she can receive state permission for an abortion. This psychiatrist, as the one at the beginning of the film, is never shown. Only his impatient voice is heard as he interrogates her disastrously, brutally. "You say that you're pregnant by your boyfriend? So why do you want to get rid of your baby? There's no reason. You know, I need a precise reason in order to give you an abortion certificate, as per Article 120 of the Swiss penal code. So, tell me, why? Why can't you keep it? Who is preventing you from keeping it? Well, lady, will you tell me the truth? Yes or no: Do you love your boyfriend or don't you? Come on, make up your mind. Ah. See? That's a precise reason. So that's why you don't want to keep the baby? Go ahead. Tell me. Why isn't that the reason? Come on, make up your mind once and for all. So, tell me why."

Running from the psychiatrist's office in tears, she seeks comfort from Bonifacio, who is even harsher than the psychiatrist. Jumping to the next scene, Gabriella has learned that the procedure is a game, and the game is simple: She must explain to the psychiatrist that she is mentally and emotionally unstable, that if she were to give birth, her behavior would put both the child and herself in grave physical danger. That does the trick. She hands Bonifacio the certificate that the doctor has just provided. Bonifacio reads it aloud and goes into a rage at all the lies it contains. Bonifacio grows ice-cold toward her, and her attempts to rekindle the romance, or at least to re-establish a rapport, are met with harsh derision and yet more screaming tantrums, as Bonifacio chases away the finest person he has ever met. Gabriella's only real fault was in being foolish enough to have fallen for Bonifacio.

Throughout the day, Bonifacio continues to debate with himself: Should he take the job or should he not? His wording, "Shall I work, or shall I not work?" seems to us to be his shorthand for taking this particular job. Soon it becomes clear that this is not shorthand at all. He simply never wants to do any sort of work. How he could possibly support himself without engaging in any form of work is a question he never asks or answers, except to fantasize about becoming a celebrity or a gloriously infamous criminal.

Halfway into the movie he visits his old friend Kim, who is portrayed by Kim, namely Franco "Kim" Arcalli, one of Tinto's friends who, at the time, was still an unknown. In a flashback, we see Kim at age 16, in the resistance and beaten by the Nazis. After the war he becomes a political activist, routinely facing violent police attacks. His mind soon enough snaps. He is now incarcerated in a lunatic asylum, where he is a model inmate most of the time, but prone to periodic screaming rants. We get to see one, and it is a terrifying thing to behold. His performance is the highlight of the film, a powerhouse example of acting.

The movie Kim corresponds to the real-life Kim, who had lost his father at age 15 to a Nazi attack. The real-life Kim had worked on only one film previously, appearing in an uncredited moment in Luchino Visconti's *Senso* as a soldier. It was Tinto who realized he would be the person to help script this film and to play a variation of himself. His work was outstanding and instantly won him a career as writer and editor.

Another notable but brief appearance is by Tino Buazzelli as Claudio, dubbed by Tinto himself in order

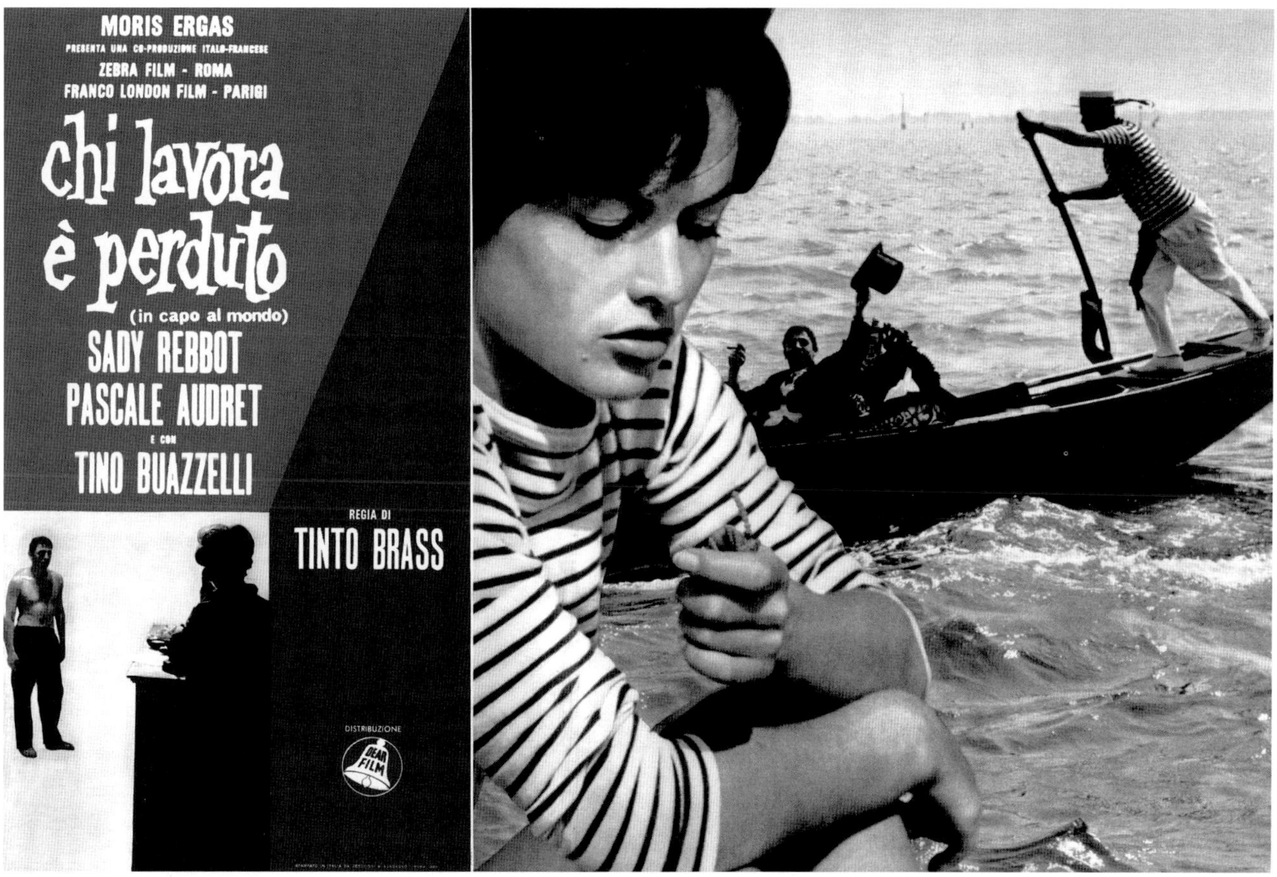

Italian Fotobusta poster, 1963

Italian Fotobusta poster, 1963

to give the character a Venetian accent. Who precisely is Claudio? A hunting buddy, not close but cordial, and we witness what will surely be one of their final chats, as Claudio is quite obviously losing patience with Bonifacio. Claudio himself went through what Bonifacio went through, and the corporate psychiatrist rejected him as schizophrenic. Still unemployed, he'll try for a job whenever he can. Claudio, devoted Communist, has spent some time in Russia and loved the place. "Either you put your faith in it or you shoot yourself," he gleefully explains. Bonifacio declares that the job at AG is not for him, that he would be considered interchangeable with any other employee, he would not be seen as having his own unique set of talents. Claudio mocks the thought and walks away with the excuse that his manager is calling him back to work. He gives Bonifacio advice: "In Russia, they say to people like you: March, get to work!"

Remembering the time his parents happened to return when he had three prostitutes in the parlor (a scene from Tinto's own life), he fantasizes about opening his own brothel, or robbing banks, or forging, or becoming a celebrated sportsman, or about going to work for AG after all, or getting a special dispensation from Christ who allows him never to work. It's all for naught. When he remembers the legend above the gate at Auschwitz, ARBEIT MACHT FREI (Work Makes You Free), he stops thinking, and the film abruptly stops, having resolved nothing.

The film, which has many points to make, pretends to have none. Because the film never spells out any conclusion, it is not easy for an audience simply to get up at the close of curtain and put it out of mind. The film leaves one a bit puzzled, tantalized, and desirous of making sense out of what was just experienced on the screen.

Presenting us with appealing characters, it turns them inside out and reveals them as empty. Presenting a work of fiction, it reveals instead actual candid glimpses of real people going about their real lives in a real Venice, and the sense of immediacy is stunning; it is almost as though we are there, too, in that time, or it seems as if we are actually remembering having been there. The film concentrates on smaller-than-life characters exclusively, but surprisingly it is not at all negative. It's life-affirming, and it achieves that result by means of a trick: Tinto and his cowriters agreed that those who have small, petty lives of no seeming importance can have great potential. If Gabriella were to think a little bit, she could associate with finer people and really make something of herself.If Bonifacio were simply to decide to put his comical musings to use, he could easily become influential. If Claudio were not so brainwashed by Soviet Communism, he could be a force for good. If Kim were to distance himself from his problems, he could make sweeping changes across Italy and beyond. None of this is spoken or explained, but it becomes evident upon some reflection, and that is a large part of what Tinto was trying to express—if not to us, then at least to himself. Also evident in this movie is the problem of intimacy, for there is none. The main characters are all warm, but they draw the line at any emotional communion, as though their greatest fear is love. That is their principal tragedy. Deeply influenced by Wilhelm Reich's books, Tinto put the theme of the fear of love in nearly every film he ever made.

There is no condemnation of these individuals. They can hardly help themselves. There is condemnation, though, in the structure of the society that molds people in this way. In all the endless images of real life, there is not a single glimpse of people basking in one another's warmth. There is not a single moment of a mother entirely lost in enchantment, looking into her child's eyes. Everyone we see is, or at least tries to be, a bit reserved or even cold.

The movie opens with a mockery of AG. Did Tinto have a bad experience with that company? Or did he just choose it at random as an exemplar of Italian firms? He probably expected some resistance from AG. Perhaps he was hoping for it, thinking he might be able to get some publicity out of the conflict. What Tinto surely did not expect was the hostility the film received from official quarters. Tinto showed Bonifacio's family in a bad light. He showed a schoolteacher in a bad light. He showed the church in a bad light. He showed military training in a bad light. He showed psychiatrists in a bad light. He showed the law in a bad light. He showed office jobs in a bad light. Broad-minded people would not bat an eye at any of this, but would chuckle in recognition and nod their heads in agreement. The Italian government officials of September 1963, though, were not in any way broad-minded. They took grave offense and banned the film in its entirety. In attempting to build a case against the film, the officials noted that Bonifacio's objection to work was a violation of Article 1 of the Italian Constitution, which stated that Italy was a country based upon labor. At the hearings, the censors demanded that Tinto change the film and resubmit with a new title, as part of the procedure. Tinto had played around with two titles, *Who Works is Lost* (Chi lavora é perduto) and *To the Ends of the Earth* (In Capo al mondo). By the time he began rolling the camera, he decided upon the latter title. So Tinto changed it back to *Who Works is Lost.*

Just three months later, after elections, a new government was in office and it agreed to allow the film, even though the ban could not legally be appealed. On the pretext that the new title made it a new film, the new officials gave it the go-ahead. Only a few prints were made and the film had only a handful of bookings. Those bookings, though, turned a small profit in a mere few weeks,[141] and that small profit made Tinto a viable filmmaker. The primary funding had come from a French production company called Franco-London Film. Unfortunately, Moris Ergas got into a row with the owner of Franco-London, and so the film was never shown in France, nor was it exported to any other country at all.

Had the film been widely shown, it could have earned significant revenue. Had it been exported, it would surely have become a favorite. Had it been released to the art houses in the United States, it almost certainly would have become a staple of repertory programming. After all, two of the film's champions were Luchino Visconti and Roberto Rossellini! That was more than sufficient cachet to attract an international audience. Instead, the film was shown only in a few Italian venues, briefly, and was not seen again until it was broadcast on Italian television in the year 2000.

The film caused a few other problems, as well. Tinto's father Alessandro was in the audience at the world première at the September 1963 Venice Film Festival, and he saw that Bonifacio's father lashed out with a threat: "I'll bend you like a wire!" That was precisely the threat that he himself had routinely used. It didn't help that, in the cemetery scene, Tinto had Bonifacio mock an inscription on a tombstone: "Blackshirt of Christmas Eve." Tinto recalled:

> **...a serious and unfortunate misunderstanding arose between us because of the film. In a certain scene set in a cemetery, I had filmed the tombstone of a fascist, whose inscription—"Blackshirt of Christmas Eve"—had made me smile. In fact, in the film, the protagonist Bonifacio sneeringly comments on it. Well, that inscription had been dictated by my father. I didn't know that, of course, but he unfortunately convinced himself that I had done it on purpose.**[142]

The film gave Tinto a good reputation as a solid and responsible filmmaker. Nothing could stop him now and within the next two years four more films would emerge.

Source Notes:

140 "Introducing Tinto Brass," *Cinéma 66* #103, February 1968, p. 10

141 Ibid.

142 Mario Gagliardotto, *Obiettivo Brass: Il cinema secondo Tinto Brass* (Modena: Edizioni Il Fiorino, January 2005), pp. 15–16

II

Ça ira, the River of Revolt

(Ça ira, il fiume della rivolta AKA *Thermidor)*

THIS WAS, UNDOUBTEDLY, the strongest film that Tinto Brass made so far—and also the most perplexing.

When working at the Cinémathèque Française, searching for World War II footage for inclusion in Roberto Rossellini's *Il Generale Della Rovere*, Tinto found a mass of war footage on file, hundreds of hours' worth. His friend, François Truffaut, took him to Pathé to show him even more. Realizing that he could fashion this material into a feature film, Tinto asked Rossellini's producer, Moris Ergas, if he would wish to fund such a project. Indeed! Tinto began the work of sifting through the materials in 1962, and his goal, at first, was to put forth the Communist point of view. He admitted as much a few years later, saying it was definitely a Leftist work.[143] Yet, just one sentence before, he explained, "It is an open film that does not pretend to convey a message." That is a bizarre statement, since the film most definitely does contain a message, the strongest of his career, and the message is blatant. Three decades later, he had yet another interpretation: "It was an anarchist film. It made no reference to any political or party alignment."[144] If one keeps in mind those three contradictory statements while watching the film and being attentive to its biases, one realizes the cause of the dissonance: The creation of this film did much to destroy Tinto's faith in the Left.

Though the Cinémathèque Française and Pathé had what were probably the world's largest collections of war footage, there were critical gaps, and Tinto needed to collect more. "The material came from Ireland, Poland, America. The search and retrieval of the images was not an easy thing. Times were very long, especially for those countries with which Italy had no diplomatic ties, especially for Eastern European countries. It was necessary to deal with Yugoslavia and have all the required materials sent to them."

Though the visuals were controlled, the narration nonetheless occasionally hinted at Leftist atrocities as well. In order not to play politics, Tinto employed another trick, and that was to illustrate that the horrors are the responsibility not of the never-mentioned Left/Right divide, but of the Up/Down divide. No matter who is in charge, no matter the ideals, if any, it is those at the Bottom who suffer. The argument is less political than social; it is an indictment of civilization as inherently violent and immoral. Further to make this point, Tinto inserts popular songs, notably Edmonda Aldini singing "La ninna-nanna della guerra" and Marcel Mouloudji singing "Le déserteur."

**Sleep my little one, and I will sleep,
and then we will not see
all the evil and the violence
that is sweeping across our world.**

**Sharp cold bayonets on rifles,
which civilized people stick
into their choking victims
at the whim of their mad leaders.**

**Those who choke and those who kill
have sold out on their rich past.
They profit from a blind faith
in a god whom no one sees.**

**You men with great names!
This is a letter
to you which maybe you will read,
If you can spare the time.**

**I do not wish to offend you,
but I must tell you
your wars are criminal
and the world has had enough.**

**Since I was born
I have seen brothers die,
I have seen fathers leave,
I have seen children cry —
and I have seen the prisoners.**

**You have taken away their souls,
you have taken away their women,
you have taken away their birthright.**

Italian Fotobusta poster, 1964

The sarcastic narration and the race through countless film clips give us fleeting, often terrifying glimpses of the opening of the First World War, the Bolshevik Revolution, the Boer War, the Boxer Rebellion, the Italian invasion of Libya, the Mexican Revolution, the Irish Revolution, the Versailles Treaty, Italy under Mussolini, the Ku Klux Klan, Prohibition's Gangsters, and the New Deal in the USA, Hitler's Nazis, Gandhi's Salt March, the Shanghai Strike, Chiang Kai-shek and Mao Tse-tung, the bombing of Shanghai, the anti-war League of Nations that could not keep the peace, Franco's Spain, the Warsaw Ghetto, the Nazi death camps, Hiroshima, the Hungarian Uprising, Lumumba in the Congo, Batista and Castro in Cuba, the Mau Mau Rebellion, and Marilyn Monroe singing for the troops in Korea. The research was credited to Carla Cipriani, otherwise known as Tinta Brass, Tinto's wife. The famous Italian author Giancarlo Fusco wrote the commentary, which was narrated by three famous Italian actors, and Brass delivered the completed film in 1962, only to see it sit on the shelf for two years.

Cinematically, the film is stunning. Tinto had obviously been studying the works of the underground filmmakers, notably Bruce Conner, who in turn had been following the techniques of Abel Gance and Sergei Eisenstein. Tinto even included excerpts from Eisenstein's *Strike* and *October* amidst newsreel footage, and the fiction is hardly distinguishable from the reality. *All Quiet on the Western Front* is also excerpted, as are numerous other studio films that only experts would be able to identify. One that is easy for us to recognize is a momentary snippet from *Who Works is Lost*. Tinto further used stream of consciousness, including Étienne-Jules Marey's motion studies, scientific films of slow motion, and various novelty acts, which tie in with the narration not thematically, but emotionally. To reduce the horror of the atrocity footage, Tinto inserted distractions, such as countdown leaders and various unrelated images, for the scenes would otherwise be unendurable. After an hour of brutality, there is comic relief as Bess Truman repeatedly attempts to christen a 1942 bomber, only to succeed in denting the nose of the airplane.

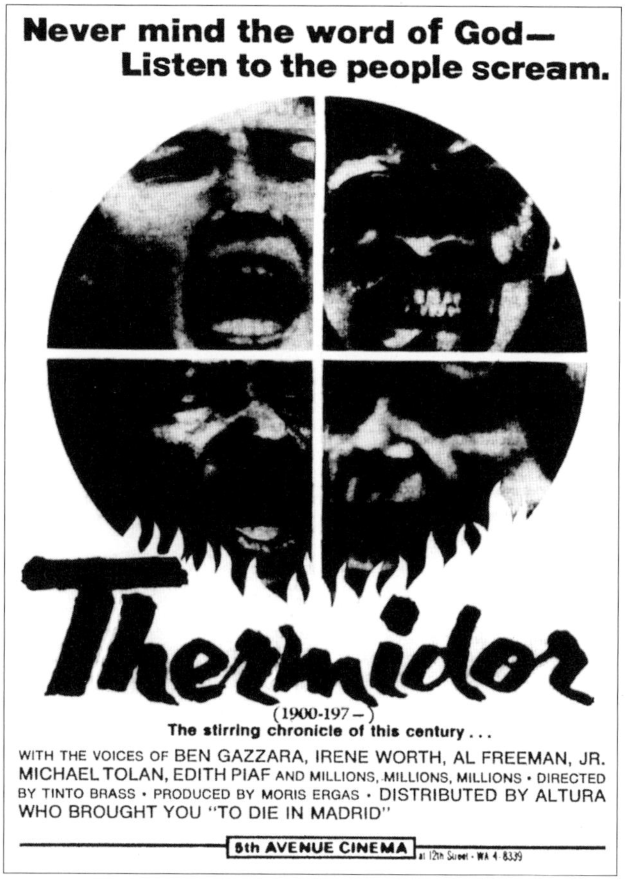

U.S. newspaper clipping for **Thermidor**, *1971*

The film makes an impression, but, alas, the impression was not the same for all viewers. *Ça ira* had its world première at the Venice Film Festival, out of competition, on Sunday, 6 September 1964. Richard Roud invited the film to have its U.S. première on Saturday, 26 September, at the New York Film Festival, but never arrived, for some reason or another.

Among other problems, *Ça ira* was not shown until after Tinto's contract with Moris Ergas' Zebra Film had lapsed, and it got only a minor release to a handful of Italian cinemas. Clem Perry of Altura Films licensed the film for the U.S., retitled it *Thermidor*,[145] and hired Ben Gazzara, Michael Tolan, Irene Worth, and Al Freeman, Jr., to record the narration in English. The American version was nearly identical to the Italian version, though there were a few minuscule trims and alterations. It played for all of one week on one screen in August 1971 and then vanished. Some critics dismissed the narration as glib and simplistic. Others dismissed the film as failed polemics. A few praised it as a worthy documentary. Roger Greenspun in *The New York Times* gave the new version of the film a mixed review:

> ...[O]ne can see how the Italian Government might feel diffident about yet another starring role for the country's modern history...
>
> ...[T]he interminable scenes of political execution, hangings and shootings... seem almost a fetish with the film—though they are meant to be, and, God knows, are, an indictment of the age.
>
> There is some unusual footage in *Thermidor*, and much of it, for example with Mao Tse tung in China in the thirties, is well worth seeing. But the best sequences are those that have an emotional logic of their own—the Loyalist campaigns in the Spanish Civil War, the liberating of the extermination camps after World War II—and these are few and far between...

Jerry Parker in *Newsday*:

> ...Nearly all of the film is interesting, some of it extraordinary. Some of it, obviously, is ghastly. A woman near me sobbed heavily as footage of Nazi concentration camps and the Warsaw ghetto was shown... *Thermidor* is more a newsreel than it is a feature film, and perhaps as much pacifist propaganda as history. But, for anyone a little vague about our recent past, it affords an excellent short course. Though it does nothing about telling us the way we are headed, nor offer much hope, it does a little to illuminate the dismal way we've come.

No critic caught the point of Tinto's exercise, which was to have us all rethink the assumptions of civilization, to rethink our ideas of political hierarchy. The film explains, embedding its effects in all of us, epigenetically. We now have the tools to create a peaceful future, and the film ends by calling us to take heed. A 16mm print was prepared for educational use, but it seems never to have been booked and is untraceable. The U.S. version has never been seen since, and one can only hope that it still survives somewhere. The Italian edition occasionally pops up on Italian television, but when it is shown, it is without fanfare.

Source Notes:

143 "Introducing Tinto Brass," *Cinéma 66* #103, February 1968, p. 10

144 Lorenzo Codelli, ed., *Nerosubrass* (Udine: Dino Audino Editore, 1996), p. 30

145 Perry at first had in mind *Tell It Like It Is* as the title, but reconsidered.

III

Work Time / Free Time

(*Tempo lavorativo / Tempo libero*)

WHO WORKS IS LOST made an impression on famed semiotician and novelist Umberto Eco, who, in 1964, was president of the Milan Triennial XIII. He commissioned Tinto Brass to create a film for the Triennial's Trade Fair, but he offered no suggestions, leaving the young filmmaker free to create anything he thought appropriate. Since Tinto had masses of unused footage left over from *Ça ira*, he decided to avail himself of that material. He gathered mostly images of people at work and people at play. He cut the images into short lengths of between two and six frames and intercut them, but, as ever, he was careful not to make a mere cut-up mess. There had to be an order and a progression.

We start with a line-up of people on a ramp, then a line-up of cars in a lot, an illuminated stick figure seeming to direct traffic, sheafs of paper emerging from a press, people leaving a building, a worker operating some sort of oven, traffic on a highway. The images continue relentlessly, about ten every seconds, constantly intercut, and when one image is abandoned, it is replaced by a new one. The general sense of directionality is more or less constant. Cars coming toward the camera are intercut with people coming toward the camera, both intercut with sheafs of paper coming toward the camera. These are intercut, though, with items moving in a different direction, and soon those are intercut with other images moving in that general direction. Images are also intercut with themselves, but upside down or flopped. Whether at work or at play, the varieties of activity are so numerous that it all soon looks like madness, and, indeed, both films, eight minutes each, end with WWII stock footage of German mental patients. Tinto's thought, consistent with his two recent features, was to show that freedom to work, freedom to play, do not in and of themselves amount to freedom at all. What should be constructive, what should be intimate, is reduced to mindless ritual. Those in the audience who could digest the onslaught of images would likely ponder that idea. Those in the audience who merely saw an onslaught of unconnected images would likely not recognize any idea behind the jumble.

The project, obviously, was time-consuming. There are about ten splices each second. The films run about 500 seconds each, and that's about 5,000 splices each. The progression had to be orderly and organized. Furthermore, the two films would comment upon each other, and so any particular moment in one film would need to correspond with that same moment in the other film. Tinto was so occupied with his work that he broke into the locked editing studio on a Sunday by climbing through a window. There was no other way to get his work finished in time.

Once he completed assembling the images, there came the question of what to do about the sound. He chose Stravinsky's *Ebony Concerto*, but ran it at double speed and overlaid it with so many other bits of music that it became almost entirely unrecognizable. On top of that cacophony, he overlaid numerous sound effects at half-speed. Five and a half minutes into each eight-minute film, he cross-faded from Stravinsky into Chubby Checker's "The Fly" and "The Twist," one after the other, at triple speed, distorted, and still overlaid with innumerable other noises.

The concept behind these two little films is not so simplistic as a verbal description would make it seem. Tinto is fascinated by people, fascinated by their activities, and, furthermore, he loves Stravinsky and Chubby Checker. He is not criticizing another group from afar; he is musing upon his own group, from within.

Those who are familiar with the works of Bruce Conner will recognize one of Tinto's inspirations. Conner had been deeply impressed by a Marx Brothers film called *Duck Soup*, in which, during a military battle, there is a call for volunteers. We then see the volunteers rushing to join. The volunteers are all from stock footage: rowboat racers, swimmers, monkeys, elephants, dolphins. Conner was mesmerized and decided to make his own films, consisting entirely of stock footage, cut together to create impressions never intended by the original filmmakers.

That is precisely the idea that Tinto had used in *Ça ira*, and he took it further in this pair of films.

How the films were presented remains a slight mystery. One story is that each was shown on continuous loop, each inside a pyramid that was lined inside with mirrors on all sides. The audience walked through the pyramid, bombarded by images from every direction, and, upon exiting, entered a second pyramid to witness the companion film. Another story is that the two films were ganged together in synchronization, shown side by side inside a single pyramid.

Who Works is Lost, Ça ira, Work Time, and Free Time are the works of youth, the works of one particular youth who was given the freedom to make what he chose, in a manner that was intended to please only himself. In this experimental work, images of death were intercut with eros, featuring footage of Marilyn Monroe, a year after her death, something we can see that Tinto would soon explore further in his future work.

Projections inside the Milan Triennial XIII

IV
The Flying Saucer
(Il disco volante)

IN 1964, TINTO BRASS RECEIVED a job offer from prominent Italian producer Dino De Laurentiis, who had a script by one of the finest Italian scenarists, Rodolfo Sonego, creator of a series of popular comedies with the popular actor/singer Alberto Sordi. They made over 50 together, all told, through the years.

This was not Tinto's story idea and it was not his script, but Sonego's script was remarkably compatible with Tinto's style. The idea of hapless visitors from other planets visiting our Earth was rather in vogue, and we can hazard a guess that Sonego had been inspired by Gore Vidal's *Visit to a Small Planet* as well as by Ennio Flaiano's short story "A Martian in Rome."

De Laurentiis had proposed the script to numerous directors, all of whom turned it down. Tinto said he would accept on one condition: Alberto Sordi must play all four of the lead rôles. De Laurentiis agreed[146] and Sordi was excited by the prospect.

Though Tinto could have shot the film in a normal way, with a cast of trained professionals, he chose instead to continue his habit from *Who Works is Lost*. He said he would shoot the film 370 miles away from the studio, in the countryside near Asolo. De Laurentiis had a fit, shouting, "What? In the country? But that's disgusting!" He demanded that the film be shot in a village near the studio, but Tinto, who had spent some of his youth in Asolo, recognized that it was the perfect location. De Laurentiis' wife, the famous actress Silvana Mangano, who was to appear in the film, stood by her director. "Tinto says we have to go to Asolo, and we will go to Asolo."[147] Alberto Sordi agreed entirely.[148] Had it not been for the support of the two legendary actors, Tinto would never have won his argument. Another notable actress appearing is Monica Vitti, who was Michelangelo Antonioni's muse in *Red Desert* and *L'Eclisse* prior to this film.

Tinto shot on natural locations almost exclusively. He employed unknown extras, many of whom were actual townsfolk with no acting experience. He shot at a real carnival and stole shots of actual festivities. Further, the more the story stretched credulity, the more realistically he staged the scenes and composed the shots. The result, truly, is an original comedy.

The story idea behind *The Flying Saucer* is only nominally science fiction. It opens with a hilarious parody of newsreels; locals in the farmlands talk of seeing flying saucers land in their fields, but their stories are disbelieved. A police sergeant is tasked with investigating why people are talking, and he discovers physical evidence and even apprehends a Martian lady, who escapes back into her spaceship. The plot is not the essence, though, for the movie is a parable about conformity and political control. A peasant woman captures a Martian and gains riches when she sells her prey to the local Count, and then loses all her riches just minutes later when the Count's mother has her servants dispose of the creature in a well and calls the police to retrieve her family's belongings. A delusional woman, under daily medical care and subject to the most elaborate fantasies, turns out to be telling the truth about the Martian lover who arrives for a nightly rendezvous. The local telegrapher, a failed poet and novelist, is zapped one night by a flying saucer, but, unable to provide proof of what he endured, is imprisoned in a lunatic asylum and forced to undergo electroshock therapy. The priest one night sees an entire troupe of Martians wandering the street, but they all vanish before his eyes. He is stone drunk at the time, and his bishop sends him away for rehabilitation. In the end, the Martians are no match for the ineptitude of the Earthlings, and they ultimately accomplish nothing.

The intricate interweaving of characters, story, and dialogue is ingenious, a credit to Sonego, and if you miss so much as a moment of the film you will lose all sense of what is happening. Every line of dialogue builds upon everything that has come before, and so there is topper after topper after topper. The comedy is influenced, it would seem, by Buster Keaton, for the actors all play it straight. There is no comical mugging or clowning around at all. The more serious the actors are, the more hilarious the story becomes.

While shooting, Tinto came up with some extra lines of dialogue and ran them by Sonego for his reactions.

Sonego refused to respond, and so Tinto added the lines anyway. They were little things, such as the telegrapher griping about how Moravia and Pasolini monopolize Italian literature. There is also the moment when Dolores, the mayor's wife, sneaking away for a tryst with the telegrapher, demands that he call her his little pig. When Sonego discovered that Tinto had thus embellished his script, he grew resentful and expressed only disappointment with the film.

De Laurentiis did not trust Tinto with the editing, because, as Tinto confesses, "De Laurentiis feared some of my narrative freedoms. I had a different language, much more edgy." He assigned Tatiana Casini Morigi to edit the film, and she did a fine job, but there are some quite obvious errors and oversights in it, as she did not understand Tinto's camerawork or intended intercutting.

Alberto Sordi claimed that while Tinto was "a genius," he was also "a little bit crazy." He regretted that the film had not been shot in a standard style in a studio, and said that was the reason for the film's relatively poor box-office returns.

What the box-office returns were, we do not know. How the costs and expenses and distribution playdates and ticket sales compared to other Sonego/Sordi collaborations, we do not know. The data are not available. We do know that the film was rushed so that it would be available for a Christmas release. We do know that the film made a profit—enough of a profit that it would be issued again the following year.

Variety reported that the trade screening at the Venice Festival was 93 minutes. By the time the film reached the cinemas, it had been censored to 91 minutes. The footage that was deemed offensive would not even raise an eyebrow today. Shortened was the brief sequence of the telegrapher wooing the mayor's wife by reciting "George Gray" from Edgar Lee Masters' *Spoon River Anthology*. The scene of the same two in the car at night was also trimmed. The lesbian couple glimpsed at the Countess' party was eliminated. The Martian carrying the Count in his arms was deleted. The image of a ballerina kissing the brigadier was shortened, because for a moment a woman's posterior enters the foreground. When the Martian lady is under arrest, a close-up of her fake rubber breasts is excised. When the film was reissued a year later, it was cut even further, to a mere 87 minutes. Original production materials reveal scenes now missing, which may have been in the original 1964 edition: more of Dolores, the mayor, and the mother-in-law; the defeated telegrapher being cared for by nuns; the psychotic Maria Meneghello dancing with her Martian lover; and, most intriguing of all, Vittoria and her children taking refuge in a Martian spaceship to head off for a more promising planet. Also, the end credits mention a lovely John Foster song, "Chi sei, amore?" which is no longer in the film. Even in this shortened edition, the film is a gem, but it is not well-known.

Why is it not well-known? Under the export title *The Martians*, the international distributor, Famous Films B.V., screened the movie at trade festivals in the hopes of licensing rights. De Laurentiis, though, had not made any foreign-language dubs, and that in itself may have discouraged distributors from placing bids. There was only one bid. Joseph E. Levine's Embassy Pictures obtained a license to show the film on television in the U.S. and Canada under the title *The Flying Saucer*. The film was never shown on a network, but was offered only in 16mm and only to local stations as filler material. Embassy created its own English dub, which had poor lipsync and was not true to the original dialogue. Despite that problem, the film was still a gem, but since it had bypassed cinemas and had instead gone straight to local television, it was largely unnoticed. Yet it played off and on in numerous markets from September 1967 through March 1998, and perhaps a little beyond those two dates. The U.S. license has apparently lapsed, and rights and materials are now with StudioCanal+ in France.

Though it was not the blockbuster success that its investors had hoped for, the movie did respectable business. Since filming lasted only a few weeks, because Tinto had been so economical and rapid, and Mangano and Sordi respected and stood up for the director, Tinto now had a solid reputation. He was pleasant, he was forceful, he was efficient, he was reliable, he was quick, he was trustworthy. Tinto would now never have trouble attracting top-tier actors for even the smallest projects.

Source Notes:

146 Fabrizio Dividi and Giovanni Spada, "Tinto Brass ci racconta 'Il (suo) disco volante,'" *Mass Medio*, 2 December 2014

147 Manlio Gomarasca and Davide Pulici, *99 donne: stelle e stelline del cinema italiano* (Milan: *Media Word*, 1999), p. 219

148 Fabrizio Dividi and Giovanni Spada, *Mass Medio*

V

My Wife

(*La mia signora*)

PARTWAY INTO FILMING *The Flying Saucer*, Dino De Laurentiis paused the production so that he could assign Silvana Mangano, Alberto Sordi, and Tinto Brass to spend a few days filming two brief comical episodes for an anthology film called *My Wife*.

La mia signora was one of a plethora of anthology films produced in Italy in the 1960s. The trend had started with the 1962 omnibus film *Boccaccio '70*, consisting of four one-hour stories by Federico Fellini, Luchino Visconti, Mario Monicelli and Vittorio De Sica, which was a major hit in Italy. The subsequent anthology films showcased brief works by established and up-and-coming filmmakers, and for Tinto Brass this was a fashionable introduction. *La mia signora* (which can be translated *My Lady*, *My Wife* or *My Mrs.*) is a fine, thoroughly enjoyable example of this genre, a compelling experiment in mood, comedy and cinema technique. The five short stories, by five authors and four directors in various combinations, all feature Alberto Sordi and Silvana Mangano as the leads.

"*L'uccellino*" (The Little Birdie), by Tinto Brass, features wifey Silvana Mangano who annoys her draftsman husband Settimo (Alberto Sordi) with her perpetual baby-talking to her canary. Hubby grows insanely jealous, murdering his feathered rival, and then all the successor feathered rivals one by one. This introduction is followed by "*Eritrea*," a screwball comedy directed by Luigi Comencini. An engineer named Sartoletti (Sordi) fails to win an endorsement from a government official until that official comes to believe that Eritrea (Mangano) is his wife. In fact, she is a prostitute, and, in order to further his career, Sartoletti hires Eritrea to seduce the official. The third episode, by Rodolfo Sonego, based on a short story by Goffredo Parise, and directed by Mauro Bolognini, is "*I miei cari*" (My Dear Ones), about a wife and mother-in-law who nag rather than comfort the bedridden husband in hospital. The loveliest episode, "*Luciana*," by Mauro Bolognini again, has a chance encounter between an unhappily married man and woman whose significant others have just boarded a plane that experiences technical difficulties and can neither proceed to its destination nor return to the runway for service until its fuel is used up. Their panic brings Luciana and Giovanni together to commiserate, but they soon discover that they are a perfect match, and spend a romantic day and night together as their spouses circle above them in the sky. When the plane finally lands, they regretfully go their separate ways. The fifth act, "*L'automobile*" (The Car), again directed by Brass, is more pointed and, breaking from tradition, was recorded in direct sound. A husband and wife file a police report about their stolen Jaguar. The badly rattled and explosively tempered husband is convinced that his wife was insane to turn over the keys to her young cousins, who surely stole the machine. World-weary wife tries to explain that the car will turn up again. She wins.

Both momentary stories were remarkably witty, smoothly directed, and beautifully acted. Had performers of lesser experience been assigned to these rôles, shooting could never have been completed so quickly and effortlessly. As Tinto was not permitted to edit his films, he "edited in the camera," so that Nino Baragli would have no choices in how to assemble the material.

My Wife is another interesting film, typical of the era but not worse off for it. It has top-tier scripts and top-tier actors who were old-school and versatile. The overall result is delightful, moving, enchanting, surprising, and insightful. Alas, few foreign distributors bid on it, and it was never seen in English-speaking countries. Interestingly, a follow-up anthology film, equally delightful, was *La donna è una cosa meravigliosa* (Woman Is a Wonderful Thing), directed largely by Mauro Bolognini, which featured Tinto Brass in an uncredited cameo part.

*Tinto Brass behind the camera for **Yankee**, 1966*

VI
Yankee

THE SUDDEN SUCCESS of Sergio Leone's *A Fistful of Dollars* (Per un pugno di dollari) spawned hundreds of copycat films, and one of the first few dozen was *Yankee.* When the producers approached the promising young Italian to direct it, Brass was delighted, for he too was a great fan of Leone's film. The script was by Alberto Silvestri and an uncredited Alfonso Balcázar, and what was in that script is anybody's guess. In all likelihood, it was a simplistic variation on *A Fistful of Dollars.* Tinto worked withSilvestri on rewrites, and the dialogue was credited to Giancarlo Fusco, who had worked on Tinto's first two features. Being handed a script along with two lead players as a nineteenth-century gunslinger and a Mexican bandit, Brass planned to do something different. He rewrote the script and based the bizarre, unreal feel and look of the film on popular Italian comic books (fumetti). Taking a visual cue from Chinese and Japanese pictographic writing, he decided to create a visual synecdoche, representing a horse by a close-up of its ear or nose, representing a gunfighter by a close-up of a gun barrel, representing an equestrian by a close-up of a boot in a stirrup.

When Tinto had completed the bulk of his rough cut, production staff entered the cutting room while he was away and looked at his work on the Moviola. Tinto recalled on the film later:

Yankee was a western, an Italian western, and I wanted to make the film with ideograms. You know, the ideogram is Chinese or Japanese writing, a detail for the totality. And it was done in that way, in my editing: When showing a horse, I showed only the horse's hoof, or only its ear. The producer saw that and became furious, and there was a big fight, actually a physical fight, and I was thrown out of the editing; so I didn't sign the film.[149]

The producers fired Tinto and hired Juan Oliver to re-edit the film in a traditional manner. Tinto sued and won his demand to have his name removed as director. In its initial run, *Yankee* was "un film di Antony Luc," an abbreviation of co-producer Antonio Lucatelli. When the film began to make a handsome profit, the producers offered Tinto a settlement: In return for an extra payment, Tinto would allow the credit to be changed to "un film di Tinto Brass." Though he refused to accept a director credit, his name appeared in several countries on the theatrical posters.

The irony is that once Tinto disavowed his film, it won international distribution. It was shown in France, Germany, and Spain, and a quite good English dub was also prepared, though it would never be released.

Some scenes were cut, for instance one with a nude girl on a horse, as could be seen in stills. Tinto once showed a deleted sequence of this film to a friend, Alan Sekers.

In the clip, the protagonist comes into the saloon and goes up to the check-in desk and rings the bell. The manageress (with a formidable bust) appears and asks what he wants.

"A room" he says.

"One dollar." He pays.

He goes up the stairs along the corridor and gets to where the room must be. There is no door. He comes down and rings the bell again.

"What do you want?"

"A room with a door."

"One dollar." He pays and goes up again, walks to the door, opens it, enters and falls down to the ground floor. He returns to the desk and rings the bell.

"Yes?"

"I want a room with a door and a floor."

"One dollar." He pays and goes up.

Yet even in its modified, blanded-down form, *Yankee* certainly comes across as an atypical "spaghetti western," exciting and innovative, and, as one of 46 Euro-westerns released in 1965, it is both a cause for celebration and a failed experiment. The film stars Philippe Leroy as the eponymous gunfighter defending

Stills photography contact sheet, 1966

the city of Pueblo from El Grande Concho (played with relish by Adolfo Celi) and his band of renegades. A stylish excursion into the western mythology, Brass' single western is both an homage to western grit and a deconstructive look at "cowboy" cinema. The film as it currently stands is passable entertainment, and has some memorable scenes of a naked girl being tied to a totem pole, and the main actor being tied to a wheel of fire. Brass would continue integrating the world of comics with cinema in future films, especially the next two.

Interestingly, *Yankee* went full circle. Inspired by fumetti comic books, it was adapted into a photonovel for a French magazine, *Star-Cine Bravoure* #127 (May 1967). These photonovel magazines are essentially comic books, but with photographs rather than drawings. The *Yankee* photonovel is notable for presenting a longer version of the film than was ever shown at cinemas, and it includes more scenes with circus performer Osiride Pevarello. In the film's current state, he is on screen only for a few moments. Pevarello and Brass quickly became fast friends and have continued to work together to this day.

For admirers of Tinto's works, *Yankee* is an engaging entry in his career, though sadly not the version he intended it to be. However, the film was recognized when Quentin Tarantino selected it for a spaghetti western retrospective at the 2007 Venice Film Festival.

Source Notes:

149 Nico B, *Tinto Brass: Maestro of Erotic Cinema*, interview conducted 3 November 2001 (Los Angeles: Cult Epics, 12 August 2014)

Italian 2-Fogli poster, 1963

Left and Right: Italian Fotobusta posters, 1963

MORIS ERGAS
PRESENTA UNA CO-PRODUZIONE ITALO-FRANCESE
ZEBRA FILM - ROMA
FRANCO LONDON FILM - PARIGI
chi lavora è perduto
(in capo al mondo)
SADY REBBOT
PASCALE AUDRET
E CON
TINO BUAZZELLI
REGIA DI
TINTO BRASS
DISTRIBUZIONE

MORIS ERGAS
PRESENTA UNA CO-PRODUZIONE ITALO-FRANCESE
ZEBRA FILM - ROMA
FRANCO LONDON FILM - PARIGI
chi lavora è perduto
(in capo al mondo)
SADY REBBOT
PASCALE AUDRET
E CON
TINO BUAZZELLI
REGIA DI
TINTO BRASS
DISTRIBUZIONE

Left and Right: Italian Fotobusta posters, 1963

SAB 24 NOV
ORE 12 13
MORIS ERGAS PRESENTA UNA CO-PRODUZIONE ITALO-FRANCESE ZEBRA FILM - ROMA • FRANCO LONDON FILM - PARIGI
chi lavora è perduto
(in capo al mondo)
DISTRIBUZIONE
DEAR FILM
REGIA DI
TINTO BRASS
SADY REBBOT
PASCALE AUDRET
E CON
TINO BUAZZELLI
AVVERTENZA Il diritto di utilizzare la presente fotografia è riservato esclusivamente al Cliente che l'ha direttamente noleggiata dalla S.A.C.

MORIS ERGAS
PRESENTA
ÇA IRA, IL FIUME DELLA RIVOLTA
UN FILM SCRITTO E REALIZZATO DA
TINTO BRASS
UNA PRODUZIONE
ZEBRA FILM
DISTRIBUITO DALLA
DEAR FILM
DEAR FILM
Vecchioni & Guadagno, Via del Casale de Merode, 8 Roma Agosto 1964
AVVERTENZA

Left: Italian 4-Fogli poster, Right: Italian Fotobusta posters, 1964

Left: Italian 4-Fogli poster, Right: Italian 2-Fogli poster, 1964

DINO DE LAURENTIIS PRESENTA
ALBERTO SORDI
DINO DE LAURENTIIS
CINEMATOGRAFICA
DISTRIBUZIONE S.P.A.
IL DISCO VOLANTE
STUDIO DE SETA
E IN ORDINE DI APPARIZIONE
MONICA VITTI
ELEONORA ROSSI DRAGO
SILVANA MANGANO
REGIA DI TINTO BRASS
SOGGETTO E SCENEGGIATURA DI RODOLFO SONEGO

Czech A3 poster, 1967

Top and Bottom: Italian 2-Fogli posters, 1964

Italian 2-Fogli poster, 1964

Left: French Grande poster, 1967, Right: Italian Fotobusta posters, 1966

un film di TINTO BRASS
yankee
PHILIPPE LEROY - ADOLFO CELI
JACQUES HERLIN
TOMAS TORRES
PACO SANZ - FRANCO DE ROSA
e con MIRELLA MARTIN
prodotto da ANTONIO LUCATELLI e FRANCESCO GIORGI
per la TIGIELLE 33 ROMA
P.C. BALCAZAR - BARCELONA
EASTMANCOLOR - WIDESCREEN
Musiche di NINI ROSSO
DISTRIBUZIONE I.F.C. INTERNATIONAL FILM COMPANY
AVVERTENZA: Questo elemento pubblicitario è di esclusiva proprietà della EDINCA s.r.l. che ne consente l'uso all'esercente che ne abbia fatto regolare acquisto dal noleggiatore di zona. Qualsiasi infrazione sarà perseguita a termini di legge.
PRIMA EDIZIONE MCMLXVI

un film di ANTONY LUC
yankee
PHILIPPE LEROY - ADOLFO CELI
JACQUES HERLIN
TOMAS TORRES
PACO SANZ - FRANCO DE ROSA
e con MIRELLA MARTIN
prodotto da ANTONIO LUCATELLI e FRANCESCO GIORGI
per la TIGIELLE 33 ROMA
P.C. BALCAZAR - BARCELONA
EASTMANCOLOR - WIDESCREEN
Musiche di NINI ROSSO
DISTRIBUZIONE I.F.C. INTERNATIONAL FILM COMPANY
AVVERTENZA: Questo elemento pubblicitario è di esclusiva proprietà della EDINCA s.r.l. che ne consente l'uso all'esercente che ne abbia fatto regolare acquisto dal noleggiatore di zona. Qualsiasi infrazione sarà perseguita a termini di legge.
PRIMA EDIZIONE MCMLXVI

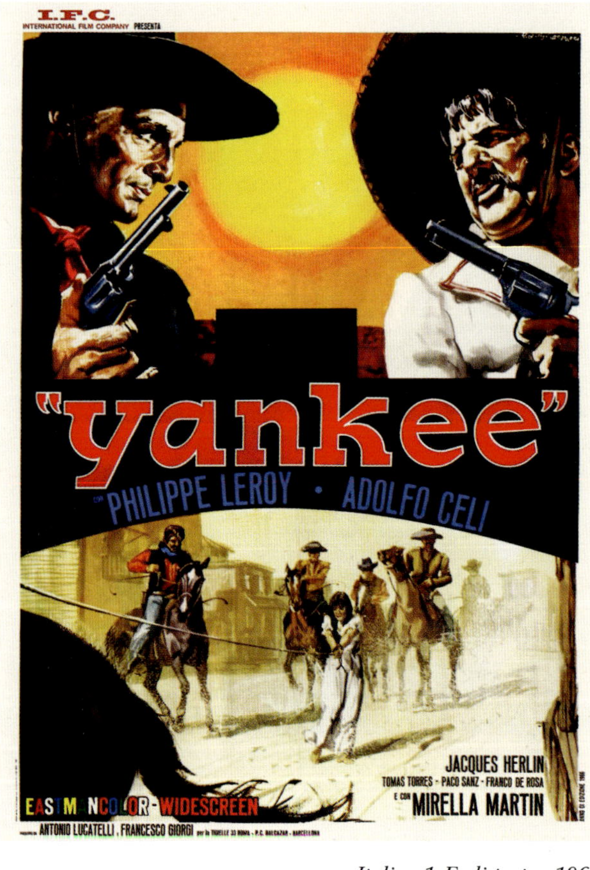

Top: Italian Fotobusta poster, Bottom: French Pressbook, 1966

Italian 1-Fogli poster, 1966

Spanish One Sheet poster, 1968

THE FILMS OF TINTO BRASS

PART TWO
EXPERIMENTAL ARTHOUSE

Newsprint advert from U.S Pressbook, 1968

VII
Deadly Sweet
(*Col cuore in gola* AKA *I Am What I Am* AKA *With Heart in Mouth*)

DEADLY SWEET, or, more properly translated, *Heart in His Mouth*, was another job offer, and the script had already been prepared. Tinto leapt at the opportunity. Of course, he was not about to turn down a job offer, even though it seems that he cared nothing for the script. He was, though, interested in turning his next movie, whatever it happened to be, into a big-screen comic book. Though the story took place in Rome, he changed it to take place in London, and he and Tinta rented a flat on Cadogan Place. Tinto commented on the change in locale:

London was a town, at that time, which gave you a kind of feeling of freedom. Things were happening there, there is no doubt—The Beatles, everything sexual as well, big freedom, sexual freedom. And so really, I had the feeling that it was much more exciting to try to live and to film there rather than in Rome, where there was a well-established industry, but where you couldn't have that kind of freedom. Also because I wanted to be as far as possible from the producer, from the one who put up the money. He was in Rome and I was in London; I could do much more freely what I wanted then.[150]

One can easily imagine that he was still smarting from his experience on *Yankee* and wanted to do whatever he could to avoid such alterations and altercations in his next project.

We know little of what brought this film about. Sergio Donati, a novelist and only recently a screenwriter, had written a standard crime tale, rather, a *giallo*, called *The Paper Tomb*, and published it in a cheap weekly called *I gialli Mondadori* (#373, 24 March 1956). Giallo, by the way, means "yellow," and it referred to the background color of the magazine covers in which these stories were published. Panda Società per l'Industria Cinematografica S.p.a. was a small production company with only a handful of insignificant films to its credit. Panda, coincidentally, was partly owned by another Donati, Ermanno, though he seems to have been no relation to Sergio. By 1967, Panda attempted to begin a series of finer films. "PANDA: Producers Donati and [Luigi] Carpentieri are no longer grinding out quickies for others and their current list of pix to come is decidedly more impressive. Tinto Brass is directing *Heart in the Mouth*, on extended London locations with Jean-Louis Trintignant and Swedish newcomer Ewa Aulin..." (*Variety* weekly, 26 March 1967).

That deserves comment. In order to hire more reputable directors and actors, Panda forged a partnership with a French production company, Les Films Corona, which had a good track record stretching back decades. As for Jean-Louis Trintignant, he had been impressed by Tinto's work and let it be known that he would be most interested in working with the young director. When Tinto heard that, he contacted the actor with an offer. In all likelihood, this was the offer:

This is the story of a strange and brief encounter between a disappointed man and a girl with no illusions.

It is strange because it takes place in the presence of the body of a dead man, and brief because it lasts only a day and a night.

However, this short interval of time is sufficient to give back the man his mechanism for life, rusted by disappointment, and to kill in the girl any other feeling except the purely biological one of surviving.

This is favoured by the objective circumstances in which Jane and Bernard find themselves living their love-story, in the London of today, with all its most typical contradictions.

So the reality which surrounds them weighs with all its familiarity on their story, thrusting them towards a tragic conclusion.

In other words, the re-born illusions of Bernard are revealed as powerless to change the course of the thriller in which he too is involved, just as Jane's lack of illusions is revealed as being useless to save the love-story in which she had believed for a minute. (*Unitalia Presents Italian Production*, 1967)

Trintignant was pleased to accept the job offer, and one would suppose that he even reduced his price to standard union scale in order to appear in this film. He was then puzzled when he received the script, which bore no resemblance to the film he thought he had agreed to.

The female lead, Jane, was Miss Teen International winner Ewa Aulin. Tinto was indifferent about who would play this part, and he hired Aulin only because she was available. That was a stroke of luck. She was perfect for the part, entirely unlike the traditional *femme fatale.* Other performers were mostly from Central Casting. Assistant director Alan Sekers recalled the line-ups.

For the extras in *Col cuore in gola* we worked with Central Casting, which was as boring for Tinto as it was for me. We used Central Casting for the bit parts, and Tinto was horrible. We would go to the production office in Wardour Street in Soho, and all the Central Casting extras came in at the same time. Sometimes Tinto would swear at me in front of them. "Why did you get me such ugly people?" he would ask, right in front of them. If he was happy, he would say "Yesssah!" with his big cigar in his mouth.[151]

In order to have some control over the film, Tinto paid half the budget himself, out of his own pocket. He did that by a trick. Tinta drew out the budgets, and made sure that they were double the actual cost. With the leftover, Tinto purchased 50% of the next film.

The script remains mysterious, as no draft of it is available for inspection. What we do know is that, apart from one setting and one character name, the final film had nothing at all to do with Sergio Donati's original story. It seems that the original draft was written by Francesco Longo and Pierre Lévy-Corti, and that Tinto worked with those two scenarists on a polish. It appears, further, that Tinto made little use of the script once he began shooting. As Alan Sekers recalled:

In retrospect, I believe that for Tinto, scripts were initially ways of raising cash and channeling his thinking. Perhaps he later used them to some extent in the cutting room.

When shooting, he preferred lightweight unblimped cameras and did not bother with sync sound, although he sometimes had a guide track recorded. His crew was always quite small in number. The camera crew, the grips, the electricians and costume people, were regulars and became like a family. They were all very skilled, very loyal, and could cover for each other as required. Altogether, this setup gave him an extraordinary flexibility in how he worked.

Typically, he would set up a scene and then shoot it with two Arri's, with 10:1 zooms, at right angles to each other. With that setup, he could shoot a whole scene in two or three takes. He printed it all in color, and he had a shooting ratio of 90:1 or 100:1, which was very rare in those days. It was expensive, but he wasn't spending money on anything else. The minimum was spent on locations, studio, and crew. He was supremely confident in his skills as an editor, and knew that with the amount of film he shot, he could make the scenes work as planned and even find new and unplanned ways to make them work in edit.

Tinto invented a way of working based on his own skills and his relatively limited financial resources. He always said he was not very good at directing actors, but he was sensationally effective in the editing suite. He was extraordinarily disciplined and lucid working with tape splicers at the Steenbeck table.

I can't remember seeing a script on set. Tinto knew what he was doing. Sometimes he didn't know in detail until the day before, and sometimes he didn't know in fine detail until he was setting up the shot.[152]

To turn the film into a live-action comic book, Tinto hired comic artist Guido Crepax to draw the story boards and to add decorations to the sets. Tinto followed Crepax's visuals slavishly, down to in-camera split frames. Incidentally, to date, nobody has identified the actor who portrayed Mr. Leris. This unidentified actor bore an uncanny resemblance to Guido Crepax, though he looked about 20 years older than the cartoonist. Could it be that the actor actually was Crepax in heavy makeup? We may never find out.

The greatest virtue of *Deadly Sweet* is that it is a record of the London of 1967, a London that no longer exists. The film was shot on actual locations in five to six weeks, without permits. Some of it in black-and-white, when not enough light was available, or documentary-style in London streets and B&W comic-style, intercut by express, being Silvano Ippoliti's first feature with Tinto as cinematographer. We see extensive exteriors of various parts of the city, and we also see some culturally significant establishments. The nightclub at the beginning of the story, where Bernard first sees Jane and her family, was Samantha's, a small basement club, quite hip, 3 New Burlington Street, W1. Prescott's office was shot at the flat rented by Janet Street-Porter and her husband Tim. (Prescott, who appears as the corpse, was portrayed by Tinto's driver, Sam Dorras.) Prescott's house was shot at Bob Monkhouse's house. There are shots taken in and in front of a famous tailor shop called Granny Takes a Trip, 488 Kings Road, Chelsea. Most significant is the happening that closes the film. At David's flat we see an "it" (*International Times*) flyer displayed on a door. This was thematically appropriate, since it was the "it" that sponsored the happening, which was called the

"14 Hour Technicolor Dream," a poster of which is also on display at David's studio. It was this happening that was a defining moment in British counterculture. The film concludes at the "14 Hour Technicolor Dream," and, as Simon Matthews discovered when he researched his book *Free Your Mind*, it was Tinto who made that happening happen!

Tinto would frequent the screenings by David Curtis at the London Arts Lab. Recalled Alan Sekers, "He put on the most fantastic nights of films. There were no cinema seats, just mattresses. He would show Cocteau, Warhol, experimental stuff. Brilliant programming, every night. Tinto would go there regularly in the daytime, because there was a book shop there as well, which sold J.G. Ballard's pamphlets, *Why I Want to Fuck Ronald Reagan* and so forth." The hippie counterculture was also just coming into existence at the time, and Tinto was fascinated by it. He heard that the "it," *International Times*, was attempting to get a happening off the ground, a massive event at the Alexandra Palace, but that the financing was short by £3,000. Tinto took £3,000 from his film budget and handed it to the *International Times*, with the agreement that he would be allowed to shoot his movie in the midst of it. If for nothing else, Tinto's name should be remembered as an important and integral part of the London scene, but he never publicized his involvement, and so now his participation is forgotten.

Ewa Aulin spoke English on camera, while Jean-Louis Trintignant usually spoke French, as he did not know a word of English. Trintignant did, though, deliver one important scene entirely in English. He must have learned his lines phonetically. Vira Silenti (Ermanno Donati's wife) portrayed Martha, and she spoke Italian on camera, as did Luigi Bellini, who portrayed a gangster named Jelly-Roll. The intention was to create an English original as well as an Italian original, and to dub the dialogue into other languages as well. Tinto appears not to have been involved in the dubbing process, and his active involvement ended with the creation of the Italian edition.

This is all by way of background, by way of what little background is available to us. What of the film itself? It is a violation of every concept of narrative, a violation of every established rule of filmmaking. To begin with, its story is well-nigh incomprehensible. Even after multiple viewings of this gangster tale, few people would catch on who was murdering whom and why. Stylistically, the film seems chaotic, but intentionally so: It is suspense, intrigue, comedy, absurdism, and pop art all at the same time. As with previous films, Tinto shot much of *Deadly Sweet* with hidden cameras, capturing glimpses of real people going about their actual lives. One of his most intriguing coups was to capture footage of busker Ronnie Ross, of The Happy Wanderers, dancing in the middle of the street in Piccadilly Circus. One of the most pleasing aspects of the film is its eccentric editing, which occasionally evolves into intercutting flashes only two or three frames long each, with splicing tape visible everywhere.

The International Times

Flyer for the International Times, *1960s counterculture newspaper and sponsors of the "14 Hour Technicolor Dream" in Alexandra Palace, London, 1967*

It seems that crucial scenes are missing. Nonetheless, enough remains for more astute viewers to piece together the few surviving fragments of the story. Suffice it to say that the story deals with rival gangs. A Mr. Burroughs is killed by a speeding car that gets away. It becomes clear that it was Mr. Leris who ordered that killing, as he is having an affair with Mrs. Burroughs. Another gang is operated by a nightclub owner named Ruby Prescott, who is blackmailing Mr. Leris. Prescott is murdered, apparently by Leris' gang. Prescott's gang, meanwhile, are wrongly convinced that an unsuccessful French actor, Bernard, murdered their boss. Leris orders his gang to kidnap Mrs. Burroughs' daughter, Jane, and they are fully prepared to execute her. So far, we have the makings of a standard crime thriller. Yet the film usually skirts past the criminals, ignoring them except to show flirtatious Bernard and Jane constantly crossing paths with them and getting into ever more confusing and dramatic situations. At the end, Jane is wrongly convinced that Bernard has been the cause of her troubles with the gangsters, and Bernard is wrongly convinced that Jane murdered Prescott.

The intricate plot is not the focus of attention. As a matter of fact, it goes almost unnoticed and it is never explained. Rather, we are treated to nearly two hours of pop art, mod culture, hip music, psychedelic imagery, the occasional bout of relentless editing, countercultural hippies who were just then making their presence known, flashy visuals, and the atmosphere of a London that is long gone. In all his films so far, Tinto had been remarkably playful, but in *Deadly Sweet* he allowed playfulness to overpower every other aspect of the film. As a character talks, the screen shows us a close-up of toy lips opening and closing. As Bernard and Jeremy race down the street to rescue

French Lobby Card, 1967

Jane, the camera links the noise of the roaring engine with a pan across a poster proclaiming that Exxon is GRRRRRRRRRRREAT. When Jane Burroughs performs an impromptu strip in a photographic studio, Bernard swings on a cable yodeling like Tarzan. When characters get into fistfights, we see not their violent action on screen, but zooms to cartoon bubbles: SLAM, BWING, SLOUGH.

Most coincidental is the scene that is universally accepted as an homage to *Blow-Up*. That is when Jane and Bernard, in the photographer's studio, roll around in the diffuser paper. Tinto was quite proud of that scene and thought it marvelously inventive. Just one day after shooting it, he, his wife, and Alan Sekers attended the London Pavilion to see Michelangelo Antonioni's new film, *Blow-Up*, which had recently opened. Tinto's heart sank. The scene he was so proud of had already been done! Fearing that audiences would conclude that he had copied Antonioni's film, he seriously considered deleting his scene, but eventually decided to retain it, come what may. In his film, he added a poster of *Blow-Up* from the front of the London Pavilion, and he also included a quote from Antonioni, to convert the coincidence into an homage.

Tinto added a second homage as well. He had just seen the film version of *Marat/Sade*, which had opened at the Odeon Haymarket on 8 March, and he was quite impressed by it. So, when Leris is murdered, Tinto made sure the sequence would parallel the assassination of Marat. Leris is murdered in a bathtub, above which is a display ad for that film, showing Marat murdered in a bathtub. That is yet another example of an amusing joke taking precedence over the narrative. The film was also intercut with war footage, from Vietnam and elsewhere in the world, as a historical reference, taken from *Ça ira*.

Most breathtaking is the lengthy scene at the 14 Hour Technicolor Dream, held at the Alexandra Palace, or Ally Pally as it was nicknamed. We see elaborately costumed funsters enter by sliding board, play with a gigantic inflatable tube, groove to the rock bands, smile at the camera as it wanders by. We see two other film crews also capturing the events of the night. We catch glimpses of the bands, and, underneath the thousand sound effects and the other overlaid music, we can hear Mick Jagger and the Rolling Stones belting out a tune, the only instance of production audio surviving to the final cut.

A number of sequences consist of multiple images on screen at once. Alan Sekers explained how:

> **The split-screen sequences were done in the camera to save money and using a very ingenious technique. At that time, the usual way to do split-screen sequences was to film normally and then to scale and superimpose in the lab after filming, using a black border to separate the screens to allow for inaccuracies in printing.**
>
> **Tinto and Silvano devised another technique (or maybe resuscitated it from silent film days?). To do this, they used an Éclair Cameflex camera for these sequences. Although rather noisy, it was unique because the viewfinder allowed you to look through the gate, and because it was designed to use either 35mm or 16mm film, "with the insertion of a 16mm film gate into the camera body and using the appropriate film magazine."**[153]
>
> **Tinto and Silvano exploited this by having special photographically matched shaped gates made that could be inserted and removed as needed. This meant that when, for example gate [A] was inserted, just that shaped part of the screen would be exposed, and you could see the masking effect. When you put in one of the negatives of gate [A], you would see the matching masking effect. The lab could print from the exposed films and the screens would match perfectly without needing borders.**

Since *Deadly Sweet* perfectly captured the time, it looked like a guaranteed success. It needed to be released in England in an English version, right away, and it needed to be publicized by "it" *International Times*. That would have put it over the top and ensured its popularity with the in-crowd and the mod crowd and the hippies. Though an English dub was prepared, it was never seen by the public, as the film never opened in England. It had a small success in Italy, due to Trintignant's popularity at the time there. When Tinto's friend, the famous novelist Alberto Moravia, saw the film, he was puzzled. As he mused to Tinto, "I recognize the signifiers, but I don't understand what they signify." That, of course, was the point.

The film was later dubbed into German, French, and Spanish, and the alterations in the German edition were particularly egregious. Again, it was given small releases in those territories.

Two years later, after it was too late to capitalize on the hippie subculture that was so startlingly new in 1967, Paramount Pictures licensed the rights in the U.S. and several other territories. Rather than use the previous English dub, Paramount hired an American crew to record a new dub, not always well, and with unconvincing British and French accents. Paramount altered much of the dialogue, added new dialogue, re-edited some of the music, deleted a hilarious scene halfway through, and chopped the final scene short, resulting in an abrupt stop rather than a finish. Paramount hired Technicolor to make an imbibition dye-transfer matrix from an Eastmancolor duplicate. Why? Ewa Aulin's third feature, *Candy*, had just opened in Manhattan and had performed remarkably well in its first few weeks. Paramount wanted to hop onto that bandwagon and was hoping to make a good profit on a small investment. Paramount gave the movie a trade screening in Kansas City and received not a single bid. Realizing that it would never be a hit, Paramount dumped the film off with a subsidiary, Films Releasing Corporation, which offered it to the exploitation market with no publicity. It played at only a handful of tenth-rate cinemas and drive-ins, on double and triple bills, and a year later Paramount withdrew the film from release altogether.

It is tempting to guess that Paramount had actually invested in the production. The reason to suspect this is that the Paramount edition includes some nude footage not included in any other edition. When Jane emerges from the shower, the scene is discreetly composed. Yet uniquely in the Paramount version, the nudity is fully revealed. Two separate takes were spliced together, in mid-shot, to achieve that continuity. When Bernard swings on a cable, yodeling like Tarzan, the scene, again, is quite discreetly photographed. In the Paramount edition, there is an extra shot revealing nudity, once again, and a few frames of the soundtrack are blank, with splices, lab marks, and damage clearly visible. Both flashes of nudity are degraded.

All that survive of the Paramount edition are three prints, nothing else. One is at the archive of the Academy of Motion Picture Arts and Sciences' Pickford Center for Motion Picture Study in Hollywood, and the other two are in the Paramount Pictures Archive Building in Hollywood, which are missing scenes from the original Cult Epics video release and vice versa.

Curiously, *Deadly Sweet* begat a child. Les Films Corona, which had co-produced, decided to co-produce a follow-up, also featuring Trintignant and Aulin, and edited by Tinto's old friend Kim Arcalli, who later became known for the films *The Night Porter*, *The Conformist* and *Novecento*. It was called *Death Laid an Egg*, directed by the auteur filmmaker Giulio Questi—a bizarre concoction that had few sales, and was re-edited and released as a giallo following the success of Argento's *The Bird with the Crystal Plumage*, though word of mouth obtained for it a cult following decades later, when it was released in 2018 by Cult Epics in the U.S. and Nucleus Films in the UK.

Though *Deadly Sweet* was buried before it could find an audience, it was a turning point for Tinto. It was his freest film, an experiment, and in it some nudity which he would explore more later on. He just shot whatever he felt like, wherever he felt like, however he felt like, taking full advantage of whatever happened to be going on around him. He edited the material together not in a way that would make sense, but just in a way that he found amusing. He shot without permits, without interference, and without oversight from the production office. It was a delightful experience, one that he found liberating. On the audio commentary of *Deadly Sweet* he expressed years later:

> **The film is not really realistic or surrealistic, imperialistic. It is in the same line of the other films I have done, *L'urlo*, *Nerosubianco*, *Ça ira*, in a certain way. Films where in a way I was searching my style, I wanted to find my expressive style. They're full of experiments, elements in any situation what I could do to express myself. I didn't have many communication problems, I didn't care if people would understand or not. I was trying to find my own expressive type. This is a thriller, but also a parody of a thriller.**[154]

For his next film, he would go further yet, and create a singular masterpiece.

Source Notes:

150 Nico B, "Tinto Brass: Maestro of Erotic Cinema," interview conducted 3 November 2001, Torcello (Los Angeles: Cult Epics, 2014)

151 Alan Sekers: telephone interview, 26 January 2019

152 Ibid.

153 *collection.sciencemuseumgroup.org.uk*

154 Audio commentary by Tinto Brass, *Deadly Sweet* DVD (Cult Epics, 2009)

U.S. One Sheet poster, 1969

VIII
Attraction

(*Nerosubianco* AKA *Black on White* AKA *The Artful Penetration*)

THIS IS A TRULY IMPRESSIVE FILM that, like most of Tinto Brass' works of the 1960s, flew under the radar, the indirect victim of a tax seizure and numerous other bureaucratic complications.

Tinto Brass now founded his own production company, Lion Film, so as to have full control over his work. He retrieved a story he had written in 1964, immediately upon completion of *Who Works is Lost*. He called it *Nerosubianco*, a Joycean play on words. "Nero su bianco" is generally used the way English uses "black and white" in reference to paperwork: "Get it all down in black and white." In Italian, though, the phrase has a different flavor, as "su" is "on" rather than "and," and the reference can thus become the impression made by an African man upon a Caucasian woman. Tinto ran all three words together to emphasize EROS in the midst of the term. The story was a female version of *Who Works is Lost* but with even less narrative. It was to be a musical comedy consisting of the thoughts that race through a housewife's mind when she spots an African man on the street. That was the entire plot. The original treatment, in English translation, is available for viewing at AMPAS' Margaret Herrick Library in Beverly Hills. In 1964, when other job offers materialized so quickly, Tinto was compelled to put *Nerosubianco* aside, but it was always on his mind, and he was determined to make the film. Tinto explains how it got made:

During the shooting of *Deadly Sweet* arrived a phone call by Dino De Laurentiis, the tycoon, the big producer in Italy. I had written a short script called *Black on White*. The love story between a black guy and a white girl. He had at that time under contract a black girl, so he phoned me and said can you change the plot. No, I can't change, I can not make the story of a black girl and white guy. It was a mythology of the sexual power of a black guy, on that I based my script. He said, when you come back, let's see and let's talk. Anyway, he accepted to do *Black on White*.[155]

It hardly needs saying that De Laurentiis would not use his own money, but would instead raise funds from yet other investors, and the available evidence suggests that it was Columbia Pictures in Hollywood that agreed to pay the remaining costs, in return for a right of first refusal on distribution. The funds were funneled through its Italian branch, Columbia C.E.I.A.D. (an amalgamation of Columbia and Compagnia Edizioni Internazionali Artistiche Distribuzione). We may be confident that the Hollywood connection required an English-language original version of the film.

Again, Tinto shot the bulk of the film in and around London. He enjoyed London, the "Scene," the excitement of the city. He certainly liked being far away from his financiers. There is one idea, though, that becomes frightfully obvious: He realized, from before he shot the first frame of film, that his movie would never clear the Italian censor board. He planned, from the first, to create two versions: a bowdlerized edition for Italian release and a full version for export. Once the Italian authorities were to approve the expurgated edition, he would export the full version, but under a different title. The title he chose was *Attraction*.

He and Franco Longo drafted a full 120-page script filled with the minutest details, but almost entirely devoid of dialogue. Here is the opening sentence: "Over the first lyrical and somewhat abstract images, quick panoramas of sea and sky, of trees and lawns, we superimpose stroboscopic images of male seeds in a frantic race towards the female egg." Once the script was complete, Tinto forever afterward completely ignored it, and instead had his crew photograph any odd sight that caught his fancy.

Music had been matched to image from the earliest days of the movies, but what Tinto would do in *Nerosubianco* was startlingly original, for music and image would link abstractly. This film would be loosely structured, so much so that nearly any meaning could be extrapolated from any part of the proceedings. In his original conception, he wanted the music to be on par with Jerome Kern, but the world of 1967 was nothing like the world of 1964. Popular culture was changing by the hour, fashions were changing by the hour, music was changing by the hour, responses to the war in Vietnam were changing by the hour. Few realized, though some did suspect, that the counterculture was evolving at a pace far too fast to be organic. It was heavily influenced by CIA PsyOps and by the FBI's COINTELPRO, which created instant new rock idols who were all the sons, and sometimes daughters, of military intelligence officers and who thus were never at risk of being drafted. These rock stars encouraged by example drug use and irresponsible behavior in an apparent attempt to coöpt and discredit the peace movement.[156] Against all odds, these newly minted rock idols were able to collaborate with phenomenally talented musicians, and almost overnight they burst forth with a wave of creativity that was sensationally popular. This new musical culture could not be ignored, and so Tinto decided to have a new rock group serve as a Greek chorus to his wandering players.

Before he could hire a band, he was faced with an emergency: The film needed scenes of hippies relaxing in a park, but it was already the end of September, cold and wet.

Woburn Abbey Park had just hosted a "Love In" at the end of August, and it is possible—unknown, but possible—that Tinto grabbed some shots of that event and included them in the final film. The story opens with Barbara wandering through Woburn on a warm, sunny day, surrounded everywhere by flower children. That must have been shot on the final two warm days of 1967, 27 and 29 September. Woburn was the property of the Duke of Bedford and filming was strictly forbidden without a permit, which Tinto did not have and had no intention of getting. Tinto and his crew of 15 simply descended upon Woburn unannounced with a pair of lightweight unblimped Arriflex 35 II cameras. What happened next is not recorded, but it is evident that a policeman noticed the intrusion and approached the crew, asking, "Who is in charge?" Tinto either somehow convinced that policeman to record that statement into a tape machine, delivering the line in various ways, or he had someone mimic the policeman, and used that line to open the film.

Journalist Nerio Minuzzo detailed a little bit how Tinto and his crew managed to capture park scenes and city scenes without permits:

He starts at impossible hours, because he is a corpulent man who wakes easily. He often leaves, hunting for images, when it is still dark. Four cars and a van: all fifteen people, including the actors, squeeze inside, together with the Arriflexes, the tripods, the lamps, and the film magazines. There is an abundance of film. We start from Cadogan Place, where an apartment serves as an office, an interior set, and a dormitory for half the crew. No one knows where the day will end. Sometimes the director jumps out of the car, looks around, finds that the light is right, the place is good. In two minutes the tripod is in place, the reflectors are in position, and one of the troupe kindly offers to divert passers-by. Often, there is no permission to shoot, and if a suspicious policeman arrives, the order is to lie: We're Italian journalists; we're making a TV documentary. As an excuse, it wouldn't mean anything, but the explanation is rather unusual, and it is provided in English with help from Brass, a ragged beatnik who by chance bears a surname that is illustrious throughout the United Kingdom, and so it follows that if even a filthy longhair has his papers in order, he is still authoritatively Establishment.[157]

Alan Sekers elaborated a little more:

The police had a form, Form 258 or something like that, regarding permission to film in the streets. The form began with the sentence that, "We are unable to give anybody permission to film in the streets." Full stop. It went on, though, "However, we will not interfere with filming in the streets, provided that the following conditions are met."[158]

There were three lead characters: Barbara, her husband Paolo, and an anonymous American. Paolo was portrayed by Nino Segurini, an Anglophile who spoke perfect English and whose passion was performing Shakespeare. Casting Barbara was rather involved. The actress would need to be sexually at ease with herself and nonchalant in front of cameras. All in all, 80 actresses were auditioned.[159] The winner was 25-year-old Anita Sanders, originally from Sweden, with a Greek father and strikingly Greek eyes. She had appeared in Fellini's *Juliet of the Spirits*, but all that remained of her rôle in the final film was a shot of her nude torso that lasted a mere few frames. Her movie career had just begun, but she would be involved in only a few more films before her career came to an end a decade later.

The nameless American was played by an American, a rather prominent one, Terry Carter, an accomplished classical pianist. He had fallen in love with the stage as a youth and was an admirer of avant-garde films. He became a regular on *The Phil Silvers Show: You'll Never Get Rich* (syndicated as *Sergeant Bilko*). He appeared on Broadway with Eartha Kitt in *Mrs. Patterson* (1955) and he had the starring rôle in a short-lived Broadway musical called *Kwamina* (1961), of which Carter was especially fond and proud, calling it "quite different" and "extremely challenging," as well as "the most wonderful experience in my professional life."[160] Alas, the show flopped and has never been revived.

In the early 1960s, Carter vacationed in Italy, hired a language tutor, and married her. In 1965, with no background in journalism, he became a newscaster and telejournalist on WBZ-TV 4 in Boston, where he was highly regarded. Vacationing in Italy again during the summer of 1967, he informed the William Morris agency that he was open to gigs, and an offer arrived from De Laurentiis Cinematografica. It may have been significant that *Nerosubianco*, like *Kwamina*, was an offbeat entertainment that dealt with a black/white liaison. He auditioned, got the part, and applied for a 13-week leave of absence from WBZ. He was so thrilled to be performing again that he soon left journalism and decided to devote the rest of his life to acting. (Fans of American television will recognize him in *McCloud* and *Battlestar Galactica*.)

Despite the thrill of being in front of a camera again, Carter was frustrated, and it is easy to understand why. The script was not being used and the directions seemed to be entirely pointless: "Smile," "turn around," "grimace," "run," "cross the street," "shrug," and so forth. There seemed to be no rhyme or reason to anything he was being asked to do, and there was certainly no narrative.

That was how the film was shot. There was no obvious sense to anything that the cameras captured, and Tinto was improvising constantly, capturing images and sounds that caught his fancy, but always within the confines of his basic theme; he knew exactly what he was doing. As he was catching glimpses of passersby on the streets, as he was pointing his cameras at public gatherings and at odd graphics in display windows, and as he was improvising with his actors, he knew basically (not precisely) how he would piece all this disparate material together. He knew how he would sculpt a playful avant-garde exercise in free association out of many hours of random images and sounds.

Tinto and Tinta were staying at a flat on Cadogan Place. Silvano Ippoliti and his wife rented a part of a house owned by a gentleman from India. When Tinto saw that house, he arranged to have it decorated to serve as a studio. The owner let it with the agreement that it be returned to its original condition when the crew were through with it—and he was rather appalled one day to walk in and see a cow in the bedroom—a cow wearing a bra.

Publicity photo: Anita Sanders and Terry Carter, 1967

Anita Sanders, Tinto Brass and Freedom band member in the studio, 1967

Though the crew occasionally stayed at a hotel, mostly they lived in this house. The crew members painted the walls white to serve as a makeshift studio. This eliminated the necessity and expense of renting a proper studio.

Tinto continued to attend David Curtis' daily screenings of underground films at the London Arts Lab on Drury Lane, and those abstractions were exciting his imagination. Tinto could no longer conceive of *Nerosubianco* as a Kern-like musical. It would now be edgier, and the result is unmistakably a child of Bruce Conner and Maya Deren and *The Running, Jumping and Standing Still Film* and Fred Mogubgub and *An Andalusian Dog* (which is excerpted), as well as countless other works, which in turn were also influenced by pop art, and pop art frequently fills the frames of *Nerosubianco*. Indeed, Tinto once again hired cartoonist Guido Crepax to draw storyboards for the film as well as to design graphics to replace live-action sequences.

For the first week or two of filming, there was no idea of what music would accompany the rapidly flashing images. Tinto had De Laurentiis send out a request for proposal to various agents, and the quick response consisted of deliveries of new music by their clients. Alan Sekers has an amusing anecdote about this:

Tinto said he'd been sent this cassette of a band from some unheard-of person called Stigwood. It was the Bee Gees. Nobody had ever heard of them. Tinto had a pretty tin ear, and so he handed the cassette to me. I said, "I don't think it's right for the film," and so Tinto went with Freedom.

Sekers later reviewed his memory and offered a correction:

No, it was Tinto who rejected the Bee Gees. Jonathan Weston had got to Tinto by then—hence Freedom.

Bobby Harrison and Ray Royer had just recorded "A Whiter Shade of Pale," Procol Harum's première single, and the song reached the Number One slot immediately upon release. Nonetheless, Harrison and Royer were instantly replaced, which is why they began their own group, Freedom, named in honor of a Charlie Mingus song of that name. Their first hire was singer Steve Shirley, and that is when they got an offer, as Royer recalled:

We had never even played a gig when, in the autumn of 1967, our manager Jonathan Weston was approached by Italian film director Dino De Laurentiis. He was looking for a group to write and perform the soundtrack for a projected film of his which at that point was titled *Attraction*. The choice was between either us or Steppenwolf. We got the job but we had to change our keyboard player in the

Publicity photo: Members of the band Freedom and entourage, 1967

process. Our management then came back with Mike Lease, who was an absolute genius.[161]

Freedom began its very first job on Monday, 9 October. Tinto would explain the themes and concepts he wanted in each song, and Freedom would oblige with expressive word salad. Though Freedom performed on camera, the sound was not direct, nor was it playback. The songs would not be recorded until January through April 1968, months after filming was complete. The result is that the music never synchronizes with the images of the band playing, yet that hardly mattered. Realism was not the name of this game.

Paradoxically, despite the pop-art cartoons and wild fantasies, *Nerosubianco* is partly a newsreel documentary, capturing actual scenes. One day, the cameras captured Leftist activist Tariq Ali holding forth at an outdoor rally (probably 10 or 11 October) in honor of Che Guevara, who had just been killed in action in Bolívia. The tape recorder that the crew carried around captured snippets of actual conversations by random Londoners. We see storefronts of shops that are long gone, as well as the interior of a performance space called the Roundhouse, the interior of an art gallery exhibiting plastic sculptures by David Cobbold, and the Natural History Museum.

The most incomprehensible portion of the movie is also visually the murkiest. That is "Born Again," filmed in the Roundhouse. Alan Sekers kindly explained:

As for the scenes shot at the Roundhouse, it was Quasar Khanh who designed the inflatable sofa and the inflatable armchairs. I had been working on special effects for Mark Boyle and [his wife] Joan Hills, was doing light shows for the band called The Soft Machine and who had toured the U.S. with Jimi Hendrix. Mark had a project called "Son et Lumière for Bodily Fluids and Functions," and he was looking for a venue to do a new version. He had performed at the ICA, the Institute of Contemporary Arts, and he did a wonderful thing with the "Birth of Venus." It was projected on a sheet, and as the slide burned up, Joan was revealed standing there in the same pose. I put Tinto in touch with Mark, at a meeting in the hotel where the crew were staying. Mark proposed a "happening" to be held without spectators, but just "to be" for its own sake.

There was to be a randomly chosen boy and a randomly chosen girl to lie on a Quasar Khanh couch, wearing only electrodes and heartbeat monitors, connected to an oscilloscope, onto which was trained a video camera. The image of the oscilloscope would be projected by a black-and-white Eidophor television projector. All the equipment needed technicians, in white laboratory coats, and people looking after the brain monitors and so forth, and tuning the oscilloscope. Mark Boyle would occasionally dash in to get a smear of bodily fluid onto a slide, which was projected behind the couple. The boy was called [Kumo] Spyder, and he had been hired as a truck driver, who was always up for anything at all. The girl who had volunteered got slightly cold feet. Tinto was perfectly happy with the result, and then had Nino and Anita walk through all this.

When performed on stage, "Son et Lumière for Bodily Fluids and Functions" concluded with a dream dance. "The original intention was for the girl to go to sleep afterwards with a strong soporific and to be wakened as soon as the encephalogram showed that she was dreaming. She would then tell her dream, and the dancer Graziella Martinez would attempt to dance it."[162]

Graziella Martinez appears in the film in this sequence, improvising movements, but none of this is explained.

De Laurentiis received duplicate dailies for review in Rome, and when he saw "Born Again," with actual intercourse on camera, he was aghast. He flew immediately to London to confront Tinto about shooting censorable material. "Can you tell me, where can we distribute such a film? In Sweden, maybe, and then where? Are we only going to show it to friends?" Within minutes, his rage died down, as Tinto assured him, "We'll cut it, we'll cut it." It seems that De Laurentiis simply succumbed. After all, the film was so inexpensive that it was hardly worth losing one's temper over. Also, Tinto was being perfectly honest in his promise to cut the footage. He had every intention of reducing the visuals to mere suggestions, and that is precisely what he did in the end.

The film is open to nearly any interpretation. It is entirely stream-of-consciousness, but whose consciousness? We should pay attention to the impossible costume, makeup, and hairstyle changes, and the impossible appearances and reappearances of Paolo, who cannot possibly be there since he is away at a business meeting. The nameless American is a half-formed fantasy figure. He is Barbara's fantasy for a story she is making up in her mind to amuse herself and pass the time away. She is still trying to figure out if he should be enticing or threatening. Barbara's husband, Paolo, is less than half-formed, hardly more than a stick figure. Sometimes Barbara takes a break from building her story and neglects to work on who or what he is supposed to be, and that is when he freezes in position, for Barbara has not yet completed his character. She stares at him, puzzled, trying to figure out what to have him do next. She doesn't know whether to imagine him shaking his head No or nodding his head Yes, and so she tries her story both ways. Even the sets are half-formed fantasies, especially the couple's undecorated house with a sign on a wall reading "Front window of the house," through which pasted-on images of eyes suggest a peeping tom is peering in.

Barbara's mind jumps back and forth in time, jumps hither and thither in space, all the time. A specific example concerns the British campaign for dairy farmers: "Drinka Pinta Milka Day." This is mixed in with the British slang "cow," which Barbara imagines the receptionist (Janet Street-Porter) at the hairdressing salon saying. That brings to mind a momentary image seen earlier—a collage in which an ape's head is pasted onto (presumably) Jesus, and a nude woman is pasted over him, almost making it look as though he is about to spank her, as worshippers look on, with the entirety bearing an unrelated caption: "How Good Are Your Orgasms?" Put these three ideas together, and Barbara imagines that the salon's clients are wearing cow masks and speak only by mooing, and then Barbara herself becomes a cow, as the song refers to a cow for a wife who reads her husband's mail behind his back, and all this is intercut with archival footage of a bullfight. In terms of narrative this makes no sense at all. In terms of mimicking thought processes, it's quite exact.

What's more, Barbara is a fantasy figure as well, incomplete, not yet worked out in the mind of whoever is inventing this story. That is why some scenes are deliberately unconvincing, such as when she is ill in bed, not looking ill at all, but quite well and dressed and completely made-up. Is she self-destructive, is she angry, is she irresponsible, is she daring, is she frustrated, is she conventional? Her character is tried out in different ways as the story evolves, but it is never locked into place.

When Tinto first invented the idea for this film, it was 1964, when the very thought that people of different complexions could date or have any emotional intimacy was all but unheard of. In many parts of the world, such romances were illegal. That is why Tinto wanted to make the movie: No audience could be unaffected by the idea; the film would compel people to take sides. Three years later, though, in 1967, the resistance had largely broken down, at least among the younger generation. The film would not divide audiences, but it was still stimulating, with its free-form abstractions and its lightning-fast editing. Further, the psychedelic rock music was similar to that of the top-flight Procol Harum, and that was expected to help put the movie in the first or second tier of the day's box-office champions. The screen was filled with flower children and pop art, the ideas were up to date, and the film was trendy. All its ingredients guaranteed success, and so why did it all go so terribly wrong?

The reason was simple: Dino De Laurentiis had cheated on his taxes. The Italian authorities seized his studio and all his holdings, and De Laurentiis himself fled the country to take up residence in Hollywood. Italian tax bureaucrats did not know how to handle a film studio, and so *Nerosubianco*, after having gotten immense amounts of pre-release publicity, was now ignored. It had been planned for sales at the May 1968 Cannes Film Festival, but these complications put paid to that idea. That hardly mattered, since anti-war protests managed to shut the Cannes Festival down that year, anyway.

To make matters worse, Tinto understood full well that the censor board at the Ministero del Turismo e dello Spettacolo would never approve the film. The two-dimensional fantasy characters pondered sex outside of marriage, and though they never put their thoughts into action, the very idea by itself was enough to get a film completely banned. Tinto could have gotten away with it had he simply added some lines condemning the idea and showing how such a choice would lead to personal ruin, but he would never do such a thing. Further, there was some nudity as well as a scene dealing with birth control. As for "Son et Lumière for Bodily Fluids and Functions" with Kumo Spyder and his never-identified ladyfriend having intercourse on an inflatable cushion, well, that would never do. Tinto's plan was simple. First, he would complete his ideal version of the film. Next, he would cut it to please the Italian censors. Finally, once the censor board approved the bowdlerized edition, he would get an export license and sneak out the full version for international release.[163]

The first step of the plan was easy. Tinto spent from late November 1967 through probably February 1968 editing the hundred or so hours of image and sound into free association. It included scenes that were all of two frames long, too short to be perceived even subliminally. When he received the finished recordings of the 14 songs in April 1968, he mixed them in, though they never fit the lip movements. He hired Giancarlo Fusco to write lines to be spoken over the action,[164] and he hired actors to record those lines in English and to dub the characters' few lines into English as well. He then hired different actors to record all the lines in Italian. He proudly showed the result to Anita Sanders and to Alan Sekers. They were pleased with the two-hour product.[165] Probably nobody else ever saw that original version, for Tinto immediately set about massacring his own film.

First, Tinto needed to remove as much nudity as possible. One of the victims of this cutting was a song called "Decidedly Man," which was entirely deleted, though a few flashes of the accompanying images in the dress shop were moved to a different song, "The Truth Is Plain to See." Barbara's musing about the conservative fear of pubic hair was changed to the conservative fear of nudes. "Son et Lumière for Bodily Fluids and Functions" was severely shortened and scrambled, much of it was darkened almost to invisibility, and swirling misshapen concentric circles were superimposed over the images of Kumo Spyder and his ladyfriend. The swirling circles, by the way, were a joke. They were copied exactly from the opening credits of *Schichlegruber Doing the Lambeth Walk* (1941, Charles A. Ridley). He cut numerous scenes. The sequence of Barbara and the American in a screening room, probably watching Welles' *Macbeth*, with a sleeping Alan Sekers in the back row? Gone. The scene in the shoe shop? Gone. The scene in which Barbara shops for funky sunglasses? Gone. The scene at Joan Price's Face Place? Gone. The scene of the shirtless American wearing a clock necklace and snakes in his hair? Gone. The scene in the Fun House at Luna Park? Gone. The scene of Barbara presumably hooking in front of a strip joint? Gone. The opening credits prominently announce that Umberto di Grazia appears in the film. He is gone. The striptease performed by someone named Rusty has at least a minute chopped out from the middle (we can hear the splice and the jump in the music), and we may never learn what was in that material. As Callisto Cosulich explained, Tinto "prepared for use on the Italian market a fake copy with obscured scenes and others cut, still others replaced by harmless sequences. Of course, the *Nerosubianco* which was supposed to circulate in Italy would not have been 'his' film. And, in fact, Brass intended to disown it as soon as he obtained the censorship visa. A questionable way forward? Maybe. We shall see."[166]

By the time Tinto was through slashing away, all that was left of his two-hour movie was about 75 minutes, mere scrambled fragments of what had once been a visionary work. He submitted this amputated remnant to the Ministero del Turismo e dello Spettacolo, and the censor review was scheduled for Friday, 8 November 1968, a little more than a year after shooting was completed. At the time, Tinto was in London shooting his next film, *The Howl*. He flew back for the occasion and stood in the chairless lobby for 75 minutes while the screening proceeded in the auditorium. Seven censors were on duty that day: Antonio Giorgini of the Court of Cassation; Rinaldo Orecchia, a professor of legal philosophy; a schoolteacher named Iclea Picco; a psychologist named Nicola Perrotti; a movie director named Roberto Savarese; Camillo Bruno, a lawyer representing the movie industry; and Enzo Natta, film critic at *Christian Family* (*Famiglia Cristiana*). When the screening was over, they left, walked right past Tinto, and uttered not a word. It was not until after the time for appeal had expired that the censors sent a registered letter to Tinto and Lion Film. Clearance was emphatically denied:

The majority of the Commission sees in the conceptual inspiration of the film, as in almost all the scenes in which it is articulated, elements of serious offense to public morality mentioned in article 6 of the law of 21.4.1962, number 161, and in article 21 of the Constitution, offense that is understood in the sense of an attack on public morality.

It is impossible to list the innumerable sequences (many of which are inferior even as vulgarity and obscenity) detrimental to this public morality. Drawing on a pretext of the protagonist's psychological introspection, the film shows realistically and with evident complacency the most disconcerting aspects of her morbid, obsessive, exasperated sexual anguish, revealed through her soliloquies, through her behavior in erotic scenes of extreme audacity in which she is sometimes the protagonist and sometimes the spectator, through the recurrent allusions of clearly phallic symbols, through episodes of undeniable obscenity, even if sometimes shrewdly presented in the background or put in rapid "flashes" or partially but not sufficiently concealed.

The film's theme itself is extremely ruthless and immoral; she winds through the constant contrast between the erupting virility of black eros and the constitutional insufficiency of the husband, and she finds her catharsis and her sublimation in the consummation of adultery as a means of redemption for the frustrations of the unsatisfied protagonist, who only in this way is led to the liberation from agonizing anxiety and the powerful sexual charge that pervades her, and hence her redemption.

Therefore, the opinion against the issue of the clearance for his public screening is expressed.

Upon receiving this letter, Tinto got one of his wicked ideas and burst out with a guffaw. He would cut even more of the film's moments of tenderness, and in their place he would splice in war atrocities.[167] He called Nino Segurini back to do a new scene, in whiteface, to portray Paolo as a ghoulish priest who heralds the upcoming war scenes. This scene, interestingly, offers us a hint that the few lines of dialogue may have been filmed in English as well as Italian. We see Father Paolo make the sign of the cross with his poster that reads "PROIBITO." When he turns around to walk away, we see that on the reverse of the poster is a duplicate, this one reading "FORBIDDEN." Clearly, two acceptable takes were made of this sequence, but only the Italian variant is known to survive.

Italian Fotobusta poster, 1969

Tinto by now knew the pattern: Wait for the next election. Upon the election, the government was slightly liberalized and the film, with footage of war atrocities substituting for a love scene, was passed, and Columbia C.E.I.A.D. released the film to Italian cinemas on 26 February 1969.

Inexplicably, there was a blatant error in the Italian print. The credit scroll at the opening was not superimposed over the image, but was placed on the black border below the image, an area of the film that would be cropped off in projection. The laboratory then "corrected" this error by raising the image, resulting in the top of the image going missing. Most characters are thus headless during the credit sequence. More surprisingly, this identical error was replicated for the export version of the film!

Unexpectedly, *Nerosubianco* made a little bit of money, a box-office gross of IT£234,144,000, about US$373,498, which was average for a minor low-budget film.[168] As small as the profit was, it caught the attention of some executives in Hollywood.

Tinto was not able to release the full film internationally. He was foolish to have announced his plan to export the full edition. It was illegal to export even a frame of film that had not been cleared by the censors. Had Tinto simply kept his mouth shut, he could surely have packed a different version of the film into a box and shipped it out of the country and nobody would have noticed. Yet he gave his game away. He told journalist Callisto Cosulich that he planned to export a different edition of the movie, and so he was caught. The export edition of the film was only slightly different from than the domestic version. Each edition contained a little bit of material that the other was missing, each contained a song that the other was missing, but neither was even close to the two-hour original. The final Italian version was a mere 76 minutes, while the export edition was 80 minutes.[169] Both are choppy, with jumps and pops and thuds in the audio where sections were excised, a blackout to mask objectionable images, and multiple leaps from one set of images to another when they clearly do not belong juxtaposed. In its favor, the export edition at least had fewer spinning spirals and grids obscuring the image.

Columbia Pictures decided against issuing *Nerosubianco/Attraction* in the U.S. and Canada. Who was operating De Laurentiis Cinematografica at the time remains unknown. Perhaps it was still in the hands of the Italian tax authorities. Whoever was in charge arranged

U.S. newsprint advert, 1969

for a trade screening during the time of the Cannes Film Festival in May 1969. Some executives from Paramount Pictures were impressed by the movie, but the winning bidder was Radley Metzger of Audubon Films.

Radley was a fiendishly clever promoter. In addition to making his own films, he also specialized in licensing U.S./Canadian rights to risqué European films, films that straddled the border between high art and outright exploitation. Whenever and wherever he opened a film, there were lines around the block and sell-out crowds for weeks on end. When he saw *Attraction* he recognized a polished jewel. It fit his program perfectly, and, better yet, it was an exceptionally fine film that deeply impressed him. He was certain he could make a success out of it. He advertised the film as *Black on White* and opened it in Manhattan at the Trans-Lux East and at the Trans-Lux West, where he had it run for 29 days. It was a flop. The few reviews were extremely hostile. *The New York Times*: "garbage," "dull," "sickening," "idiotic," "filthy," "excruciating." *The New York Daily News*: "pornographic," "incredible garbage." *Variety*: "pretentious exploiter," "utterly forgettable rock score," "tasteless," "agonizing." It is obvious that these three critics, who were probably the only three American reviewers, were entirely unaware of avant-garde underground cinema and were oblivious to the counterculture. Radley also opened *Black on White* in Detroit and in State College, Pennsylvania, and perhaps in a few other places as well. The reception was no warmer.

After years of successes, Radley finally had a failure. He had made the mistake of aiming the film at the erotica market rather than at the psych-rock flower children. There was no crossover in those two markets. He was terribly disappointed that the film never found its audience.

To earn back his investment, he superimposed a new title onto the opening shot, *The Artful Penetration of Barbara*, and he released it as a two-bit exploitation film. It played at a handful of mainstream cinemas as well as at porn houses, usually for one-week bookings, and when the last 35mm release print wore out a decade later, he withdrew the film. Years later Radley sold Cult Epics the rights, with the only availability of a 16mm print, which was painstakingly restored.

A powerful method of promoting a film is by means of an original soundtrack album. When an OST is issued in parallel with a film, each promotes the other. A British release in the first half of 1968, targeted to the members of the London scene and the counterculture and the psych-rock fans, would have been a sensation and would have worked wonders for the Freedom band as well as for the film. The original soundtrack album for *Nerosubianco* was issued in June or July 1969 on Atlantic, ATL-LP 08028—but it was issued only in Italy, and the Freedom members did not even know about it until three decades later.[170] Despite being on the Atlantic label, Atlantic declined to distribute it, and instead sublicensed it to Rifi Records of Milan, which had little clout. The album had no commercial value in the Italian market and so only a handful of the LPs were sold. In recent years, upon the rediscovery of the short-lived Freedom, the album has become a collector's item, and the rare original copies sell for hundreds of dollars.

When Radley opened the film in the U.S., two years after it was shot, there was no album sold alongside it. Freedom disbanded in 1972, and it was not until the following year that Columbia-Warner released *Attraction* in England. It was cut to 59 minutes and played at a porno house called the Jacey Tatler on Charing Cross Road, second-billed to *Sex Is the Name of the Game*. It ran from 27 September through 31 October 1973 and it then vanished.

Columbia released the film as *Negro en Blanco* in Spain in 1969; as *Attraction* in West Germany and Austria in October 1969; and as *SEX* in Japan in 1970. Columbia also released *Attraction* in Denmark in July 1970 and in the Netherlands in September 1970. In November 1974, Columbia sent the 59-minute British version to Australia, where it played in a few minor rural cinemas for a few days, as second on a double bill, without display ads.

Nerosubianco is still a remarkable film. In its original release, it was shown to general audiences and exploitation audiences, and it left them cold. Nowadays, it is specialty audiences who show up, audiences who enjoy challenges and thoughtfulness. Those are the audiences who love it.

Nerosubianco/Attraction, despite disappearing unnoticed from movie screens, had an outsized influence. Alan Sekers worked with a schoolmate, Nick Saxton, on several pictures including *Nerosubianco*. Saxton worked as Tinto's location manager, and a dozen years later he borrowed Tinto's techniques, adapted them to the technology of the time, and made a video of a Michael Jackson song, "Don't Stop 'til You Get Enough," released in October 1979. It was one of the earliest music videos, a revolutionary work that transformed the music business and spawned MTV two years later. So, Tinto, who by luck happened to capture the birth of the flower-power movement and psychedelic rock, directly led to the birth of the music video. It was an unexpected, unplanned journey that remunerated him probably not a lira and earned him not even a moment of recognition.

Before *Deadly Sweet* and *Attraction* had a chance to fail, they were seen by Hollywood executives who recognized in Tinto an exceptional talent. Alan Sekers revealed an unpublished story:

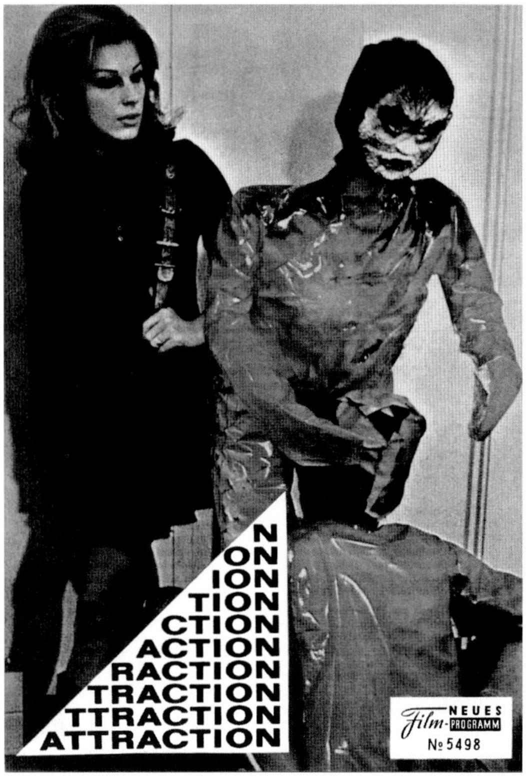

West German film program, 1967

It was after *Col cuore in gola* [Deadly Sweet] that Tinto got a call from some studio, maybe it was United Artists, who asked him to bring his new script to Manhattan. They gave him a first-class ticket from Rome, a limousine picked him up from JFK Airport, and took him straight up to the skyscraper. "Come back tomorrow," he was told. When he went back the next day, the reception desk told him to go around to the back, where a mailroom clerk, with his fingers over his nose, handed him an envelope. His return trip had been downgraded. Apparently, they hadn't liked the script.

Whether that script was *Nerosubianco* or *The Howl*, we do not know. What we do know for certain is that not long afterwards the narrative was repeated, but with a variation. Paramount Pictures at the time held an option on Anthony Burgess' novel *A Clockwork Orange*. Novelist Terry Southern was impressed by Burgess' work and tried to get a film version off the ground, with Mick Jagger as Alex and the other Rolling Stones as the Droogs. Michael Cooper was considered as a director. Cooper was unavailable, and so the film was offered to David Bailey, Nicolas Roeg, John Boorman, Ted Kotcheff, and Ken Russell. One by one, each director either dropped out or was dropped. When some Paramount executives saw *Attraction*, they thought they had at last found the perfect director for *Clockwork*. Tinto elaborates:

At that point they called me from the United States, because I did *Black on White* and they appreciated it, and they wanted me to work for them at Paramount. Then I met at this studio, great, full of memories, and I said I had this project... I wanted to do *The Howl* and I didn't have a script, just two lines. They offered me another film... and they gave me a book. For two, three days I read that book. It was not easy to read, it had a strange language, it was *Clockwork Orange*. They wanted me to make *Clockwork Orange*. I went back and when I met them again and said I like the book, surely, and I will be pleased to do *Clockwork Orange* but first I want to do *The Howl*. Then *Clockwork Orange* was done by Kubrick. But I like to do *L'urlo* next... it's a film that correspondent [*sic*] with me the most.[171]

Source Notes:

155 Audio commentary by Tinto Brass, *Deadly Sweet* DVD (Cult Epics, 2009)

156 Dave McGowan, *Weird Scenes Inside the Canyon: Laurel Canyon, Covert Ops & the Dark Heart of the Hippie Dream* (Headpress, 2014)

157 Nerio Minuzzo, "Infrange i tabù, l'ultimo film di Tinto Brass, BIANCA E NERO," *L'Europeo: set-timanale politico di attualità* Vol. 23 #45, 9 November 1967, pp. 86–90

158 Alan Sekers: email, 2 November 2020

159 Alfred Friendly, Jr., "Mama Mia! Rome Is No Place to Be a Movie Star," *The New York Times*, Sunday, 1 February 1970, sec. 2, p. 30

160 Terry Carter, "Notes During a Rehearsal Break," *The Pittsburgh Courier*, Saturday, 19 August 1961, sec. 3, p. 21

161 Claes Johansen, *Procol Harum: Beyond the Pale* (London: SAF, 2000), pp. 114–115

162 J.L. Locher, "Mark Boyle's Journey to the Surface of the Earth," *Boyle Family*, March 2001, *boylefamily.co.uk*

163 Callisto Cosulich, "Il film vietato agli italiani: Nerosubianco. Per poterlo vedere ci vorrà il passaporto," *ABC settimanale politico e di attualità*, Vol. 9 #48, 20 December 1968, pp. 33–48

164 Giancarlo Fusco, "Com'è nato Nerosubianco: Non si può non si fa," *ABC settimanale politico e di attualità* Vol. 9 #48, 20 December 1968, p. 34

165 Alfred Friendly, Jr., *The New York Times*, sec. 2, p. 30

166 Cosulich, *ABC settimanale politico e di attualità*, pp. 33–48

167 Alan Sekers: personal conversation

168 Gianni Rondolino, ed., *Catalogo Balaffi del cinema italiano: tutti i film italiani degli ultimi dieci anni* (Turin: Giulio Balaffi Editore, November 1976), p. 77

169 The common claim that the export edition was 89 minutes was the persistent result of a typographical error.

170 The discs were cut on 23 June 1969.

171 Audio commentary by Tinto Brass, *The Howl* DVD (Cult Epics, 2009)

IX
The Howl
(L'urlo)

ONCE AGAIN TINTO contacted Dino De Laurentiis if he wanted to produce his next film, with no script attached. De Laurentiis agreed to invest in the production after Tinto's convincing argument:

I convinced the financier of the film, it was Dino De Laurentiis, to make the film, with a statement that I did and it said: If history start running, the cinema can't go on walking, the time has come to blow up the screen. And the time has come to start looking at the image and the unexploited possibilities of the cinema. The time has come to make exceptional films, only in this way we can avoid losing those young people recognizing themselves in anything which is today offered by the society they live in. He was impressed.[172]

How Tina Aumont was brought on to the project, nobody seems to know. As for Luigi "Gigi" Proietti, Tinto had long admired his versatility and hired him, over De Laurentiis' objection. The objection? De Laurentiis wanted the film to be in English, but Proietti's English was hesitant at best. Tinto turned that into a joke, as Proietti's character conjugates English verbs. English conjugation is then incorporated into a song, "Break, Broke, Broken." Tinto: "Tina, she was the most beautiful woman I had met, and had an accent—because she was French her voice was dubbed by Mariangela Melato, who was a most famous actress in theatre."[173]

The title comes from Allen Ginsberg's poem "Howl," as well as from Edvard Munch's famous painting *Skrik* (The Scream). The concept of the film comes from riots. The methodology of the film comes from dreams.

The Howl is very much a companion piece to *Attraction*, as it was created in a free-form fashion. Tinto had typed a treatment of sorts, though what it included, we do not know. We do know that it was about a young woman who chose to run away from marriage and to continue by running away from society. We also know that Tinto did not use that treatment. He and his cast and crew simply chose locations when the situation arose. The basic concept of the story was clear, but not the specific episodes, which cast and crew invented in response to their locations. Tinto commented on shooting in Rome and London:

Shooting the film was very exciting because we translated our feelings day by day. I remember that we were shooting in Rome, and at a certain moment we had the feeling that it was more interesting in London, so in one week we organized everything, and went to finish the film in London.[174]

As a matter of fact, he was shooting in a studio in Rome, and Dino had heard he was not shooting a very correct scene there. Tinto: "There was a problem with shooting in Rome, as a rumor went about doing some scenes, an orgy, so then we went to London."[175] They continued to plane-hop during the shoot. Various sequences were shot at New Forest in Hampshire, in a subway tunnel in London, at Cinecittà, in Naples, in Berlin, in Paris, on the island of Santo Stefano, and perhaps in some other places, too. The result, having no continuity whatsoever, results in a sort of dreamworld.

The story opens with Anita Anigoni being imprisoned, but it establishes this not by the simple precedent of showing her behind bars. Instead, it opens with stock footage of a riot, of police charging, of police suppressing a riot, and then we hear Anita scream as we see the cover of Franz Kafka's short story *In the Penal Colony*, featuring a graphic of a man shouting. The expression is entirely abstract, but entirely understandable.

The remainder of the film continues in this vein. Because a cue of Fiorenzo Carpi's background music has a thump-thump rhythm, there is a cut to an earth rammer. When Anita is distressed, we see a detail of Diego Rivera's *Sueño en una tarde dominical en la alameda central* (1947). This technique continues throughout. As with *Attraction*, the blending of image and sound is not linear, but simply follows a free flow of thoughts and associations.

Coming to Anita's rescue is her boyfriend with a bribe at hand. He is Berto Bertuccioli, a suit-and-tie conformist, executive of PPP, or, more exactly, of PPPPP, and that is a joke that was not meant to be understood. Pier Paolo Pasolini's friends often called him PPP. Tinto found that amusing and put the sobriquet to his own use. Upon getting her released, he proposes marriage, and her lackadaisical response is "Yeah, if you like." The wedding ceremony is in what appears to be a garbage dump. The priest with an abscessed tooth wears a shrunken head on his necklace. When Anita is cued to say "I do," she spots Coso (meaning Whatshisname or Thingamabob) gazing at her. She runs off with him and immediately they begin a series of adventures, none of which makes even the slightest bit of sense. Physically consummating their affair on a commuter bus that is driving through a forest preserve, they come to a halt when the bus driver (Tinto himself) runs away screaming. The passengers alight from the bus as the Keystone Kops run in from nowhere. Somehow escaping from prison, with Coso still in striped outfit and a ball and chain, they hitch a ride in a car driven by a duplicate of Berto Bertuccioli who has a duplicate of Anita in the passenger seat. They make their way to a hotel (the sperm hotel) that proves to be a party spot, complete with baboons, a talking swan enjoying the company of Leda, and a gathering of mournful exhibitionists. A guard chases them to the woods where a tree-dwelling cannibal family intend to roast and eat the whole lot of them. Without explanation, they find themselves in the middle of World War II with a talking cannon and a clucking piano player. Coso survives a firing squad, and he and Anita assassinate the dictator, a midget dressed as Napoleon with a wind-up key on his back. That turns the tide of battle, and, upon victory, they party with a group of hippie revelers in a subway tunnel and free the all the prisoners who are guarded over by a lyre-playing officer and his pet lion. The prisoners worship Anita as their goddess until they find that the exit is open and they all flee. General de Gaulle, Karl Marx, and Malcolm X rise from their graves to give their advice, Coso chases Anita away, she dies in a car wreck and then marries Berto.

The Howl is anarchistic and sometimes surreal cinema at its best with no dialogue-driven script but scenes played out, similar to the zeitgeist of Fernando Arrabal and Jodorowsky. It was made during the unrest of 1968 and it incorporated that unrest. As with a dream, as with tea-leaf readings, as with any random stimuli, a meaning forms itself. Tinto and those who improvised with him were surely aware of their concepts and their attitudes and their outlooks, but they were unaware of any message until they were nearly finished, and they then recognized what they had wrought: an agonizing scream against convention as well as a sense of humor about it. Indeed, it is the most playful film that Tinto ever made. It remains his favorite of all his films, the one he says best represents who he is.

When it came time to write the dialogue to be dubbed in after editing was complete, there was a concerted effort to make that dialogue pointless. Says Anita as she is traveling through an overgrowth in the countryside, "Oh. An alligator just bit me," spoken in the same way she would mention a mosquito bite. When the priest finally marries Anita and Berto at the end, his words are no less meaningful than those spoken in regular ceremonies:

> **PRIEST: Can the bird of paradise strike against the annihilated consumed tree of your sap without a parachute?**
> **GROOM: Yes.**
> **PRIEST: And can the tired turtle fly fast in the months of July on Wednesday?**
> **BRIDE: Um.**
> **PRIEST: Ergo I lengthen a box on tip-toe, figs and cloves of breath. Anise.**

This is a brilliant mish-mash of word associations, signifying nothing other than the sheer joy of mixing things up.

The behavior of the performers on screen and of the creators behind the camera is like that of small children who enjoy playing grown-up. Such rituals serve to illustrate, whether intentionally or unintentionally, the pointlessness of prescribed social behaviors.

The film boasts delicious performances all around. The young Tinto had been enchanted when he saw Tino Scotti perform on variety stages, and the two worked together splendidly in this film. What Tina Aumont's talents were, we do not know, but she was comfortable in front of the camera and she perfectly understood the comedy and the absurdism. Gigi Proietti, another famous variety comic and singer, stole every scene he was in, and he invented many of those scenes himself. Even his delivery of word-salad lines was done as physical comedy, and it is nearly impossible to take one's eyes off of him. Eduardo Florio as Diogenes dressed in a barrel, the extras, the revelers, the prisoners are all magnetic.

The movie was filmed in September and October 1968, during the protests against the war in Vietnam, not long after the May 1968 protests that nearly toppled the French government, just after the failure of the Prague Spring. Anti-authoritarianism was taking strong root and protest art was in evidence everywhere. Tinto explains:

> ***The Howl*** **is about a meta reality, a reality different from the one we are living, more pleasure and to feel free. Make happen the impossible, the impossible will therefore**

become possible. If you believe deeply in something, you succeed. Typical line of students of 1968. It was a film of the time, *The Howl*, the cry of rage of that time, of the student movement. I understand now they can see a very insane story, a story to the meaning of the film, it was a story to express feelings. How we felt during these days.[176]

The Howl can easily be considered an example of that protest art, or anarchistic punk rock before such even existed. Rather, it can now be seen as poetic art, a film about 1968. He mixed the grotesque with comedy, and while most of it is hilarious it also shocks, and shows humanity at its worst, as displayed in *Ça ira*—and impossible for most people to maintain their laughter when they are suddenly confronted with wartime scenes of executions or the killing of a mouse or the butchering of a gosling. Tinto: "There was a hotel of sex, a mixture of Bosch and Brueghel paintings of all sorts of perversions."[177]

The Howl is a singular item in Tinto's filmography probably because there was no way to follow it up. It took the ideas as far as they could go, and so it is not in any way surprising that all of Tinto's future films would have coherent plots that were written out ahead of time.

As we sift through the publicity materials, we see that the bulk of the production photographs are images of scenes that are not in the final film. Many would have been deleted as a matter of course in the editing of the film, and that is perfectly normal. What we see, though, is much more than that. Because of censorship, he was unable to present it at the 1969 Venice Film Festival, and so instead he presented it at the June 1970 Berlin Film Festival, at which it was well received. A festival director told Tinto that *The Howl* would win the grand prize, but it did not, since anti-war protests shut down the remainder of the Festival. Back in Italy, the censors banned the film unless Tinto would agree to trim it. Tinto: "What offended the censorship was pure political, the attack to the violence of the institutions. It got banned, seized and not been shown."[178]

Tinto had long been amused by a Portuguese epigraph that Henry Miller included on his personal stationery: "Cuando merda tiver valor pobre nasce sem cu" ("When shit becomes valuable, the poor will be born without assholes"). Tinto took that sentence, put it into Italian,

Tinto Brass with actors Gigi Proietti and Tina Aumont, 1968

Publicity photo: Scene from ***The Howl****, 1968*

and gave the line to an actor impersonating Malcolm X, but made a change: "When shit becomes valuable, blacks will be born without assholes." The censors objected. "No, no, it's impossible. You can't say '*merda*' [shit], but '*sterco*' [dung]." There was also a scene in a Latin class with a bottomless teacher admonishing an excited student. The censors said that had to go. Tinto recognized that these were not legitimate objections, but were just pretexts. Indeed, after all the unrest around the world in 1968, the censors actually seemed to understand that the film was nonconformist, and such they could not abide. They had to search about for any excuse to condemn the work, and they succeeded. They knew Tinto would never agree to such absurd cuts, and he didn't. He refused to budge. Tinto protested in a public letter, which 21 members of his cast and crew cosigned. It was an astonishing letter. Though Tinto and his cast and crew were making a surreal comedy, once they looked at what they had crafted, they understood its meaning and they understood perfectly well its effect. Tinto wrote:

We protest with all indignation the circumstance that demanded the inadmissible abuse perpetrated against our film *The Howl*, rejected by the 4th Censorship Commission on 15 September 1969, on the pretext of "constituting an offense to morality and morality, as normally understood in the current historical moment."

We affirm with all the strength of our conviction that this motivation does not correspond to the truth, but is a cover for an act of pure and simple ideological repression.

We admit that our film may not please certain authorities; it is also undisputed that certain audiences may not like it; it may even happen that it encounters circulation difficulties; but we deny that—in the light of the laws in effect—its circulation can be prohibited on principle.

The Howl is an explosion of anger, nausea, pain from those who feel that the air of the "current historical moment" is less and less breathable, full of death, meanness, material and spiritual misery.

It is a desperate cry of joy from those who try to get out of the swamp of the "current historical moment" in which day after day we risk drowning.

It is the exhilarating spectacle of freedom and life as opposed to the humiliating daily reality of death and servility that loom over the "present historical moment."

In the film there is no offense to morality and custom; there is simply the rejection of a morality and custom, "good" or bad, which have made and continue to make

Publicity photo: Nino Segurini and Tina Aumont, 1968

the "current historical moment" an epoch of blood and violence, of intolerance and oppression, of alienation and dehumanization, of narrow consumerist materialism without ideals, without hope, without creative vitality.

There is therefore no law that can legitimately prevent us from howling; there are only hypocrisies and subterfuges, maneuvers and interpretative exploitation that can illegally attempt to gag us. Operations repressive, that is, of our right to express ourselves and that of the public to judge us. We therefore protest these abuses.

Other filmmakers came to his defense, Michelangelo Antonioni among them, penning a petition to have the film released. The censors backed down and agreed to pass the film; the film got a censorship visa with the accord to the distributor that it should not be released, and it was not until 1974 that the general public would have the opportunity to see *The Howl*, with a small release. Later on, it did get the recognition it deserved, as Tinto commented on *L'urlo* in the early 2000s:

***L'urlo* is a film now shown in many cinema institutes, including the Cinémathèque Française*, where they paid homage to me. They consider *L'urlo* really a very significant film of that period and of those days.**[179]

The Howl later gained a cult following when a special edited version under Tinto's supervision, derived from different elements, was released uncut by Cult Epics in the U.S. For the first time, a new audience finally was able to experience the film he made.

Source Notes:

172 Audio commentary by Tinto Brass, *The Howl* DVD (Cult Epics, 2009)

173 Ibid.

174 Nico B, "Tinto Brass: Maestro of Erotic Cinema," interview conducted 3 November 2001, Torcello (Los Angeles: Cult Epics, 2014)

175 Tinto Brass, *The Howl* DVD

176 Ibid.

177 Ibid.

178 Ibid.

179 Nico B, "Tinto Brass: Maestro of Erotic Cinema"

*A Tinto Brass retrospective was shown in January 2002.

X
Dropout

CURIOUS ABOUT the escalating scandal surrounding *The Howl*, a number of people in the movie business asked for a private screening. That occurred in England, probably in London, certainly in March or April 1970, though further specifics are impossible to discern. It played to an audience who mostly did not speak a word of Italian. In that audience was Jane Fonda. Also there was Vanessa Redgrave, who did speak Italian and who was deeply impressed. Just afterwards, Vanessa's boyfriend, Franco Nero, sent Tinto a letter to say that Vanessa hoped he had a script for her. Franco Nero said later:

He was an important filmmaker of that period, a popular director at that time—there was talk of "the new genius." (*IsTintoBrass* documentary, 2012)

Tinto's previous scripts had been musings, experiments, avant-garde expressionism, or, in the case of *The Howl*, free-form improvisation. This time it would be the same, he had an idea, it was simple. An escapee from a mental institution, on a search for the only witness who can prove his innocence, kidnaps a woman to help him in his quest. His victim becomes totally loyal to him, and their search takes them through the slums and into the criminal underground.

Soon Vanessa Redgrave and Franco Nero were at Tinto's house. Tinto's company, Lion Film, would produce. Lion found an investor in Carlo Ponti, who quickly withdrew his offer. Said Tinto to Vanessa and Franco, "Let's do it anyway!" Lion raised some funds by partnering with Oreste Coltellacci's company, Colt Produzioni Cinematografica. Further funds were gained by preselling Italian exhibition rights to Medusa Film and international distribution rights to Titanus International, which in turn signed a contract with Twentieth Century-Fox for right of first refusal on U.S. distribution. Tinto, Vanessa, and Franco may have topped off the total by investing some of their own money as well. Altogether, they now had about $100,000 with which they could make a 16mm film quickly on natural locations in England. Vanessa and Franco worked without pay, but with only a promise of royalties, if any. Shooting began on the first of June and was concluded before month's end.

One can recognize some spiritual predecessors. In 1931, René Clair made a film called *À nous la liberté*, which seamlessly combined naturalism, social realism, and absurdism, and was done in part as a musical. Such a feat would seem impossible, and yet it worked, brilliantly, and it has withstood the test of time. Some years later, Cesare Zavattini and Vittorio De Sica attempted the same impossibility with *Miracle in Milan*, and once again the film worked brilliantly and it is still celebrated. With such works in the background, Tinto attempted something similar. *Dropout* provides us with naturalistic scenes of slums, shot on actual locations, with locals portraying themselves. Yet the story was told as an absurdist tale, filled with preposterously comical elements.

Bruno kidnaps Mary at knifepoint and strips and strings up her husband Robert to prevent him from giving chase. He drives Mary away in her car, not to hold her hostage, not to do her mischief, but simply to help him find his witness, a certain Jennifer Johnson. He finds Jennifer's elderly landlady on the toilet, and when she attacks him in fury, he bursts into an opera aria. He imprisons Mary in an abandoned house that is ready to topple over and conveniently he falls asleep on her. She makes her way back home, where she takes the opportunity to tell her husband that she will stay with Bruno.

There follows a throwback to *Ça ira*, which frequently employed workingman's hymns on its soundtrack. Here, when Bruno and Mary ask a large group of striking workers about the whereabouts of Miss Johnson, the soundtrack provides us a different sort of workingman's song, which may well have been an actual song that Tinto happened to hear some men singing, or it may perhaps have been a joke song by Don Fraser. The tune is catchy, but most of the lyrics are buried underneath dialogue and sound effects. Some of the phrases we can catch are:

Work, work, work, work,
work brothers, work.
It's good for us, it's good for us,
it keeps us out of trouble,
a good day's work, a good day's work,
but night rate pays us double.
We're brothers all, we've brought it all,
we made the common stand,
we hate the blacks, we hate the Jews,
and we hate the bloody band.
We walk with frogs, the dirty sods,
the spastics and the queens,
but worse than them the student scum,
they're the brunt of all our tears.
The skinhead louts and layabouts,
the yellow and the blind,
we hate the lot, the loghead mob,
but worst of all mankind.

The police riot to break up the strike, and next we find ourselves in a slum where Mary and Bruno chance upon a Black Power meeting and are attacked as spies. They spend the night in a doss house where Bruno witnesses a murder and where the two find themselves again in the midst of another riot. Mary hallucinates that secret military troops in gas masks are aiming for them and to stave them off she tears Bruno's pants down. A limp Italian, Gigi the Pimp, claims that Jennifer works for him, and to find her, he and his strongman, together with Bruno and Mary and some passersby, dance to Bizet's *Carmen* to arrive at the residence of the Prime Minister, a Mafioso who expects Mary to become one of his prostitutes. Meanwhile, Gigi the Pimp lectures some meths drinkers about prostitution being corporate capitalism as one drunken meths drinker sings "Bandiera Rossa" in Italian. When Robert attacks Mary upon her return, she escapes once again with Bruno in the hopes of taking refuge in Italy. Alas, the police put paid to that idea.

There are other adventures besides. None of the adventures makes any particular sense, though each adventure is engaging, a few are hilarious, and some are strangely and agonizingly moving.

Don Fraser composed about an hour of music, but it seems that little if any of his work made its way into the final film. Two of the songs, "The Sun Is Shining" and "Do Not Cry," were composed and performed by a new Scottish group called the Middle of the Road, which

Vanessa Redgrave, Tinto Brass, and Franco Nero, 1970

at the time was based in Rome. "The Sun Is Shining" is reggae, while "Do Not Cry" takes its text from a letter to his son by Ferdinando Nicola Sacco on the eve of his execution. Both songs are marvelous, but the group soon discovered that such works did not sell, and so quickly switched to a different, more middle-of-the-road rock style that became fabulously successful. Tinto decided against using "Do Not Cry" in the film. Instead, he chose an Italian adaptation that was rewritten in honor of Giuseppe Pinelli, who had just been tossed out a window to his death by a police interrogator. Luigi Proietti sang this new version, "Non piangere," and different verses appear sporadically throughout the movie. The English original as sung by Middle of the Road was later released as a single, but only in Portugal.

A journalist, Sally K. Brass (no relation), caught up with the *Dropout* troupe and asked Vanessa Redgrave why, after turning down so many studio scripts, she chose to go ahead with this one. Vanessa was a bit startled by the question, and answered, simply, "I saw his last film. He is a fantastic director. It's the first film I've been around which is on every level that I'm concerned about, and that we are all concerned about."[180] She continued that whereas British films require adherence to a script, Italian films are freer, more open to improvisation, and allow everybody to pitch in ideas. Tinto would explain his intentions, and, as the camera rolled, the actors would invent the scenes to match those intentions. That is how we learn that the script was just a departure point, read once and then jettisoned. The cast and crew invented the details of the story as they discovered the characters and situations.

Tinto also spoke of Vanessa:

She is "the" actress par excellence. After working with Vanessa, any other actress seems... well, you know what I mean. She was the best, absolutely. Watching her acting was a unique experience, and a real pleasure—whatever she did, she was great. I remember shooting *Dropout*—by the end of the film there's a scene where Vanessa and Franco Nero, both fugitives, are waiting to board a ship as stowaways at Southampton beach. She asked me, "What's my character's mood now?" I did not use a script then, just tiny little treatments on which we used to improvise day by day. I did not know exactly what to say, so I replied vaguely, "Think about

Italian Fotobusta poster, 1971

two beaten dogs licking their wounds." Just those few words. Lights, camera, action. They are sleeping, covered with old newspapers as sheets. Vanessa wakes up and looks at Franco by her side. Then she starts licking him, literally, passing her tongue on his eyes, his nose, his ears, all over his face. My metaphor had become reality, yet it wasn't something pretentious or over-ambitious. She managed to turn a simple suggestion into something strong, powerful, and violent. I was absolutely shocked. That scene had become so real and effective, without a single jarring note... simply shocking, and I mean it... Vanessa would catch me off-guard every time, changing a bit here and there.[181]

Tinto has frequently said privately that he is not a great director, though he is convinced, rightly, that he is the world's best editor. He would rescue bad direction and poor performances in the editing. He even rewrote the dialogue by mixing syllables from the original sound tapes to create entire conversations that the actors had never spoken. While some actors fully concur that Tinto's approach leaves a great deal to be desired, other actors do not agree at all with Tinto's low assessment about his directorial skills. A few months after shooting was completed, Vanessa Redgrave explained:

We knocked it off in three and a half weeks, and I'm just dreading the 17 weeks of working in a studio for *The Devils*. Brass knew exactly what he wanted, he simply told us what to do, and without any discussions or nonsense, we did it. It was just that simple. I like working with Italian directors. They don't depend on an actor acting up a storm and carrying on with boring, stupid rehearsals and infinite discussions about motivations and meanings. The Italian director tells you what to do—and of course you have confidence in him or you shouldn't make the film—and you do it![182]

This is a legitimate style of directing that was employed by many of the best. Such a director assumes that the actors know their job and entrusts them to do their job, without endless discussions and without rehearsals.

Tinto again engaged in his hobby of mixing fiction and reality. When he needed a scene with meths drinkers, he wandered about and found some meths drinkers.

We have used a lot of real people there. The other night I saw some rushes from a scene we did in a hideaway under Tower Bridge. It was with a lot of drunks. They were meths drinkers—we gave them not real meths, just some alcohol colored like meths. It is incredible how they played this scene. More true than if I took an actor. The truth is that they didn't play it at all. They helped and gave suggestions. I knew the area where they hang out, also I went into two or three doss houses and mercy houses, but once you have found one, you have found the lot because the rumor goes around.[183]

It is also obvious that the film as we have it has been gouged. There are jarring jumps in the story that render various points of the narrative incoherent. Clearly the censors and/or the distributors had a go at the film.

Tinto made a point of shooting the bilingual film in direct sound, and yet little of that direct sound survives in the only copy currently available. Italian law requires that films be spoken in Italian, and so what Italians saw was a dub. The Italian dub deprived the story of some of its coherence, since we in the audience need to know who is speaking which language and when.

Tinto and his cast and crew skirted the edge of danger. A story such as this needs a disciplined structure, but *Dropout* does not have much of a structure at all, disciplined or otherwise. The plot synopsis above illustrates that the film is largely a series of surreal sketches with barely even a linking device. A narrative employing such a technique risks being dull and tedious. Amazingly, the film manages to hold an audience's attention. The problem was that the film never had much of an audience. It was barely released in Italy and in Latin America, and was shown at a few small college screenings in the UK, but it was not seen elsewhere. Twentieth Century-Fox apparently exercised its right to refuse a distribution contract, and so Scotia American attempted the U.S. release, but abandoned the idea after a single test screening in January 1975. Further information about that is unavailable. The film has rarely been seen since that time and has never been issued on home video. It is not available for cinema screenings, and became one of the most rarely-seen films of his directing career.

Source Notes:

180 Sally K. Brass, "Director's Quest for Reality," *Los Angeles Times*, Wednesday, 2 September 1970, pt. IV, p. 13

181 Manlio Gomarasca and Davide Pulici, *99 donne: stelle e stelline del cinema italiano* (Media Word S.a.s., 1999), pp. 219–220

182 Bernard Drew, "No Other Star Is Like Vanessa Redgrave" (Gannett News Service), *The* [Nyack, NY] *Journal-News*, Saturday, 23 January 1971, p. 12

183 Sally K. Brass, *Los Angeles Times*

XI
Vacation
(*La vacanza*)

VANESSA REDGRAVE, Franco Nero, and Tinto Brass had so enjoyed working together that they embarked upon another venture, also for $100,000, also without pay, also in 16mm. They returned to Italy, specifically to the countryside in the Veneto along the Adriatic Coast. Tinto told Lorenzo Codelli where he got his idea.

It stemmed from a visit I had made to an asylum near Naples. There were women locked up there. It was terrible. They had affected me very much, so the idea of making a film of them was born. These women had given me poems, which are the songs in the film. I later went back to the asylum with Vanessa, because she wanted to see with her own eyes how these women lived. And a very strong thing happened: They filled her with notes. I didn't notice it, and neither did she. Someone who had accompanied her had noticed it, and so they undressed her and found them. On the notes were written things like, "Tell the President of the Republic how they treat us."[184]

As with *Dropout*, naturalism and absurdism are both on display in equal measure. The visuals are of real landscapes, real edifices, ofttimes real residents, and the look of the film is quite gritty as shot on 16mm. The story, though, flies off into the world of fantasy. Immacolata Meneghello, on an experimental leave from an asylum, is returned to her family farm. Her father is not much above the age of 20. Her grandmother is a man in drag. Her siblings are midgets who are more than a generation older. The Meneghello family immediately give Immacolata to their landlord in lieu of back rent, and he accepts her as a mare. She escapes into the woods where she meets up with Osiris the Poacher. The two are jailed for poaching on Count Claudio's estate. Gigi the Englishman, a bicycling salesman, invites her to squat with him and his four friends, a kazoo player, a mute woman, a blind woman, and a feeble-minded woman. They are captured by Nazis and imprisoned in a sewing factory. Upon escaping they are attacked by the police.

The film plays like a fairy tale. It is enchanting, sad, funny, preposterous. It is filled with bizarre imagery, such as Osiride Pevarello wearing a dress and interrogating a donkey. There is a scene in a courtroom in which the witnesses testify in rhyme and rest their case by performing a conga dance around the judge. A psychiatrist treats his patients by having them wrapped in cloth sacks to hop around in the countryside.

This was Tinto's most assured work to date. Tinto was obviously in love with the countryside in the Veneto region, and everywhere he looked, he saw stories form. The more natural the settings, the more absurd the stories. This film was an improvement over *Dropout*, for it did not rely as much upon improvisation. The script was strictly structured in the standard three-act format. Unlike *Dropout*, there was nothing here that was haphazard about the development of the narrative or of the characters. In part that was due to the problem of having Vanessa Redgrave deliver her lines in the Venetian dialect, in which she was not fluent. Osiride Pevarello trained her on each of her lines, and so improvisational departures could not have been as frequent or as free.

Vacation is entirely unlike anything else; every moment of it is engaging, it is breathtakingly beautiful, it is as delicate as a flower, and the songs would melt any heart but an ogre's.

Vacation received its world première at the Venice Film Festival on Friday, 3 September 1971. Most Italian filmmakers boycotted the festival that autumn. Tinto was one of the few to show up. Some in the audience objected furiously to the film. They took offense at the scene in the factory near the end of the story, in which the women prisoners orgasm to the vibrations of the sewing machines. The brief scene is done in an entirely inoffensive way and it is so ridiculous that it becomes hilarious, but a certain section of the audience disagreed and began screaming out "DISGUSTING!" and "ENOUGH!" They drowned out the remainder of the film. Tinto, predictably, shot back. As the curtain closed, he stomped to the front of the auditorium and greeted the hecklers with a *bras d'honneur*. Nonetheless, *Vacation* won the award for Best Italian Film of the Year.

Once again, the film went nowhere. The distributor, Italnoleggio, just sent it to a few Italian cinemas, without ballyhoo, without any meaningful publicity, and business died before it could even begin. The film was not seen elsewhere. That is how Lion Film came to an end. That is how Tinto's career ground to a halt. His four films for Lion remain four of the finest and most inventive films in cinema history, but they have not been widely distributed upon its release.

The sad irony is that, of all the films Tinto ever made, *Vacation* is artistically the most accessible. It would be a perfect fit at any museum series of great films from around the world. With even minor publicity, it would undoubtedly win acclaim everywhere. Yet it remains an undiscovered secret.

Tinto had now made his most interesting films of his career: *Deadly Sweet, Attraction, Howl, Dropout,* and *Vacation,* all which failed to reach general audiences for a number of reasons. After these, Tinto directed a few stage plays. He made a beautifully lyrical two-minute TV commercial for Vespa motorscooters. He wrote some scripts for which he tried and failed to find funding. For most of the next three years, though, he earned a living by working for his in-laws at their Locanda Cipriani on the island of Torcello. It seemed that restaurant work was to be his destiny. His next feature film would however change everything.

Source Notes:

184 Lorenzo Codelli, *Nerosubrass* (Udina and Rome: Dino Audino Editore, 1996), p. 82, 84

Publicity photo: Colin Redgrave, Franco Nero, and Vanessa Redgrave, 1971

XII
I Miss Sonja Henie
(*Nedostaje mi Sonja Henie*)

ONE OF THE ODDEST and rarest entries in the Tinto Brass filmography is a short to which he contributed only about three minutes. The movie was the brainchild of Karpo Ačimović Godina, a Slovenian who had dreamed of becoming a filmmaker but who had to settle, at first, on being a cameraman. When he did break out to make a series of short films, he found himself in trouble. The government labeled him a member of the Black Wave, the several filmmakers who made what were then called "amateur" films, or what we would now call *avant-garde*. These were films made not as commercial investments but rather for the sheer joy of making them. The Yugoslavian authorities were not pleased and banned Godina's movies, one after another. One they even went so far as to destroy with axes, and we are fortunate that a single copy escaped the massacre to be unearthed decades later, after the government fell. What was the offense? Playfulness.

Godina and Tinto were opposites in technique. Godina preferred a static camera, whereas Tinto preferred never to let the camera stay still. In terms of imagination and outlook, though, they were kindred spirits.

At the 1972 Belgrade Film Festival, Karpo Godina stood at the entrance to stalk his prey. He had contracts at the ready, and whenever he recognized a filmmaker's face, he approached with a contract about creating a short film together. Buck Henry showed up to promote *Catch-22*, Miloš Forman was there to promote *Taking Off*, Dušan Makavejev attended to promote *WR: Mysteries of the Organism*, and Tinto arrived to present *Vacation*. Others that Godina recognized and approached were Frederick Wiseman, Paul Morrissey, Bogdan Tirnanić, and Mladomir "Puriša" Đorđević. All of them agreed to the project, and Godina explained the rules. He would supply an actor and actress, Branko Milićević and Dobrila Stojnić, he would supply a room, and he would supply the camera. The focal length was fixed and the camera must not move. In a *Peanuts* comic strip of December 4, 1967, Snoopy, the beagle, pined for Sonja Henie. Godina liked that line and required that each filmmaker incorporate it (Paul Morrissey forgot to do so). The script for the final film was credited only to Snoopy. In Tinto's film, Dobrila scratches herself and feels like fucking, then Branko uses the toilet and then sticks his face in a pie.

Godina was curious what different filmmakers would create within those limits, and what they created was 13 minutes' worth of precious absurdities, most of it truly indescribable. As the eight invited filmmakers improvised their sketches, Godina captured 100 minutes' worth of them engaged in work, and he later edited that 100 minutes of raw footage into a 26-minute behind-the-scenes making-of, revealing a sudden flowering of creativity, recording it for posterity.

The Belgrade festival itself was far more dramatic than any of the films on screen. The Yugoslavian military brass were singularly unamused by *Catch-22* and Buck Henry was truly afraid that they would have him killed in retaliation. Then Makavejev learned of a government plot to kidnap Forman and extradite him to Czechoslovakia to face political charges. Makavejev exchanged identities and arranged for Forman to flee by train in the nick of time.

After the festival, back in his studio, Godina merged the several small films into a single 15-minute extravaganza, but, predictably, the authorities banned it on the grounds that it was decadent and, worse, a collaboration with Westerners. *I Miss Sonja Henie* and its making-of remained locked away and not even the people who had worked on it were permitted to see it. Then in 1998 or thereabouts, after the breakup of Yugoslavia, there began to be occasional screenings for special occasions. The movie was twice issued on DVD as part of a Godina set, in Slovenia in 2006 and then in the U.S. in March 2010 when it was inserted into a magazine called *The Believer*. Each release went out of print almost immediately. The film, like all of Godina's films, remains difficult to find, but it is definitely worth the effort to seek it out.

Italian 2-Fogli poster, 1967

Left and Right: Italian Fotobusta posters, 1968

JEAN-LOUIS TRINTIGNANT • EWA AULIN in
COL CUORE IN GOLA
Liberamente tratto dal romanzo IL SEPOLCRO DI CARTA di SERGIO DONATI edito dalla ARNOLDO MONDADORI EDITORE S.p.A.
UN FILM DI TINTO BRASS
con ROBERTO BISACCO - CHARLES KOHLER - MONIQUE SCOAZEC - LUIGI BELLINI
e con VIRA SILENTI
EASTMANCOLOR TECNOSTAMPA
PRODOTTO DA ERMANNO DONATI E LUIGI CARPENTIERI
co-produzione italo-francese PANDA SOCIETÀ per l'INDUSTRIA CINEMATOGRAFICA S.p.A. Rome - LES FILMS CORONA Paris
PRIMA EDIZIONE ITALIANA ANNO MCMLXVII
DISTRIBUZIONE RANK FILM

JEAN-LOUIS TRINTIGNANT • EWA AULIN
COL CUORE IN GOLA
UN FILM DI TINTO BRASS
ROBERTO BISACCO
CHARLES KOHLER - MONIQUE SCOAZEC - LUIGI BELLINI
VIRA SILENTI
EASTMANCOLOR TECNOSTAMPA
PRODOTTO DA ERMANNO DONATI E LUIGI CARPENTIERI
RANK FILM

JEAN-LOUIS TRINTIGNANT • EWA AULIN
COL CUORE IN GOLA
UN FILM DI
TINTO BRASS
ROBERTO BISACCO
CHARLES KOHLER - MONIQUE SCOAZEC - LUIGI BELLINI
VIRA SILENTI
EASTMANCOLOR • TECNOSTAMPA
PRODOTTO DA
ERMANNO DONATI E LUIGI CARPENTIERI
RANK FILM

JEAN-LOUIS TRINTIGNANT • EWA AULIN
COL CUORE IN GOLA
UN FILM DI TINTO BRASS
ROBERTO BISACCO
CHARLES KOHLER - MONIQUE SCOAZEC - LUIGI BELLINI
VIRA SILENTI
EASTMANCOLOR TECNOSTAMPA
PRODOTTO DA ERMANNO DONATI E LUIGI CARPENTIERI
RANK FILM

JEAN-LOUIS TRINTIGNANT
EWA AULIN
COL CUORE
IN GOLA
UN FILM DI
TINTO BRASS
ROBERTO BISACCO
CHARLES KOHLER - MONIQUE SCOAZEC - LUIGI BELLINI
VIRA SILENTI
EASTMANCOLOR • TECNOSTAMPA
PRODOTTO DA
ERMANNO DONATI E LUIGI CARPENTIERI
RANK FILM

THE RANK ORGANISATION présente
JEAN-LOUIS TRINTIGNANT / EWA AULIN
DEAD STOP
EN 5ème VITESSE
REGIE · TINTO BRASS
LE COEUR AUX LEVRES
WITH ROBERTO BISACCO AND VIRA SILENTI · EASTMANCOLOR
IMPR. LICHTERT · Bruxelles 7

Left: Belgian Window Sheet poster, Right: French Moyenne poster, 1967

West German A1 poster, 1968

Japanese B1 poster, 1968

R. CASARO
LA CEIAD COLUMBIA PRESENTA UN FILM DI TINTO BRASS
NEROSUBIANCO
CON
ANITA SANDERS · TERRY CARTER · NINO SEGURINI
MUSICHE COMPOSTE DAL COMPLESSO
FREEDOM
PRODUZIONE E ARRANGIAMENTO
JONATHAN WESTON E MICHAEL LEASE
PRODOTTO DALLA
LION FILM
CEIAD COLUMBIA
ANNO DI EDIZIONE 1969

Left: Italian 2-Fogli poster, Right: Italian Fotobusta posters, 1969

CEIAD COLUMBIA PRESENTA UN FILM DI
TINTO BRASS
NEROSUBIANCO
CON
ANITA SANDERS
TERRY CARTER
NINO SEGURINI
MUSICHE COMPOSTE DAL COMPLESSO
FREEDOM
PRODUZIONE E ARRANGIAMENTO
JONATHAN WESTON E MICHAEL LEASE
PRODOTTO DALLA
LION FILM
CEIAD COLUMBIA
PRIMA EDIZIONE ITALIANA 1969

Italian Fotobusta poster, 1969

Left: Italian Fotobusta posters, Right: Italian 4-Fogli poster, 1969

CEIAD COLUMBIA PRESENTA UN FILM DI TINTO BRASS
NEROSUBIANCO
CON ANITA SANDERS TERRY CARTER NINO SEGURINI
MUSICHE COMPOSTE DAL COMPLESSO FREEDOM
PRODUZIONE E ARRANGIAMENTO JONATHAN WESTON E MICHAEL LEASE
PRODOTTO DALLA LION FILM
CEIAD COLUMBIA

FORBIDDEN.
Therefore Irresistible.
ATTRACTION
ATTRACTION
ATTRACTION
COLUMBIA PICTURES Presents A Film By TINTO BRASS "ATTRACTION"
with
ANITA SANDERS · TERRY CARTER · NINO SEGURINI
Music composed by FREEDOM · Production and Arrangements JONATHAN WESTON and MICHAEL LEASE
Produced by LION FILM

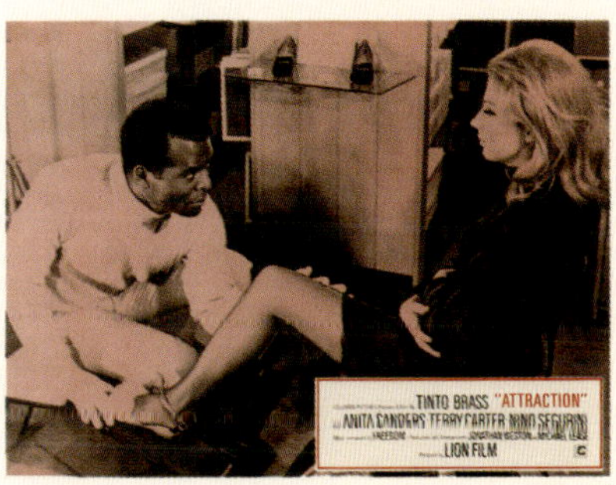

Left: U.S. One Sheet poster, Right: U.S. Lobby Cards, 1969

Left: U.S. Lobby Cards, 1969, Right: Italian 2-Fogli poster, 1974

Titanus
TINA AUMONT
LUIGI PROIETTI
L'URLO
UN FILM DI
TINTO BRASS
ANNO DI EDIZIONE 1974
PRODOTTO DALLA LION FILM S.R.L.
EASTMANCOLOR
TECHNOSPES

Left and Right: Italian Fotobusta posters, 1974

Titanus
TINA AUMONT · LUIGI PROIETTI
L'URLO
UN FILM DI TINTO BRASS
PRODOTTO DALLA LION FILM S.r.l. EASTMANCOLOR - TECHNOSPES

Titanus
TINA AUMONT · LUIGI PROIETTI
L'URLO
UN FILM DI TINTO BRASS
PRODOTTO DALLA LION FILM S.r.l. EASTMANCOLOR - TECHNOSPES

Titanus
TIN
L'O
UN FILM DI
TINTO BRASS
EASTMANCOLOR - TECHNOSPES
PRODOTTO DALLA LION FILM s.r.l.

Italian Fotobusta poster, 1974

UNA .... FATTA BENE, FA PIACERE E SBLOCCA IL RENE
MEDUSA DISTRIBUZIONE PRESENTA
FRANCO NERO E VANESSA REDGRAVE IN
DROPOUT
UN FILM DI
TINTO BRASS
CON LUIGI PROIETTI E FRANK WINDSOR
FOTOGRAFIA DI SILVANO IPPOLITI
MUSICA DI DON FRASER
PRODUTTORE ESECUTIVO ORESTE COLTELLACCI
EASTMANCOLOR - SCHERMO GIGANTE
LE CANZONI: "DO NOT CRY" E "THE SUN IS SHINING" SONO CANTATE DAI MIDDLE OF THE ROAD - SU DISCHI RCA

Left: Italian 2-Fogli poster, 1971, Right: Italian Pressbook, 1971

Mexican Lobby Cards, 1975

Left and Right: Italian Fotobusta posters, 1971

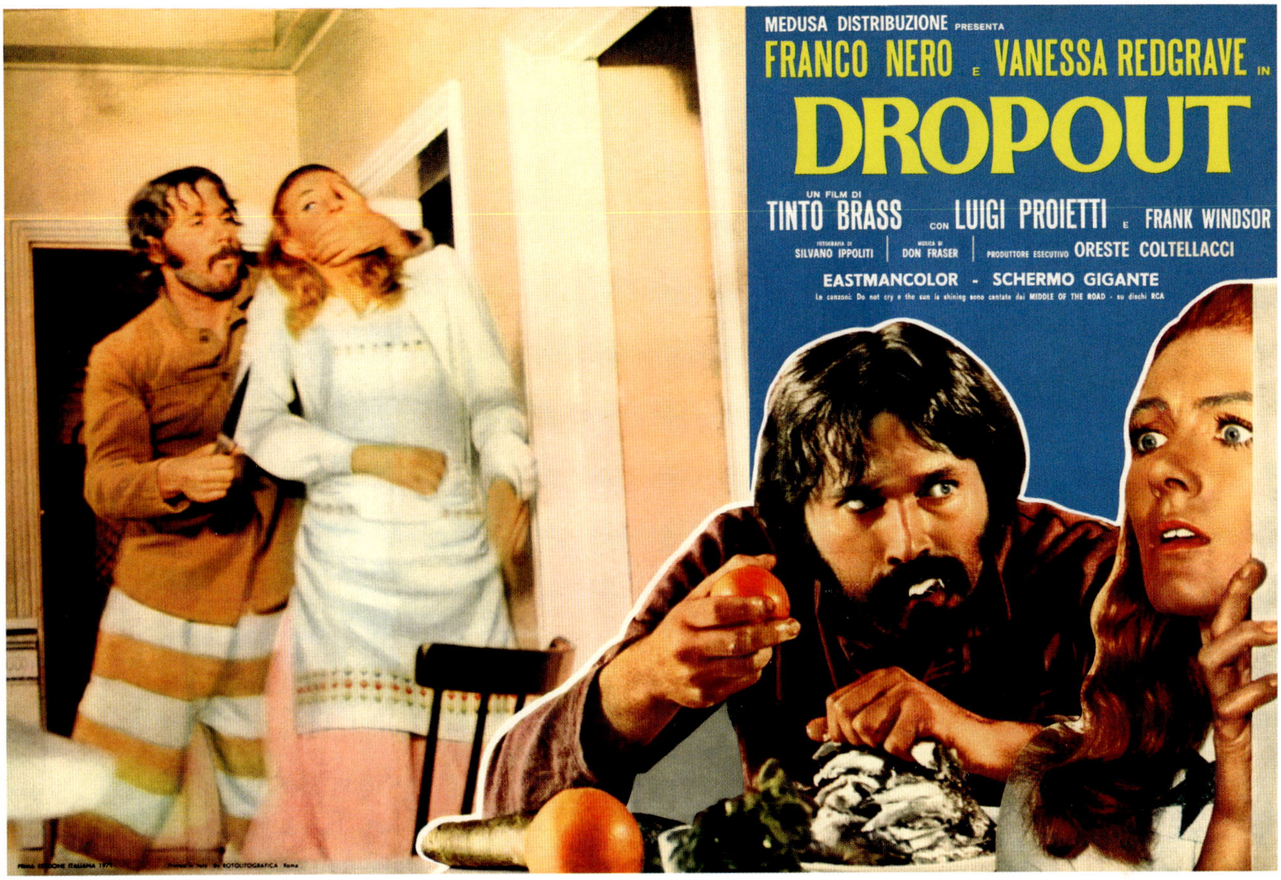
MEDUSA DISTRIBUZIONE PRESENTA
FRANCO NERO E VANESSA REDGRAVE IN
DROPOUT
UN FILM DI TINTO BRASS CON LUIGI PROIETTI E FRANK WINDSOR
FOTOGRAFIA DI SILVANO IPPOLITI
MUSICA DI DON FRASER
PRODUTTORE ESECUTIVO ORESTE COLTELLACCI
EASTMANCOLOR - SCHERMO GIGANTE
Le canzoni: Do not cry e the sun is shining sono cantate dai MIDDLE OF THE ROAD - su dischi RCA

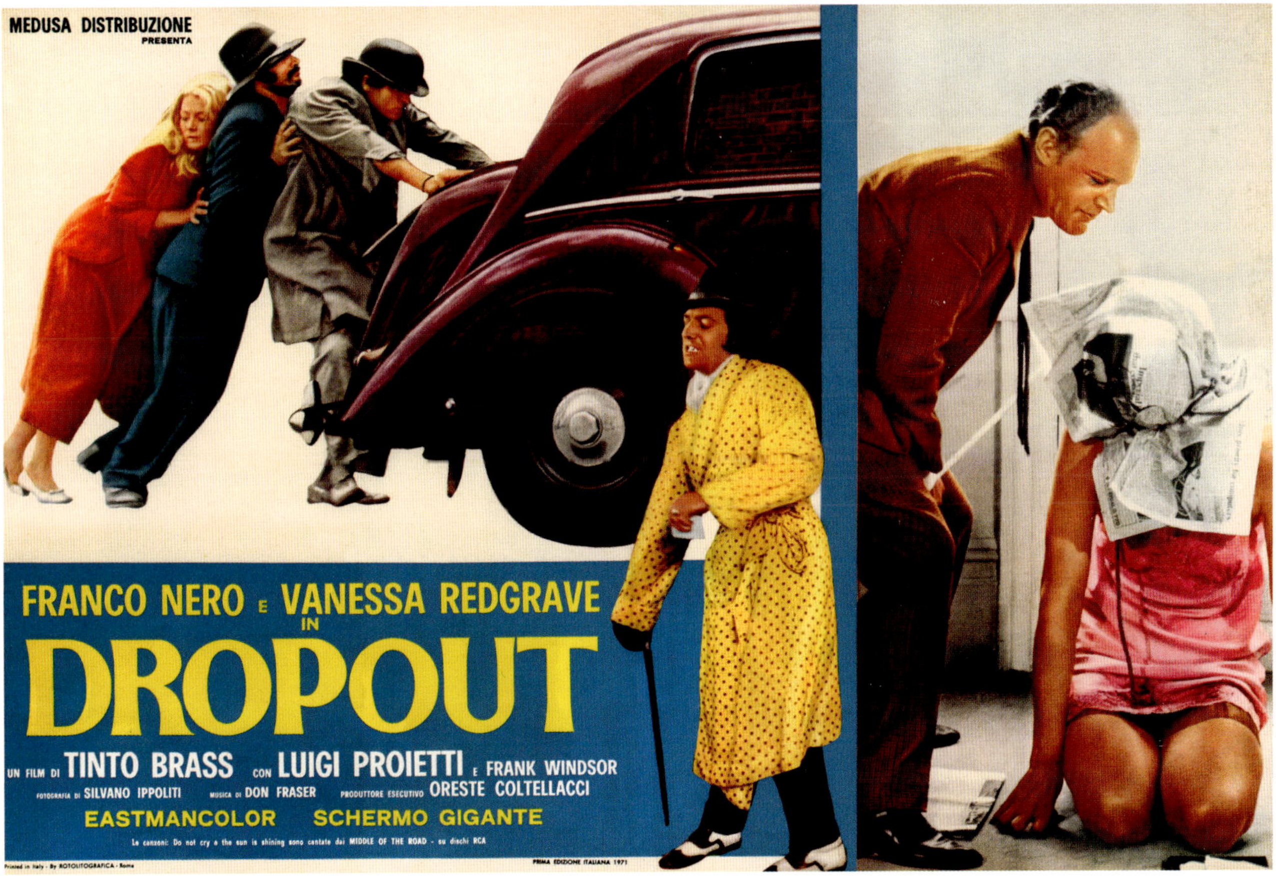
MEDUSA DISTRIBUZIONE PRESENTA
FRANCO NERO E VANESSA REDGRAVE IN
DROPOUT
UN FILM DI TINTO BRASS CON LUIGI PROIETTI E FRANK WINDSOR
FOTOGRAFIA DI SILVANO IPPOLITI
MUSICA DI DON FRASER
PRODUTTORE ESECUTIVO ORESTE COLTELLACCI
EASTMANCOLOR
SCHERMO GIGANTE
Le canzoni: Do not cry e the sun is shining sono cantate dai MIDDLE OF THE ROAD - su dischi RCA
Printed in Italy - By ROTOLITOGRAFICA - Roma
PRIMA EDIZIONE ITALIANA 1971

Italian Fotobusta poster, 1971

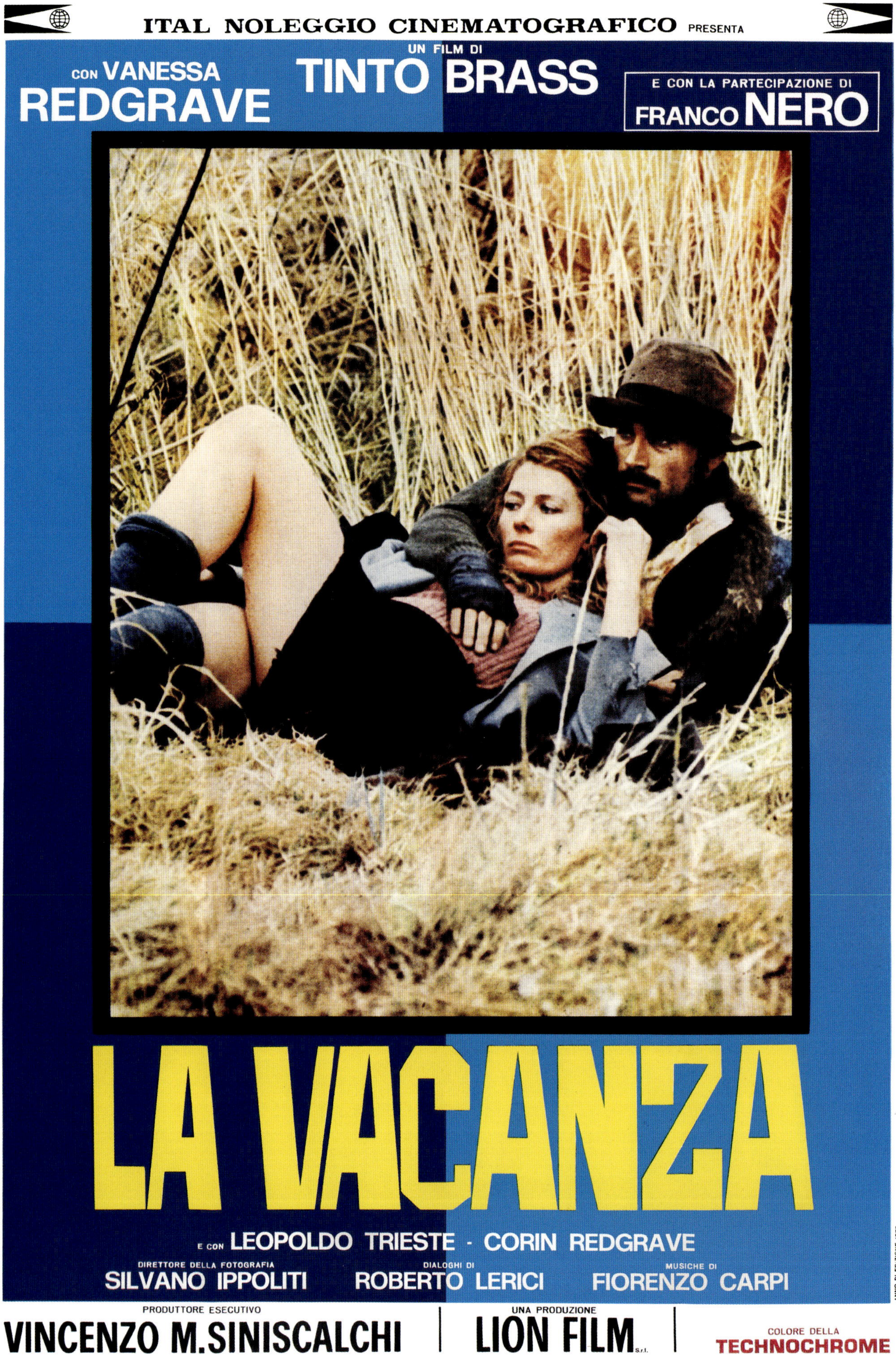
ITAL NOLEGGIO CINEMATOGRAFICO PRESENTA
UN FILM DI
TINTO BRASS
CON VANESSA
REDGRAVE
E CON LA PARTECIPAZIONE DI
FRANCO NERO
LA VACANZA
E CON LEOPOLDO TRIESTE - CORIN REDGRAVE
DIRETTORE DELLA FOTOGRAFIA
SILVANO IPPOLITI
DIALOGHI DI
ROBERTO LERICI
MUSICHE DI
FIORENZO CARPI
PRODUTTORE ESECUTIVO
VINCENZO M.SINISCALCHI
UNA PRODUZIONE
LION FILM S.r.l.
COLORE DELLA
TECHNOCHROME
ANNO DI EDIZIONE 1972

Left: Italian 2-Fogli poster, Right: Italian 1-Fogli poster, 1972

TINTO THE FILMS OF BRASS

PART THREE

SEX & ANARCHY

Italian 4-Fogli poster, 1975

XIII
Salon Kitty
(*Madam Kitty*)

IT WAS 1974. Dino De Laurentiis had by now sold much of his assets to La Titanus Distribuzione. Titanus thus found itself with an unreleased film called *The Howl* and decided to release it. First, it cut the film to meet the censors' objections, but the film went nowhere. It had been a direct response to the widespread unrest of 1968, but 1974 was not 1968. Flower power was no longer on anybody's mind. Of more concern was the anarchy in Italy and the terror unleashed by the Red Brigades, who were locked in battle with the Mafia-riddled right-wing government. Many people were too afraid to leave their houses, and so a comic ode to hippies met nobody's needs.

Though it did almost no business, *The Howl* caught the attention of critics and producers, who recognized a significant film made by a brilliant talent. It was only a matter of time before some producers would decide to hire that brilliant talent, but not to be brilliant or talented. The producers hired him to be a technician-for-hire, nothing more.

This new project began with a German researcher named Peter Norden, who devoted 20 years to investigating the Salon Kitty, a brothel in Berlin that was taken over by the Nazis, who assigned spies to be prostitutes and who also bugged each room. As soon as the owner, Madam Kitty Schmidt, got wind of what was happening, she tried to leave Germany, but she was apprehended and put right back to work. Norden dug up countless documents and he was even able to listen to some of the recordings, which were then archived in East Berlin. Then, unaccountably, rather than a history, he published a book. The book, *Madam Kitty*, was soon enough slashed to half its original size and the abridgment was issued in translations around the world. The German publisher, Robert Schafer of Südwest-Verlag, licensed film rights to Dieter Geissler Film Produktion, which would co-produce with Roberto Infascelli of Rome. Together, they flipped the property to Giulio Sbarigia of Oceania in Rome, and Oceania, in turn, received funds from Les Productions Fox-Europa S.A., which was the French subsidiary of Twentieth Century-Fox. When we untangle all this, it appears that *Salon Kitty* was in actuality a Twentieth Century-Fox production, but run through various subsidiaries and disguised as an Italian production in order to reduce costs. With legal registration as a film of Italian nationality, the total budget would eventually amount to US$1,724,618.40. Had it been registered as of U.S. nationality, the budget would have been probably five times higher.

Since it was a Fox film, it would of course be shot in English. Originally, the film was to have been directed by Giuseppe Patroni Griffi. He either resigned or was dismissed, and his replacement was Sidney Lumet. Then Sbarigia sold half his interest to Ermanno Donati of Coralta Cinematografica, and Sidney Lumet either resigned or was dismissed. The producers approached George Pan Cosmatos, who was not receptive. In need of a director, the producers contacted Tinto Brass, whose *The Howl* had just been issued. He read Ennio De Concini's script, found it banal, said he was not interested, and left.

What happened after that, we do not know. Tinto said that the idea of 20 young women being so horribly pressured began to capture his imagination, and so he reapplied for the position. Tinto went back to Sbarigia and Donati and offered his services, on the condition that he and his friend, Maria Pia Fusco, could work with De Concini on a rewrite. He thought the script was too sensational; he preferred a political focus. As he put it in his usual obtuse terms, "eroticism as a provocation and not as a trade, a cultural and political operation in the first place and secondly a show."[184] His wish was granted. Coralta Cinematografica hired him and paid $30,000, the first real salary Tinto had received in years. The contract called for Tinto to be a director-for-hire who would create a film of no longer than 120 minutes. The contract stipulated that shooting would begin on 20 April 1975 and would be completed ten weeks later. In fact, shooting began on 12 May and lasted 12 weeks, a typical delay.

As with the true story, the institution at the center of it was indeed called Salon Kitty, in Berlin; the madam's given name was Kitty, the Nazis did place spies as prostitutes, and the rooms were bugged. Apart from that basic premise, there is no other correlation with the true story. We do not have access to the treatment written by Antonio Colantuoni, nor do we have access to De Concini's draft scripts or to the later rewrites. We cannot determine who is responsible for which aspects of the film.

It is difficult to know what was on the producers' minds. They cast Ingrid Thulin and Helmut Berger as the leads. They had not long before appeared together in another Nazi story, Luchino Visconti's highly regarded drama, *The Damned*. Whether they were cast in *Salon Kitty* to capitalize on the earlier film, or whether they were under contractual obligation, or whether this was mere coincidence, we do not know. The producers were also deeply impressed by a musical called *Cabaret*, set in Nazi Germany as well. It was an international success that was still earning massive profits two years later. Consequently, the producers hired songwriters to turn *Salon Kitty* into a musical and hired Annie Ross to spend a day in a sound studio recording those songs. *Salon Kitty* would further copy some images from *Cabaret* almost exactly.

One may wonder why *Salon Kitty* bears almost no relation to the book upon which it is supposedly based, and why it similarly has no connection with the true story. It turns out that *Salon Kitty* was inspired partly by an exploitation film called *Love Camp 7*, which in all likelihood Tinto has never seen or even heard of. Someone in production certainly knew about it, though, and its ideas trickled in. *Salon Kitty*'s Nazi whoring bears some unmistakable resonances to the earlier film, and even the composition of a few shots is reminiscent. So, to all appearances, Fox, or whoever was truly in charge, was hoping to attract the audiences that had enjoyed *The Damned*, *Cabaret*, and *Love Camp 7*. Those three films have almost nothing in common, and to adapt a new film from all three made for an uncomfortable amalgam.

This was the first time that Tinto was in charge of a large production, and he was not intimidated. Directing two separate camera crews, delegating authority, brainstorming with designers and artists and variety performers and all manner of technicians came naturally to him. In previous films, he would hardly direct his actors at all, but gave them brief suggestions, at most. In *Salon Kitty*, probably for the first time, he consulted with the actors, even going so far as to explain motivations and psychology.

As with any job he performs, Tinto put his heart and soul into it. He and the other two writers polished the script. Tinto began casting, and for a leading part, he championed an unknown, Teresa Ann Savoy, and managed to hire her over production's objections. He was also deeply impressed by another unknown, Jost Jakob, and again hired him over the objections of production. Jost would design the ladies' costumes. For the music, Tinto hired Fiorenzo Carpi, who had created the bouncy soundtrack for *The Howl* and the beautiful score for *Vacation*.

For the sets, Tinto found himself working with Ken Adam, who had designed *Dr. Strangelove* and some of the James Bond films, among many others. Adam's technique was to exaggerate but never so much as to be unconvincing. His sets had to be plausible. He had grown up in Berlin, but left in his early teens to escape the Nazis. He had just suffered a nervous breakdown when working on *Barry Lyndon*. The film's producer, Stanley Kubrick, was not sufficiently prepared, and would, without any notice, demand locales and designs that nobody had even thought to mention earlier, and he demanded them instantly. Adam lost all confidence in himself and thought his career was over. Tinto revivified him. The two men had similar ideas, and Tinto, unlike Kubrick, was outgoing, positive, encouraging, and helpful. Working with Tinto was the best therapy that Adam could have hoped for.

> **...Tinto Brass was wonderful. He'd got me on the rebound from *Barry Lyndon* and he realized I had gone through absolute purgatory, so he was very sensitive about it. My sketches were a bit small—I was afraid to do big ones—but Tinto loved them. In fact, he kept all the originals. I have only a few bad photocopies. He came up with all these brilliant ideas for shooting. He's an extraordinarily talented director, but he's got this sexual obsession which is really unfortunate in some ways.**[185]

The narrative structure is different from any of Tinto's previous films. The film opens not with a story, but with brief vignettes that seem to have little connection: a cabaret song, then nude men exercising in the Berlin Sportforum, then a family watching *Triumph of the Will* at a cinema, then a scene in a medical theatre, then Nazi officers playing raucous games inside a slaughterhouse, then a political argument at a family dinner, then a Jewish couple and their grandson defying a prohibition by entering an aquarium, then a precision military orgy at the Sportforum, then sexual-performance tests at a hospital. Only later on are we meant to see how these separate events converge to form a story.

The convergence comes when young women, having been successfully brainwashed by Nazi ideology, volunteer to become prostitutes at the Salon Kitty in order to report back on the high command who pay for their services. These young recruits are unaware of the basement, in which audio technicians record everything that happens in each room, courtesy of hidden microphones.

One would probably be right to guess that Tinto's contribution was the emotional breakdown that the SS prostitutes begin to suffer when they could not harmonize the contradiction of affection and treachery. One would certainly be right to guess that Tinto also contributed the visual tricks to make the various scenes engaging. Were it not for his lighting, composition, and editing techniques, the film would have been deadly dull, and therein lies the problem. Parts of the story are outright risible. One can think of Kitty's outburst when one of the prostitutes suddenly gets rabies. The lines are overwritten and the acting is hopelessly unbelievable. Tinto rescued that by turning it into farce. The whole concept of the cat-and-mouse game between Untergruppenführer Wallenberg and Madam Kitty stretches all credulity, as does the game between Untergruppenführer and Margherita. Further failing the credibility test is the naïveté of many of the characters, in addition to which there was plenty of cornball dialogue. The entire premise of the story falls apart, for it is inconceivable that the authorities would have left any room at all for subterfuge, and yet, in the film, subterfuge runs unchecked.

Tinto did his best to get around these problems by constant cosmetic applications of clever camera moves, unexpected lighting, unexpected pacing. He would play one scene as a farce, the next as a melodrama, the next as kitsch, and he invited entertainers to appear on camera. The real Salon Kitty provided no music or song or dance or entertainment of any kind, apart from the ladies in private rooms. That did not deter the producers from showcasing the Salon Kitty as a place of merry musical routines. Bedroom proceedings are interrupted nightly to delight the guests with four homosexual cabaret artists. Where Tinto found those four men we do not know, but we do know that right after this movie, three of them joined forces to create a drag show called Le Sorelle Bandiera, also known under their English name, The Fabulous Flag Sisters. They are now legendary.

When Tinto had completed filming the script, he had a massive mess. A moment of lyrical beauty would be immediately followed by a moment of ridiculously bad dialogue, followed by intrigue, followed by a moment of preposterous comedy, followed by a moment of effective drama, followed by an entertaining musical number, followed by a bloody murder, and mixed throughout is an immense amount of nudity and simulated sex, with a stream of sexual frustrations that border on insanity. In previous films, Tinto conveyed his ideas subtly, beneath the surface, but the *Salon Kitty* script allowed for no subtleties at all. The antifascist message screamed from every scene in its contemptuous displays of an entire society brainwashed with hatred.

Though he had at first dismissed the project, once he had begun work, he became passionate about it. "We are performing an operation," he explained to his actors. "Plastic surgery, but in reverse, because, instead of patching and improving noses, thighs, or breasts, this plastic surgery tears the connecting flesh of Nazi society; it tears the wounds wide open to the limits of emblematic monstrosity. This is a film made of lurid, garish inlays; it is a coffin made of marble and mirrors. It is not the story of Kitty and her whores, but the story of a brothel in Nazi Berlin used for spying and blackmailing. We are bent on showing a violated reality."[186]

Tinto began editing the film sometime around Monday, 4 August, and the job occupied him until mid-September. It seems that he edited the Annie Ross songs first, simply because the visuals needed to conform to the sounds. The remainder of the film he mostly edited silent, as was his usual practice. He did, though, spend a few minutes amusing himself with the sound. He would put the image of one take of Ingrid Thulin and synchronize it to the audio of a different take, and it would match perfectly, since the actress delivered her lines identically each time. Because of the schedule and the massive amount of work, he had to delegate duties. As he completed each reel, a duplicate was sent to Fiorenzo Carpi, who would write the music for it. Another duplicate was sent to Luigi Proietti, who directed the Italian dubbing. A third duplicate was sent to the Foley crew to add sound effects (clinking glasses, automobile engines, a barking dog, room ambience, flying airplanes, and so forth). As Carpi completed writing music for each reel, he would send his work to Bruno Nicolai to conduct it. The process operated smoothly, efficiently, and quickly. This was likely a first for Tinto, who, in his previous films, seems to have done much of the work himself. Once the effects, music, and dialogue were recorded, the recordings were all sent to Tinto, who would mix the result.

Some of Tinto's editing and mixing choices were rather odd. The scene of the precision military orgy took place in 1939. Nonetheless, a military band unexpectedly enters and begins playing "Wenn die SS und die SA Aufmarschiert," a song that had been outlawed in 1934. When Kitty sings her cabaret song (or, rather, lipsyncs it to Annie Ross' recording) about "It's strictly geld that counts in very large amounts," the choreography is intentionally sloppy, satirically so. Tinto, in his editing, deliberately made it even worse for comical effect.

Tinto presented his completed film, and it was in breach of contract, as it was 133 minutes rather than 120. It seems that the producers and investors waived that contractual term, accepted the extra length, and did not demand any abridging. The full film was immediately sent to a different dubbing crew to record the English dialogue. Thulin, Berger, Ireland, and Steiner recorded their own voices. Anonymous staff dubbers supplied the remainder of the voices. Though the film had been shot in direct sound, and though most of the cast had spoken English on camera, their dialogue was mostly unusable, as the mix of accents destroyed what little plausibility the story could claim. Except for a few bungled lines, the quality of the English dub was outstanding, far superior to the Italian dub.

The problems began when the completed film, in its Italian dub, was scheduled for release in early December 1975. The censors seized it and demanded cuts. Giulio Sbarigia, rather than call Tinto in to adjust the film, just went ahead and instructed his crew to make the cuts and to destroy the negatives and master tapes of the deleted materials. Tinto was livid and he sued to have the film withdrawn rather than be seen in a censored form. The suit was based on a law that permitted authors to have their books withdrawn if publishers make unauthorized changes. That law applied only to books, but Tinto argued that *Salon Kitty* was a literary work and that he was the author. The law, though, also required the author filing suit to purchase back the rights and reimburse the publisher all the costs. Tinto simply did not have the nearly two million dollars needed, but he did win the right to show his uncut edition privately. The rupture in relations between Tinto Brass and Giulio Sbarigia put an end to Tinto's next project, *The Borgias*, tentatively to have starred Marlon Brando as Pope Alexander VI and Mick Jagger as Cesare Borgia.

When Tinto agreed with the inevitable, the censored film could finally be released. That was in early March 1976, after a three-month delay. It was a massive hit in Italy, a box-office sensation. One can be forgiven for suspecting that the sole reason for its popularity was its two-hour parade of undraped flesh. Its scenes were more extreme than probably anything that had come before, more extreme even than most exploitation films. It is quite possible that Twentieth Century-Fox and Coralta had instructed Tinto to push the envelope further than anyone had ever pushed it before—which he did, but surely further than the Fox and Coralta bureaucrats could have imagined. That is likely why Twentieth Century-Fox declined to release the film in the U.S. and Canada, for fear of jeopardizing its reputation. Fox instead sold its U.S./Canadian interest in the film to an exploitation distributor called American International Pictures. Yet not even American International Pictures wanted its name associated with *Salon Kitty*, and so it released the movie through a subsidiary called Trans-American Films.

The edition released by Trans-American was 111 minutes and included an introduction falsely claiming that everything depicted in the film was accurately copied from the history books. Figures are not available, but research suggests that the movie turned a big profit despite almost unanimously hostile reviews. It was in release from January through August 1977, and then remained available through the end of 1982. What happened to the prints and materials remains a vexing mystery.

The current rights owner, Surf Film S.r.l., has only the abridged 112-minute negative. The other 21 minutes' worth of negative and audio masters seem to have vanished. Tinto's personal print of the Italian dub is complete. Note: The later Blu-ray versions from Blue Underground in the U.S. and Argent Films in the UK included an uncut director's cut, pieced together from different elements.

Salon Kitty, in various dubs of various running times, at the time was also a sensation in England, France, Germany, Sweden, Australia, Japan, and surely numerous other countries as well. Tinto had established some credibility as an efficient director with his first few films. His reputation was largely ended by the four films he had produced on his own, which to this day remain almost entirely unshown and unknown. When *The Howl* got a belated release in Italy, Tinto was once again known to movie executives as a competent director. Once *Salon Kitty* smashed records right and left around the globe, Tinto's reputation was golden. He was famous. Everybody respected him. Nothing was in the way of fame.

Source Notes:

184 Enrico Nassi, Fabian Cevallos, *Salon Kitty: storia d'un film* (Rome: Bei Editore, 1975)

185 Christopher Frayling, *Ken Adam: The Art of Production Design* (London: Faber and Faber, 2005), p. 204

186 Enrico Nassi, Fabian Cevallos, *Salon Kitty: storia d'un film* (Rome: Bei Editore, 1975)

XIV
Caligula

CALIGULA, one of the most infamous, reviled, and ridiculed films ever made, is also one of the most mangled films in history. Its writers, its director and many others who were involved have gone to great trouble to distance themselves from the end result. Oddly enough, *Caligula* is also a rather popular film, surely because of its status as a curiosity item, being the first—and last!—big-budget film with major actors that included numerous scenes of hardcore sex. It is unfortunate that in much of the world, certainly in North America, Tinto Brass is known mostly for *Caligula*, which bears little resemblance to the film he had actually intended. Whether fact or fiction, or who said what, the story behind it is fascinating.

In the 1940s, a revolutionary filmmaker named Roberto Rossellini came to prominence with a trio of stunning films about the Second World War. By 1947 he was contemplating a film about Claudius and Messalina but could not get funding. By 1962, his ideas had evolved. He decided to make the film about Caligula instead. Rossellini had an aversion to writing anything down. In his younger years, he had been a scenarist and hated the work. Now that he had some control, he would instead have lengthy discussions about story ideas with several scenarists, and when they would all agree on the conception, he would send them off to type up what they had spoken about. The resulting treatments and the scripts that would be developed from them were used to get funding. They were not final drafts, and cast and crew invented their own material as the filming progressed. The final films could and did veer dramatically from the original screenplays.

We may never learn who actually wrote the *Caligula* treatment in 1962, but its ideas are largely Rossellini's. Jean Gruault then developed that treatment into a full screenplay by the close of 1963. It was Rossellini's idea that Caligula was a republican who committed atrocities only to illustrate how corrupt the system was. The emperor's dream was to engender sufficient outrage to cause a revolt and his own assassination. In order to chase down funding, Rossellini began to chase down potential actors. He hoped that 43-year-old comic Alberto Sordi could be induced to portray the 19-year-old Caligula. Later he approached Woody Allen, who agreed to star in the picture, but only if he would be permitted to wear his trademark horn-rimmed glasses.[186] Rossellini later convinced Lou Castel to accept the offer, but there were delays, and in 1970 he found that Vittorio De Sica's son, Christian De Sica, was agreeable. The production company withdrew from the project, and that is when Rossellini jettisoned Gruault's script and started all over again. He worked either with Luciano Scaffa or with Marcella Mariani, or possibly with both, and their lengthy discussions produced an entirely new treatment, which was ready in 1971.

Roberto Rossellini's nephew, Franco Rossellini, after about six years of working as a film producer, now established his own company which he named after his dachshund, Felix Cinematografica S.r.l., and no sooner had he founded his new company than he found himself with funding from Warner Bros. Franco and Roberto flew to Burbank for discussions, but the ideas clashed. Warner Bros. wanted a big-name cast, with someone of the caliber of a Dustin Hoffman to play the lead. Roberto was horrified. He wanted a small film with a cast of unknowns.[187] Neither side would budge, and Roberto refused to negotiate any further. He canceled the film rather than see it turned into a standard Hollywood epic.

In 1975, underground filmmaker Paul Morrissey was in Italy, where he had recently made several films. He became friends with Franco and found him one of the funniest people he had ever met. Franco, ever on the lookout for screenplays, asked Morrissey if he had any movie ideas. Indeed, he did. Morrissey revealed that his ambition was to make a film about Caligula, without any epic scenes or crowd scenes. He wanted to shoot a small film with a small cast, showing only the behind-the-scenes of the emperor's life, and they need not even build sets. They could use Roman-style buildings that were already standing throughout Europe.

Franco said that he already owned such a project. He handed Morrissey his uncle's treatment. The filmmaker read it, thought it was garbage, and then regretted his next statement. Rather than offer to write his own screenplay, which he could have done quite easily, he suggested that they hire a well-known scenarist to do the job. He suggested his friend Gore Vidal, who, it turns out, was also Franco's friend.

The two of them visited Vidal in his apartment in Rome in June 1975. Though a U.S. citizen, Vidal spent half of every year in Italy, sometimes at his apartment in Rome, sometimes at his house in Ravello. Franco and Morrissey asked if he was perchance working on a new project. Indeed he was. He said he was preparing to write a piece about Caligula. After a discussion, Vidal agreed to write his piece as a screenplay. He and Morrissey spent some time together sifting through Suetonius' *Twelve Caesars* and Tacitus' *Annals*, deciding which episodes to use and how to use them. Vidal then started to write a three-hour screenplay. In the meantime, Franco was able to presell Italian distribution rights to La Titanus Distribuzione, and so he found himself with sufficient funds to make a small film of court intrigues to be shot on existing locations.

Morrissey had the idea that his Caligula should be short, and so in June 1975 he went to Sorrento to approach the touring Mikhail Baryshnikov about appearing in the film. Baryshnikov was agreeable, though he could not speak a word of English. Morrissey did not see that as a problem. Franco, on the other hand, approached Mick Jagger. When negotiations stalled, Franco tried for Christopher Jones, who had just fired his agent and was unreachable. In the meantime, Morrissey, back in New York, saw Peter Firth's performance on stage in *Equus* and thought he would be splendid. He introduced Firth to Vidal and to Franco, and all were in agreement.

At the end of June, Vidal discussed the project with his agent, Alain Bernheim, and together they decided that he should charge his standard price of $225,000 for the screenplay. Franco and Morrissey were crestfallen. Morrissey saw that any hope of a small, low-budget film was now tossed out the window.[188] Franco realized that the film project was dead. Italian law forbade such a high price being paid to a foreigner for a mere screenplay. What's more, Vidal insisted that, as with *Gore Vidal's The Best Man*, his name be included in the title: *Gore Vidal's Caligula*. Franco and Morrissey were confused but did not object to that second demand. Vidal would not reduce his price, and so he put his raw draft of the script back on the shelf and forgot about it.

To rescue the project, Franco understood that he needed to ally with a U.S. firm, so that the money could flow to Vidal through the U.S. rather than through Italy. He hired a New York firm called ParaGroup to be his exclusive agent, and he approached Warner Bros. once again about *Caligula*. Warner Bros. was no more receptive to the Morrissey/Vidal version than it had been to the Roberto Rossellini version.

Then, in early July 1975, Vidal received a phone call from Jack Silverman. Silverman was a prominent Madison Avenue advertising executive who lived in an apartment in one of the Manhattan skyrises that Vidal owned. The two had worked together in the past. Now Silverman had some news. He had resigned from advertising and was about to begin a new career as a film producer for *Penthouse*, a skin magazine. *Penthouse* founder Bob Guccione was looking for "properties" and was hoping for a film that would be both serious and sexy. Vidal responded that he had just what Guccione was looking for.

Silverman and Guccione flew to Vidal's gigantic cliffside house in Ravello, and Guccione had an almost impossible time figuring out what Vidal was talking about. Vidal tried repeatedly to explain that Caligula's life consisted not only of political intrigue, but of sexual intrigue as well. When Guccione finally caught on, that is the only thing he understood.

Guccione was ready to withdraw when he found out that the film already had a producer, Franco Rossellini. He did not wish to work with anybody else, and insisted upon producing the film entirely on his own. Yet Franco by contract already had the rights. If Guccione wished to proceed, he would have no choice but to work with Franco. He could buy out Franco's interest and turn the production into an American film, but that would necessitate a Hollywood crew on top of an Italian crew and double taxation as well. The costs would be prohibitive. After a week or so of hesitation, he agreed to join forces with Franco, but he quietly planned to dump him once the film was completed.

Guccione's first order was that Paul Morrissey be fired. He told Vidal that he did not want involvement with anyone associated with Andy Warhol, but that was a spurious pretext, and Guccione and Warhol had worked together cordially in the past. A good guess is that he simply did not want a homosexual man to direct a film featuring nude models from his magazine. It was now Vidal's turn to be crestfallen, since he had had his heart set upon Morrissey directing the script.

Franco, Vidal, and Guccione now began the tedious search to replace Morrissey. They approached Nicolas Roeg, who was interested but who could not work it into his schedule. They approached Peter Medak, who had a few years earlier been hired to direct a film of Vidal's, *Julian* (a later Roman emperor), which never got off the ground. He too was unavailable. They then approached Lina Wertmüller, who reached into her desk drawer and pulled out a screenplay she had written in 1965. It was entitled *Caligula*. She read Vidal's script, found it "disgusting," and explained that she would direct only her own script.

Another name kept popping up in conversation. Vidal's friend, an Italian assistant director named Guidarino Guidi, suggested that a fellow by the name of Tinto Brass might be right to direct the script. At the same time, Giancarlo Badessi, a friend of Franco, had just completed his work on *Salon Kitty* and sang Tinto's praises. More curiously, Vidal was a customer at Harry's Bar in Venice, and Harry's Bar was owned by Tinto's brother-in-law Arrigo. Perhaps he heard about Tinto there, too.

Franco had met Tinto in the 1950s when they had both been crew members on the same film. Franco had kept up with Tinto's career and found his films to be marvelously intelligent. He paid a visit to a screening room at the Fono-Roma studio where Tinto was about to run a completed seven-minute reel of *Salon Kitty*. The seven-minute reel was the seven-minute scene of the precision military orgy at the Berlin Sportforum, in which a massive line-up of naked Nazi ladies copulate with a massive line-up of naked Nazi soldiers as a Nazi military band provides musical accompaniment. Franco had by now learned enough to realize that Guccione would approve of this seven-minute reel. He had a duplicate air-expressed to Guccione's London Penthouse Club. Guccione sat back to watch it and as soon as it was finished, he leapt up to thunder forth, "I want this man to direct *Caligula*!"

Guccione flew to Rome immediately and met with Tinto. He turned on the charm, as he did only when he needed to, and the two got along. Tinto was already familiar with the Caligula story, and he agreed that the standard textbook summaries were naïve and misleading. We need to remember that he had remained friends with Roberto Rossellini and chances are strong that the two had discussed the project back in the mid-1960s. Tinto was not impressed with Vidal's script, though, which he found distinctly uncinematic.

Nonetheless, Tinto won Guccione's heart, at least for the time being. Alan Sekers explains:

> **Tinto used to define himself as a pornographer (and Guccione, hearing this, took him literally), but in the original sense from the Greek *pornographos* ("writing about prostitutes"). But for him, prostitution was not an activity confined to sex workers and not inevitably about selling sexual favors. Politicians, lawyers, and other members of the establishment were just as capable of prostitution—selling favors of other kinds, and he would write about them.[189]**

Guccione and Silverman arranged a screening of *Salon Kitty* at the Rizzoli screening room in Manhattan on the evening of the 1st of December. Franco Rossellini was invited, as was Guccione's girlfriend, Kathy Keeton, and Vidal's boyfriend, Howard Austen. Guccione and Silverman paid for flights to have Ken Adam and Tinto attend as well. Since the English dub was not yet printed, it was the Italian dub that was shipped over for this private screening. Franco, Guccione, Keeton, and Silverman were overwhelmed by the film and they had a contract prepared for Tinto to sign. Vidal and Austen had a different opinion. Vidal agreed that, technically, the film was fine, and he agreed that its feeling for 1939 Berlin was quite good, but, overall, he thought it was one of the worst films he had ever seen. He understood that Guccione liked it only because of its "emetic sexuality." He urged Franco and Guccione not to hire Tinto so hastily. They did, though, hire Ken Adam that very night. On that score, there was firm agreement. It seems that Vidal and Tinto did not so much as exchange a Hello that evening.

Ken Adam resigned as soon as he read Vidal's script.

Peter Firth proved unavailable, and so Vidal suggested that Malcolm McDowell could play the part, despite his "sinister eyebrows." Franco contacted McDowell, but not through his agent. He had in the past dated Florinda Bolkan and remained on friendly terms with her. Bolkan had just featured in a film called *Royal Flash*, in which she played against McDowell. Franco had Bolkan contact McDowell, and McDowell, a great admirer of Vidal, was thrilled. The two men met in London and got along famously. McDowell had a serious concern, though. He hated girly magazines and he hated pornographers. He didn't feel right about involving himself in such an endeavor. Vidal assured him, "Think of Guccione as the Warner Bros.; he just signs the checks." McDowell backed down, but only because he so much wanted to work with Vidal.

Vidal handed McDowell the script, with a suggestion. "It needs cutting," he said. He knew that actors are splendid script editors, and so he asked McDowell to suggest ways to condense the script. McDowell came back the next day—with all of Tiberius' scenes deleted. That was not what Vidal had meant by condensing or cutting. Vidal immediately phoned Guccione to demand, "Get rid of Malcolm." Guccione would not budge. McDowell was hot, and to have him as the lead was a feather in Guccione's cap. Guccione insisted, though, that Vidal work with Tinto on the script, even though Tinto had not been hired and was not on payroll. Tinto's first suggestion was that Ennia be introduced by showing her in sexual congress with some slaves.[190] Vidal phoned Guccione again, saying essentially to get rid of Tinto.

Guccione encouraged Vidal to give Tinto another chance, and, to the writer's surprise, Tinto proved to be a marvelous script editor. They had discussions on how to condense, how to tie loose ends together, how to make the dialogue punchier, how to make scenes more visual, how to make the characters more consistent. Vidal furiously scribbled notes into his copy of the script to keep up with Tinto's suggestions. This process lasted from December through the first week of April, when they finally had a draft that both agreed upon, fully. Fifty pages altogether were deleted, and the story had a relentless forward drive that it had not had previously. It is unfortunate that almost nobody ever saw that final script.

Penthouse's coproduction contract with Felix proved to be illegal, since there was no treaty between the two countries that would allow such a business arrangement. A new contract was drawn up, one that met the demands of Italian law, by which Felix would be the sole producer, while Penthouse would be an investor with full command of artistic decisions.

Salon Kitty was then released in early March and proved to be one of the biggest box-office sensations of the year. Guccione instructed Franco to hire Tinto immediately, without telling Vidal, who was back in the U.S. at the time. When Vidal learned that Tinto had been hired behind his back, he felt betrayed and sidelined.

It was at about this time that a Penthouse executive (most likely it was Guccione himself) made Tinto aware of some interviews that Vidal had given to the press, in which he said he was including his name in the title "to strike a blow for the writer" and against the idea that a director is an *auteur*. Unless the director writes the script, he said, the director is naught more than a technician, a hack, a plagiarist, sometimes useful, usually useless.

It was on Monday, 10 April 1976, after work, that Tinto paid a visit to Vidal's apartment in Rome to discuss this matter. Tinto's reputation was on the line. He could not be seen to agree with the accusation that he was nothing more than a hack technician and a plagiarist. He and Vidal had a lengthy discussion that evening. Vidal explained his point of view, and Tinto explained his, but the two were speaking almost different languages. Vidal had come from the worlds of the American stage theatre and early American television, in which the writer's say was final. Tinto came from the European cinema tradition, where a screenplay was a departure point and in which the director's word was final. Further, Tinto had grown up in a cinematic culture in which the screenplay writer and the director were generally the same person, quite the opposite of the Hollywood tradition in which the two tasks were typically separated. Further to the point, Vidal was busy on numerous television projects and publicity tours as well as a novel underway, on top of which he was an active political commentator. He would have no time to be on set to oversee the production, and he had already made that clear.

If Vidal declined to involve himself with the day-to-day tedium of making the film, why would he insist on the writer being the primary or sole creator of the movie? Anyone who has worked in any kind of theatre understands that lines, routines, actions, and new ideas are invented constantly during rehearsal and even during actual performance, and that ideas that had seemed sure-fire during the writing can prove to be duds in delivery. Vidal had spoken of this in the past, and in the past he had been on set to adjust his scripts on the fly, a task he now refused to perform on *Caligula*. Vidal asked Tinto who would adjust the dialogue when lines proved unplayable. Tinto replied that he would do that himself. Vidal responded that he was too famous to allow anyone else to alter his words. Tinto then said that he would not allow Vidal on the set. As far as we can determine, the disagreement never grew heated. As far as we can determine, Vidal and Tinto continued to hold one another in rather high regard, at least for the time being. Yet that meeting was terminal. The two men never spoke again. Tinto recalls later on:

The original title was *Gore Vidal's Caligula*. I said, "No way; Gore Vidal's, not at all; only *Caligula*." And there was some discussion with Gore Vidal. I must say that professionally he was perfect. I asked him seven times to rewrite the script, and he did it, absolutely; there was no problem. But then he wanted to have some kind of control And I said "No, nobody puts his feet on the set except me." And then the fights started, with him and the producers, etc. It was rather, very *vivace*, a very exciting production. But I had big means to do it.[191]

Just after that terminal meeting, a highly unusual event occurred, and to this day we do not know who was responsible. Guccione hired an Italian to rewrite the script. This Italian ignored the final script upon which Vidal and Tinto had agreed. Instead, he took several early rejected drafts, mixed them together, jumbled scenes and dialogue, spiced the lines with foul language, made countless alterations, almost all for the worse, and added offensive scenes, one of which depicted a slave woman masturbating a horse, another of which depicted Caligula proudly standing astride the gigantic phallus of a statue of himself, another that showed Tiberius urinating. On Sunday, 4 July 1976, someone handed this atrocity to Vidal, explaining that it was Tinto's rewrite. Vidal immediately resigned from the film, demanded that he not be credited with the script, and demanded further that his name be removed from the title.

The following day, Monday, 5 July 1976, McDowell touched down in Rome, and someone from *Penthouse* handed him this script, explaining that it was Vidal's latest rewrite. McDowell asked to meet with Vidal, but was told that he had just resigned. McDowell had accepted this job only so that he could collaborate with Vidal. Now he felt betrayed and abandoned. He read the script, and was horrified. He demanded that production hire a playwright friend, Ted Whitehead, to fly to Rome to repair the disastrous screenplay. Whitehead did what he could to fix the mess, but nothing he could invent even began to approach the fine work that Vidal had performed in his final draft. When Vidal was sent the revision, he got slobberingly drunk, phoned McDowell late at night, and howled that his beautiful script was being ruined. Since all McDowell knew of the beautiful script was the sickening forgery, he told Vidal that the original script was unplayable. The two ceased speaking.

Once McDowell agreed with Whitehead's revisions, *Penthouse* said that a "top secret" script was forthcoming from the unidentified Italian author and would arrive only at the beginning of the shoot. Again, it made not the least bit of sense. Vidal went to the press to denounce McDowell and especially Tinto in the harshest terms. At this time, Vidal still had not transferred his author rights to Franco Rossellini's Felix Cinematografica, and so production could not proceed. Vidal, at that moment, held all the power. All he needed to do was refuse to assign the rights unless his conditions were met. Unaccountably, he signed over all his rights, explicitly granting Felix full authority to alter his script however it saw fit, while still using his name in the credits and publicity, and then immediately thereafter he sued the production for altering his ideas and thereby impugning his reputation.

Some background shots were filmed at the end of July 1976, and then shooting proper began in early August. Because John Gielgud would be available only for five days, all his scenes had to be completed first, and they were among the most complicated scenes in the film, filled with countless extras, all performing special actions. Famed designer Danilo Donati had been hired when Ken Adam left, and his plans were grandiose. Given the budget to create nearly anything he could dream of, he turned the film into the most elaborate visual fantasy of his life, and nothing he designed matched anything in the script. The "top secret" script had few stage directions and almost no details. It consisted almost entirely of dialogue and only the most perfunctory directions. It could be filmed only by improvisation. Further, the "top secret" script was an illiterate disaster that could not possibly have been filmed as written. Tinto, the cast, and the crew were forced to improvise. When Penthouse headquarters in Manhattan was alerted that the crew were all improvising, Penthouse sent an ominous threat to Felix demanding that improvisations cease and that the script be filmed exactly as written, a sheer impossibility.

Peter O'Toole arrived to play Tiberius, a major character who takes up the first quarter of the story. He was furious that Vidal's script had been changed and he placed all the blame on Tinto. To get his revenge, he routinely showed up late. Scheduled to begin at 8 a.m. to undergo three hours' worth of makeup applications and dressing, he would keep the entire company waiting until 4:30 in the evening when he finally arrived in street clothes. The entire cast and crew would be put on overtime as he spent the next three hours getting made up and costumed. He would come out to perform scenes for 30 minutes, disappear into his dressing room, and re-emerge in street clothes. He kept up his antics for a full month. He later told interviewers that he had worked only six days, and he further claimed that the only English Tinto could speak was "Roll over" and "Are you finished?"

Maria Schneider, cast to portray Caligula's sister Drusilla, walked off the set before the cameras rolled on her, and she had a good legal case to resign, but she too was guilty of antics that would have made filming impossible. Tinto replaced her with Teresa Ann Savoy, who had performed so well in *Salon Kitty*.

Other than those problems, most of the filming proceeded rather smoothly. The sets were so gigantic that they could not be completed in time, and so production was delayed by a little over a month. Outdoor summer scenes, performed in light see-through fabrics, had to be performed at Christmastime in the freezing cold, and the actors had to keep ice cubes in their mouths to prevent their breath from fogging the air.

The point Vidal had wanted to make with *Gore Vidal's Caligula* was that, given the right circumstances, anyone can turn into a Caligula. He once explained that the apostrophe in the title was not a possessive but a contraction: *Gore Vidal is Caligula*, and, by extension, each one of us is a potential Caligula. He saw Caligula as a small child who liked to break his toys, only in this case the toys were the Roman empire and the people in it. Once Vidal left the production and once his script had been so mutilated, Tinto reverted to Roberto Rossellini's point that Caligula was a damaged young man, an idealist who hoped to provoke his underlings into open rebellion. Both views are historically and psychologically incorrect, though either could work dramatically.

Though the Rome it depicts bears no resemblance to the real Roman empire, it is so far removed from reality, so profoundly alienating, that it seems like an ancient and unknown world.

Despite the delays, despite the overtime, the film came in wildly under-budget. Felix and Penthouse had expected to expend about $7,000,000 but the entire production ended up costing them a mere half that. (The claims that the production cost $17,500,000 and that Guccione fronted all the money were blatant lies.) Guccione and Franco Rossellini had raised funds by preselling to various distributors throughout the world, and they paid themselves commissions from the leftover funds.

Then the problems began. From the very first, Jack Silverman had been lobbying Guccione to get rid of Tinto and all his crew. He considered them talentless know-nothings who were hopelessly incompetent. He couldn't understand why Tinto was using so much film. Other productions, he had been assured, did not generate so much film. A typical two-hour movie used no more than about five or six hours' worth of film. Tinto, to make a three-hour movie, burned through 97 hours' worth of film. Silverman did not understand even the most basic of the basics of filmmaking. *Caligula* was not a typical potboiler. It needed three camera crews to capture all the actions. To have shot with a single camera would have tripled the shooting time, as scenes would need to be performed even more times in order to capture all the details. Further, improvisation was necessary, and the actors were discovering their rôles as they were creating them. In those circumstances, such a high ratio of film shot versus film included is normal and to be expected. Buster Keaton, Charlie Chaplin, Stanley Kubrick, and Federico Fellini all had similarly high shooting ratios, and they could not have made films of quality without expending and tossing so much footage. Silverman, who had never worked on a film before, saw this as waste and ineptitude.

Silverman, who was strictly homosexual, was also confused by the actresses. This was a Penthouse film, and so why did the actresses not look exactly like the *Penthouse* models as they posed for the images in *Penthouse* magazine? He claimed that the actresses thus looked "ugly." In his view, Helen Mirren, Teresa Ann Savoy, Mirella d'Angelo, and the rest all qualified as "ugly." When Guccione first heard this complaint, early in the shooting, he flew in some *Penthouse* models to be added to the film—after casting had been completed—and then complained that they did not have major rôles, even though they were not cast as characters in the script, and even though Italian law forbade so many foreigners from having speaking rôles. All the rushes were sent to Guccione for review, but the only parts Guccione reviewed were the shots with his *Penthouse* models, and he could not understand why they were not featured stars.

Partway through the filming, Tinto found that he could no longer review the rushes because they had all been packed away to London. He couldn't understand why. He wrote a letter to Silverman to ask for an explanation. Silverman met with the Penthouse and Felix executives, expressed outrage at such unreasonable "blackmail," and refused to provide any response. Since the film was legally an Italian production, controlled by the Banca Nazionale del Lavoro which had sole authority over the storage of the rushes, Felix got into significant legal trouble for shipping the footage out of the country.

The bulk of the filming was completed on 24 December 1976, and then a few pickups were shot on 31 December 1976. Tinto now took the opportunity to sue Vidal for defamation of character. Unbeknownst to anybody except his intimates, he began to edit *Caligula* at a studio in Rome. How? He had surreptitiously made a duplicate either of the 97 hours of rushes or much more likely of the nine-hour preliminary assembly. That was his practice run. Alan Sekers served as his apprentice. In mid-February, Tinto flew with his wife and editing crew to cut the film at Twickenham Studios in London. He was shocked upon arrival to discover that a British crew under Russell Lloyd was already at work editing the film. The contract was clear that Tinto would perform the first cut. No one else was to touch the film until he had submitted his first cut. It was Silverman who had hired Lloyd, in open defiance of the contract, because he did not want Tinto anywhere near the film any longer.

Lloyd's crew were editing a black-and-white copy, while Tinto's crew edited the original color footage. While Lloyd was struggling to make sense of the footage, Tinto was rushing right through easily.

Tinto's crew and Lloyd's crew refused to speak with one another. Each regarded the other with contempt. As Tinto continued to work, Silverman continued to send his volleys of memos to Guccione to complain. Silverman disliked Fiorenzo Carpi's musical score. He didn't understand that Fiorenzo Carpi had not yet written the musical score, and would not until the film was finished. He had written only a series of beats so that the actors could dance to them. Silverman apparently thought those simple beats constituted the entire score. So Carpi was dismissed. Silverman continued to plead with Guccione to dismiss Tinto and to let Lloyd take over completely. At long last, Guccione responded. He wrote a letter to Franco Rossellini, furious that Tinto had gone so insane as to refuse to allow Lloyd any footage to edit. That accusation was entirely false. Guccione demanded that Franco fire Tinto for breach of contract, and one Monday morning, Tinto and his crew arrived at Twickenham to find his personal Prevost editing machine outside in the snow, the lock to the editing suite changed, and a summons attached to the door.

Tinto had edited only the first 84 minutes of the film, and he had edited only the image, silent. His work would now be for naught.

Tinto knew he could win this case. The law was entirely on his side. Felix and Penthouse had violated Italian law by exporting footage of Italian nationality. Felix and Penthouse had violated their contracts with the Banca Nationale del Lavoro and the various investors. Felix and Penthouse had breached their contract with him. He took them to court in England, which dismissed the case for lack of jurisdiction. He then took the case to Rome, where he easily and instantly won a temporary restraining order as well as an order that all the footage be returned to Italy. Guccione then had an injunction placed on the footage pending the outcome of further legal actions that he planned to file.

Back in London, at his favorite Hyde Park Hotel, Tinto was chatting with his longtime friend Alan Sekers. He told Sekers the story of Roman Polanski, who was in the news at the moment. How true Tinto's version of events was, we do not know. We do know what he claimed, and what he claimed was stunning. He said that the studios had protected Polanski, who had a predilection for underage girls. After making *Chinatown*, though, there was a change. *Chinatown* was a Paramount Pictures/Penthouse coproduction. Penthouse had not been involved in the day-to-day production, but had invested heavily. Paramount then received an offer from some investors to make a film (probably *Hurricane*), but only on condition that Polanski direct it. Polanski read the script and said he was not interested. He then got a message from Paramount: "Either you do what we want, or you get fucked." That is when Dino De Laurentiis phoned Polanski to say, "I hear you're having troubles with Paramount." Polanski responded, "No, I'm not having any troubles with Paramount. They just want me to make a movie that I don't want to make. That's all." De Laurentiis continued, "Look, you know me. You trust me. Paramount knows me. Paramount trusts me. Come to Hollywood. We'll work it out." Polanski flew to Hollywood, where it was arranged that he would photograph a 13-year-old girl—who was the daughter of a Mafia judge. At that very moment in the telling of his story, Tinto's phone rang. He answered, and Alan Sekers was surprised to see his face turn white. Sekers knew Tinto as a big burly man who was not afraid of anything, but now, for the first time, he saw Tinto appear frightened. A few minutes later, when Tinto hung up the phone, he said to Sekers, "You'll never guess who that was." "Who was it?" "It was Dino De Laurentiis. He said, 'I hear you're having troubles with Guccione. Look, you know me. You trust me. Guccione knows me. Guccione trusts me. Come to Hollywood. We'll work it out.'" Tinto went silent for a few moments, and then said, "I've lost the film."

Tinto reluctantly accepted defeat and agreed to withdraw from the film in return for a payment and on condition that he not be credited as director. What should have been his quick and decisive victory turned into a protracted two-year delay. No producer would now have anything to do with him. Tinto was no longer known as a competent filmmaker, but only as a litigious troublemaker who would delay a film's release.

Though Guccione's lawyers had placed an injunction on the footage, forbidding anyone at all from getting near it, that did not stop Penthouse and Lloyd from accessing and printing it. The editing continued. Lloyd's crew disassembled Tinto's cut of the film and spliced it back into the preliminary assembly. (After they had cut it apart, but before they spliced it back into the preliminary assembly, someone snuck into the editing suite and made a 16mm black-and-white copy of the fragments. That is how a record survived of most of Tinto's work.) Lloyd and his crew now did their work over again, this time in color. Lloyd moved the beginning of the film down by about 30 minutes, to link the dialogue with a different scene. He found most of the scenes with Caligula's horse, which were spread throughout the story, and put them all together as one continuous stretch, which made total nonsense of the narrative. Lloyd deleted the humorous dialogue and most of the other bits of comical business. Worst of all, he seldom intercut the footage from the three cameras. That decision was ruinous. For instance, at the beginning, with Caligula and his sister Drusilla in bed together, Tinto had made sure to have the second and third cameras catch all the various servants who were standing guard around them. Lloyd almost entirely chopped out those extras, denuding the story of its context. He continued thus throughout. His ideal in other films was to have each scene be a single shot. He was unable to edit *Caligula* in that manner, considering the way Tinto had shot it, but he tried to get as close as he possibly could. The result was deadly dull and made no sense.

When he had completed his cut of the film, Silverman watched the result, and he was not happy. He ordered that numerous scenes be deleted. All the scenes in the Temple of Jupiter had to go. Caligula smashing his statues had to go. The few remaining slapstick comedy scenes had to go. Lloyd obeyed and dutifully chopped them all out.

Guccione then came by with more than two hours' worth of hardcore "additional scenes" that he and Giancarlo Lui had shot on two of the sets after filming had been completed. He asked Lloyd to pull up the storm scene, explained which images of the servants to delete, and he pointed out where to add in the scene of the hardcore lesbian duet between Lori Kay Wagner and Anneka DiLorenzo. Satisfied, he asked Lloyd to pull up the reels of the Imperial Bordello. He watched it, told Lloyd which shots to delete (about one minute in total), and then he told Lloyd which shots of the hardcore "additional scenes" to splice in. When the session was over, Guccione left, still not having watched the remainder of the film.[192]

Eventually, Guccione did arrive for a viewing on the Steenbeck. Lloyd loaded the 16 reels, one by one, and Guccione was mortified. The gigantic sets had cost a fortune, but they were only in the background, while actors were in the foreground talking to one another. When the film came to an end, he walked away quietly, and he told his longtime friend, Giancarlo Lui, to dismiss Russell Lloyd.

Lui not long afterwards explained reality to Guccione. He was probably the only person to whom Guccione would listen. Guccione had in the past angrily rejected Tinto's assertions that he had shot the film in such a way that only he would be able to piece it together. Lui now explained to him that Tinto was absolutely right. He had shot the film in multicam, and Tinto, and Tinto alone, knew how to make the disparate pieces fit together. Still, though, there was a possible solution. There was an Italian editor who was accustomed to editing multicam films, and he could possibly rescue *Caligula*.[193] That is how Nino Baragli came to be hired. Baragli spoke not a word of English. He was in the midst of an emotional crisis and would periodically retreat to a corner to whimper to himself. He and Lui gathered every frame of footage, edited and unedited, and studied it all. He decided that for the first half of the movie, about half of Lloyd's work was acceptable. He discovered that all but a few shots of Tinto's original cut were still available in the 16mm black-and-white dupe, but they were entirely out of sequence. Baragli noticed that Tinto's splice marks showed through in that duplicate. If he could match the splice marks, he could reconstruct most of Tinto's work. Apparently, he had enlargements made of the first and last frame of each shot and then shuffled the photos until he managed to piece the puzzle together. He used about half of Tinto's work. For the second half of the movie, Baragli pretty much let Lloyd's edition stand, though he did delete some of the horse scenes, presumably because he couldn't figure out where they originally belonged. Then, after maybe a week or two of work, he flew back to Italy, considering his job completed.

The editing crew, now under the command of Peter Krook, set about recording the dialogue, much of it entirely rewritten, as well as the Foley. When it came time to compose the music, Franco Rossellini came to the rescue. He hired his friend, Franco Mannino, who promised to have a full orchestration ready in just a few weeks. Alfred Weiler Crown, Senior VP of Penthouse Films, explained that such was impossible. It would take many months to score a film of the complexity of *Caligula*. Mannino had his score ready in several weeks, but it had little to do with the film. It seemed to be a hodge-podge of disused leftover pieces that Mannino had collected throughout his career. The Penthouse executives pronounced his score "crap." Under pressure to submit official credits to the Italian authorities, Franco or his crew invented a false name, Paul Clemente. Shortly afterwards, Penthouse hired a composer, Bruno Nicolai, who was thus forced to use the Paul Clemente pseudonym. He composed some lovely music, but some of his cues did not fit with Tinto's intentions. When Guccione, Franco, and Tinto reached a settlement at the beginning of February 1979, Guccione announced that the unions, or "sanctimonious bastards" as he called them, were about to impound the film, and so he arranged a "midnight raid" on the vaults. Actually, it was a daytime removal into vans. The film was then sent to GTC-CTM Laboratories of Joinville-le-Pont in France. What precisely happened there is a matter of conjecture, but the physical evidence suggests that Guccione had even more of his "additional scenes" cut into the Imperial Bordello scene, which now ran 25 minutes. The music and effects were lengthened artificially with cuts and duplications and remixings and sampling, as well as a new piece of music by Bruno Nicolai. All these extra bits were clustered together into two lengths of film that could easily be spliced out and spliced back in whenever needed. This extra-long version was shown only once or twice, privately, before vanishing forever.

Guccione premièred the movie at three invitation-only screenings at a studio screening room during the time of the Cannes Film Festival in May 1979. It garnered some bids.

Franco submitted the Italian dub to the Italian censors, who at first demanded that Franco delete about six minutes. Franco happily agreed. Then, just to be safe, Franco cut three more minutes out of the film. He previewed the movie for a week in August and, predictably, there was a citizen complaint. The court dismissed the charges and issued an unappealable ruling that the film could be legally shown in Italy. The movie opened in November and did record-breaking business, but only for six days. Italian law being what it is, the unappealable ruling was appealed and the film was condemned in its entirety. It was taken off Italian screens, permanently. Franco would eventually be allowed to reissue the film under a different title and with even further deletions, but by then all interest had died.

Guccione slowly opened the film in the U.S. beginning in February 1980, and he faced legal challenges in numerous localities. At first, he gathered his dream team of lawyers, joined forces with the exhibitors, and valiantly prevailed, proudly pronouncing to the press that this is how he would fight for the film, that this is how he and Penthouse would side with the exhibitors "one thousand percent" and do whatever it would take to win the case and to counter attempts at censorship. After he made his point, he decided against putting up a fight any further. Exhibitors were jailed and fined, and Guccione simply hung them out to dry.

Franco never bothered to watch the movie, and so he did not notice that his company's production credit had been scrubbed. Yes, his name appeared in the credits, but his company's name, Felix Cinematografica S.r.l., had been deleted (except in France). The film was falsely announced as a Penthouse production. Franco did notice, though, that he was not getting his royalties. He sued, Penthouse presented forgeries in court to counter his claims, and Penthouse usually won the proceedings. When Franco would win a judgment, he found himself in the hospital with broken bones, or he found that his car was set afire, or he found that his bodyguard, Enzo Natale, was in surgery after having his skull smashed in.

The cases were heard in the U.S., in England, in Italy, in France, and in Germany for a full decade. During that time, all the evidence suggests that some of Franco's lawyers were sabotaging his efforts and rigging the cases to favor Penthouse instead. Indeed, one of the lawyers, who accepted Franco's case and who examined Franco's evidence and spoke with him at length, did not bother to reveal that he was Penthouse's lawyer as well. When Franco found out, he was livid. Soon he was penniless, but there was one final case, in Italy, at the Supreme Court of Cassation, that would issue its definitive ruling. Franco had by now won several suits, and the rulings were unappealable. He had proved that his company had produced the movie, that his company alone had the chains of title, and that he and his company were owed their share of the profits. The three-judge panel at the Supreme Court of Cassation reversed the unappealable rulings and pronounced that Penthouse alone had been the film's producer. Franco died shortly thereafter.

For years, *Caligula* had been a box-office sensation in the places it played.[194] The reviews were almost unanimously hostile, and many critics placed the bulk of the blame on Tinto.That is how Tinto earned his reputation in the U.S. and Canada. Apart from the uncharacteristic *Salon Kitty*, his earlier films were unknown in the U.S. and Canada. Americans were introduced to him through *Caligula*. Journalists dismissed him as a "porno slob."[195]

Amazingly, there were rumblings in 2016 and 2017 that *Caligula* would be rescued. Penthouse had been sold several times over, and the new owner, Kelly Holland, who had herself been a filmmaker, discovered that nearly all the rushes were still in storage. She retrieved them literally one business day before they were scheduled for destruction for lack of rental payment. Inside the Hollywood vault were hundreds of hours of film, nearly every frame that Tinto had shot, numerous various cuts of the film, production audio, post-sync, and numerous audio mixes, together with over 10,000 unit stills and numerous unused music recordings. She began the process of raising funds to have the collection digitized so that Tinto would be able, at long last, to piece the film together properly. Then Penthouse was seized by a creditor and sold several more times. After a few brief talks about continuing Kelly's project to restore the film, the new owners decided that they were not interested in Tinto's version and made the MMXX edited cut under the supervision of filmmaker Thomas Negovan in partnership with Kirkendoll Management, LLC—in which not a single frame from the original released film was used, following Vidal's original script. In response to the new version named "The Ultimate Cut" that premièred at Cannes in 2023, Tinto responded online:

"I distance myself from the version of the film *Caligula* that will be screened at the Cannes Film Festival. After numerous and fruitless negotiations that have followed over the years, first with Penthouse and then with other unclear figures, to edit the material I shot and which had been found in the Penthouse archives, a version was created [in] which I did not take part and that I am convinced it will not reflect my artistic vision."

The 90-year-old Tinto Brass says this to ANSA referring to his 1979 film, written by Gore Vidal, which is shown in the Classics section of the festival in an extraordinary version lasting two hours and fifty-three minutes.

"As you know," continued the director, "the editing gives the film my very personal style and if I can't edit my film I don't recognize it and I haven't acknowledged its paternity. There are numerous versions of *Caligula* edited by others, including that of Bob Guccione, but none corresponds to my original project. The Cannes public will therefore be misled by the arbitrary use of my name."

Source Notes:

186 Renzo Rossellini, "Filmografia completa di Roberto Rossellini," in *Roberto Rossellini, Islam: im-pariamo a conoscere il mondo mussulmano* (Rome: Donzelli Editore, 2007), p. 134

187 Llinas and Marias, "A Panorama of History," in *Adriano Aprà*, ed., *Roberto Rossellini - My Method*, (New York: Marsilio, 1993), p. 185

188 Vidal: personal conversation, 18 December 2006; Morrissey: telephone conversation, 22 September 2007

189 Alan Sekers: email, 2 November 2020

190 Vidal: personal conversation, 18 December 2006; Melton Davis, "Cinema: *Caligula*," *I Am: The National Magazine for Italian-Americans*, Vol. 1 #8 (June 1977), p. 48

191 Nico B, "Tinto Brass: Maestro of Erotic Cinema," interview conducted 3 November 2001, Torcello (Los Angeles: Cult Epics, 2014)

192 The behind-the-scenes stories of the editing room come mostly from Russell Lloyd's assistant, Peter Krook, who kept a diary of many of these events and who, in conversation, filled in the gaps.

193 This information comes largely from Giancarlo Lui, over several years' worth of personal conversations and email interviews conducted by James Chaffin, Thomas Ryerson, and RS.

194 While playing on only a single screen in the U.S. at one small cinema, it ranked in *Variety*'s "Top 50" box-office champions nationwide. Though it played usually in small cinemas, only in relatively few localities, it remained in the Top 50 for well over a year.

195 James Wolcott, "Domesticating the Dragon Lady," *Esquire* 97, #2 (February 1982), pp. 103–104

On the set of ***Caligula*** *with Malcolm McDowell, Peter O'Toole, and Tinto Brass, 1976*

XV
Action

ACTION WAS a return to Brass' avant-garde style of *Dropout* and *La vacanza*. Like them, it was self-financed and shot in 16mm.[196] On location in England with some of his previous British crew members—though shooting in Italian rather than English—Brass crafted one of his most personal films, which was also one of his most surreal and idiosyncratic. *Action* is the only film on which Brass collaborated with both of his favorite co-authors, Giancarlo Fusco and Roberto Lerici. It would be the last film for which Brass felt free to improvise, to explore the landscapes which surprised him as much as his audiences.

Lion Film was defunct, and so Tinto now set up a new corporation, Ars Cinematografica. *Ars*, of course, is Latin for "art." It is also a homonym of an English word. He would make *Action*, a story that had been rattling around in his mind for the past eight years or so. He raised funds by preselling distribution rights to CIDIF, Consorzio Italiano Distributori Indipendenti Film, not a major distributor, but a minor one devoted only to independent films made off the beaten path.

The small production was a family affair. Tinto's daughter Beatrice took two rôles in the story, and his son Bonifacio was a unit photographer. This Italian story, with Italian characters, forceful and poetic Italian dialogue, filled with references to Italian culture and Italian history, was filmed entirely in England. The story could be seen as a companion to *Dropout* and *Vacation*, dealing as it does with society's underbelly and the misfits who are left behind. The dialogue is fast, furious, wildly creative, and generally angry, reminiscent of *The Howl*. The characters are all off-the-wall, and the situations, initially somewhat convincing, gradually meld into an alien world that bears no resemblance to reality. Parts of the story were surely based upon dreams and other parts were free-form fantasies. The result is indescribable. The film simply must be experienced, and a single viewing will not suffice, because it is impossible to keep up with all the ideas, which race by at breakneck speed. Maybe ten screenings would allow a viewer to catch the bulk of the events. It is, beyond argument, Tinto's most mature work up to this time. The actors, given strong lines and even stronger personalities, deliver strong performances.

Bruno Martel, a movie actor with a background in the French New Wave, is reduced to taking a job in an action movie directed by Angry Dog (portrayed by Tinto Brass). He ruins a take by improvising a dance after he is shot with multiple machine guns, and his agent finds him a new job in porn. Before he takes his first scene, he is so offended by the crew's treatment of an actress that he destroys the set and walks away. The actress, Doris, follows him. Wandering through a city dump, she and Bruno are attacked by punks (a clear reference to Burgess' novel *A Clockwork Orange*) and are rescued by an old man who is convinced he is Garibaldi. They take refuge in a disused fire station with countless other derelicts, and they are all rounded up by the police who deposit them in Mercy House, an insane asylum in which the sadistic doctors encourage their patients to act like maniacs. Convinced that she can fly, Ophelia leaps out a window to her death. Bruno and Garibaldi escape in a stolen automobile and are hired at a filling station in the middle of nowhere. The police from the opening scene reappear and shoot Bruno dead once again. Angry Dog calls "cut" and the film is over.

This shallow description of the story does it no justice. Quotes from the dialogue would be pointless, since the lines, almost all of them bizarre, come to life only by their unexpected delivery. The style of the film is indescribable. As were so many of Tinto's previous films, it is a blend of actuality and absurdism, but this time he took the concept further. It opens as an action/crime story, which turns out to be a film within a film. The fired actor is kicked off the set, but we do not realize until the very end that the whole movie was a film within a film.

There had long been a tradition, especially in Europe, of contemplative cinema. Ingmar Bergman is perhaps the best examplar. Takes are slow and long, many shots are studies of faces lost in thought. There was hardly a moment in his career in which Tinto borrowed that style. If anything, he reacted against it. In his films, events proceed quickly, dialogue is rapid, characters are larger than life and eccentric rather than subdued. In *Action*, the little talk about the purpose of life is a few lines spoken by characters who are emotionally unbalanced, though what they say is true enough. The porn film (entitled *L'albero delle zoccole*, The Tree of Sluts, a play on Olmi's recent film *L'albero degli zoccoli*, The Tree of Wooden Clogs) requires Bruno and Doris to perform together. Before the cameras roll, Bruno tries to talk to Doris, who pretends not to hear. After a minute, she breaks her silence and explains that she won't react. She'll tune everything out and she'll tune him out as well. Her dream, she says, is to play Ophelia in *Hamlet*, and she begins reciting. When she discovers that Bruno would beat up the crew, smash the set, and lose his job rather than see Doris mistreated, she follows him around like a shadow. We soon learn that she is delusional, incapable of distinguishing reality from imagination, a concept that the entire film explores in its various ways.

Action is also a reaction to *Caligula*. Tinto plays the director of the film within the film, and he also portrays the director of *Action*. His name is Angry Dog, a reference to the various nicknames that the Penthouse staff had bestowed upon him. When auditioning for the porno film, the director, Woodruff Vandenberg Scott, launches into a tirade against auteurism and the *Nouvelle Vague*, as Gore Vidal and Bob Guccione had done on *Caligula*. Tinto explains his reason to make *Action*:

Action is another 16mm film, not a big production, because after _Caligula_ I was so upset with all the problems that happened on the shooting of _Caligula_, with the producers, with the actors, everything like that. I wanted to do a very personal, very easygoing film, without all these big producers on my back. And that is why I did _Action_. It is an anarchistic film for sure. In it I put a little bit of my sadness concerning the film industry. I mean, "action" is the word the director says to start the shooting. It is all about fiction and action, everything—life is not true but it is always cinema. I put in the film many personal dreams, nightmares, obsessions, like the scenes of the men with the phallic noses and the women with the vagina mouths. It was a dream that I had; so I just realized it in the film.[197]

The characters in *Action* are frequently in rages. Some speak solely in insults. Others speak only in screams. Yet *Action* itself is not an angry film. It is about anger, the anger that Tinto was feeling in response to having had *Caligula* swiped from him and altered beyond recognition. It was creative anger. With *Action*, Tinto wanted to show the world how massively creative and original he could be, without big-name actors, without studio sets, on natural locations, without a budget, even in 16mm. He proved his point. *Action*, together with *Vacation*, is far more imaginative than almost anything else. The performances are all top-notch, as they had to be, since they are mostly driven by rage. Luc Merenda, known for action films in France, is especially outstanding. His character blazes across the screen in a charismatic performance. He is as gifted at physical comedy as he is at dramatic and action scenes. He is also perfectly comfortable with performing in the nude.

Alas, as with his previous four independent films, Tinto did not get a good distribution deal. CIDIF barely released the movie at all. The film played probably only a few days in Italy. It also briefly appeared in Germany under a new title, *Sodom 2000*. Then it vanished for some 20 years until an abridgment was issued on VHS. *Action* is not standard entertainment, a way to sit back and relax for two hours after a busy week at the office. *Action* is extremely demanding. It's extremely funny, too, but challenging. Its characters are not the everyday folk we know from our neighborhoods. Its situations are not those that most of us would ever experience in a month of Sundays. It is not a film for a mass audience. It is a film for a select audience, which it never found at its time of release, for those who enjoy eccentricity and off-beat stories. Never again would Tinto create avant-garde works. *Action* was Brass' final attempt at making an uncompromisingly personal film. In the future, he would make films that would strictly follow fully developed novel-like scripts. The second part of his career as the Maestro of Erotica started at 50.

Source Notes:

196 *Action* was shot with a crop in mind, and the 35mm release prints were cropped in the lab not at the traditional Italian 1.85:1, but at the less severe 1.66:1 ratio common to much of the rest of Europe. It was at about this time that Italy began a gradual conversion to 1.66:1.

197 Nico B, "Tinto Brass: Maestro of Erotic Cinema," interview conducted 3 November 2001, Torcello (Los Angeles: Cult Epics, 2014)

U.S. One Sheet poster, 1977

DEPRAVED
DECADENT
DAMNED
NAZI
GERMANY
1939
SEX IS
NOT ONLY
AN ART
BUT A
WEAPON
WITH
MADAM
Kitty

DEPRAVED
DECADENT
DAMNED
NAZI
GERMANY
1939
SEX IS
NOT ONLY
AN ART
BUT A
WEAPON
WITH
MADAM
Kitty

DEPRAVED
DECADENT
DAMNED
NAZI
GERMANY
1939
SEX IS
NOT ONLY
AN ART
BUT A
WEAPON
WITH
MADAM
Kitty

DEPRAVED
DECADENT
DAMNED
NAZI
GERMANY
1939
SEX IS
NOT ONLY
AN ART
BUT A
WEAPON
WITH
MADAM
Kitty

DEPRAVED
DECADENT
DAMNED
NAZI
GERMANY
1939
SEX IS
NOT ONLY
AN ART
BUT A
WEAPON
WITH
X
MADAM
Kitty
HELMUT BERGER
and with JOHN
with the participation of
Production Designer

Left and Right:
U.S. Lobby Cards, 1977

Top: Mexican Lobby Card, 1980, Bottom: Japanese poster, 1979

Left: French Grande poster, 1977, Right: French Moyenne poster, 1976

20th CENTURY-FOX presenta una producción CORALTA CINEMATOGRAFICA S.R.L.
HELMUT BERGER · INGRID THULIN
TERESA ANN SAVOY
SALON KITTY
un film de TINTO BRASS
El Tercer Reich encontró
en Madame Kitty
y sus chicas la más diabólica
red de espionaje.
Un film clasificado «S»
COLOR
Se advierte al publico que
esta pelicula, por su tematica y
contenido, pudiera herir
la sensibilidad del espectador
con JOHN STEINER · SARA SPERATI · MARIA MICHI · ROSMARIE LINDT
PAOLA SENATORE · JOHN IRELAND · TINA AUMONT · ALEXANDRA BOGOJEVICH
y con la participacion de STEFANO SATTA FLORES y BEKIM FEHMIU.
IN CINE
Guión de ENNIO DE CONCINI - MARIA PIA FUSCO - TINTO BRASS - Director de Fotografía SILVANO IPPOLITI.
Dirección TINTO BRASS - Música de FIORENZO CAPRI.
20th CENTURY FOX

20th Century-Fox présente une production de CORALTA CINEMATOGRAFICA S.R.L.
HELMUT BERGER • INGRID THULIN
dans
SALON KITTY
les "damnées" du 3ème Reich
Un film de TINTO BRASS
Ferracci
avec TERESA ANN SAVOY
et avec JOHN STEINER • SARA SPERATI • MARIA MICHI • ROSMARIE LINDT
PAOLA SENATORE • JOHN IRELAND • TINA AUMONT • ALEXANDRA BOGOJEVICH
et avec la participation de STEFANO SATTA FLORES et BEKIM FEHMIU
Scénario de ENNIO DE CONCINI - MARIA PIA FUSCO - TINTO BRASS - Directeur de la photographie SILVANO IPPOLITI
Décors de KEN ADAM - Musique de FIORENZO CARPI
Mise en scène de TINTO BRASS
Eastmancolor - Tirage Stacofilm - Distribué par Fox-Lira
INTERDIT AUX MOINS DE 18 ANS

Left: French Grande poster, Right: Italian Fotobusta posters, 1976

Left: Spanish Lobby Cards, Right: Australian One Sheet poster, 1978

THE CALL GIRL SYSTEM AS IT APPLIED IN NAZI GERMANY. DURING THE WAR THE BROTHEL 'SALON KITTY' REALLY EXISTED AS DID THE MONITORING OF BEDSIDE CONVERSATIONS WITH THE TOP ECHELON OF THE DAY / SUPERB PERIOD RECREATION IN COLOUR, STYLE & COSTUMING WITH HELMUT BERGER AND DIRECTOR TINTO BRASS.
SALON KITTY
HELMUT BERGER INGRID THULIN
SALON KITTY
R
Un film de TINTO BRASS • TERESA ANN SAVOY • JOHN STEINER • SARA SPERATI • MARIA MICHI
ROSMARIE LINDT PAOLA SENATORE • JOHN IRELAND • TINA AUMONT•ALEXANDRA BOGOJEVICH
STEFANO SATTA FLORES BEKIM FEHMIU
20th CENTURY FOX

Left: West German Lobby Cards, Right: West German A1 poster, 1976

Salon Kitty
Ein Film
von
Tinto Brass
Mit
Helmut Berger
Ingrid Thulin
Geheime
Reichssache!
John Ireland
Tina Aumont
Therese Ann Savoy

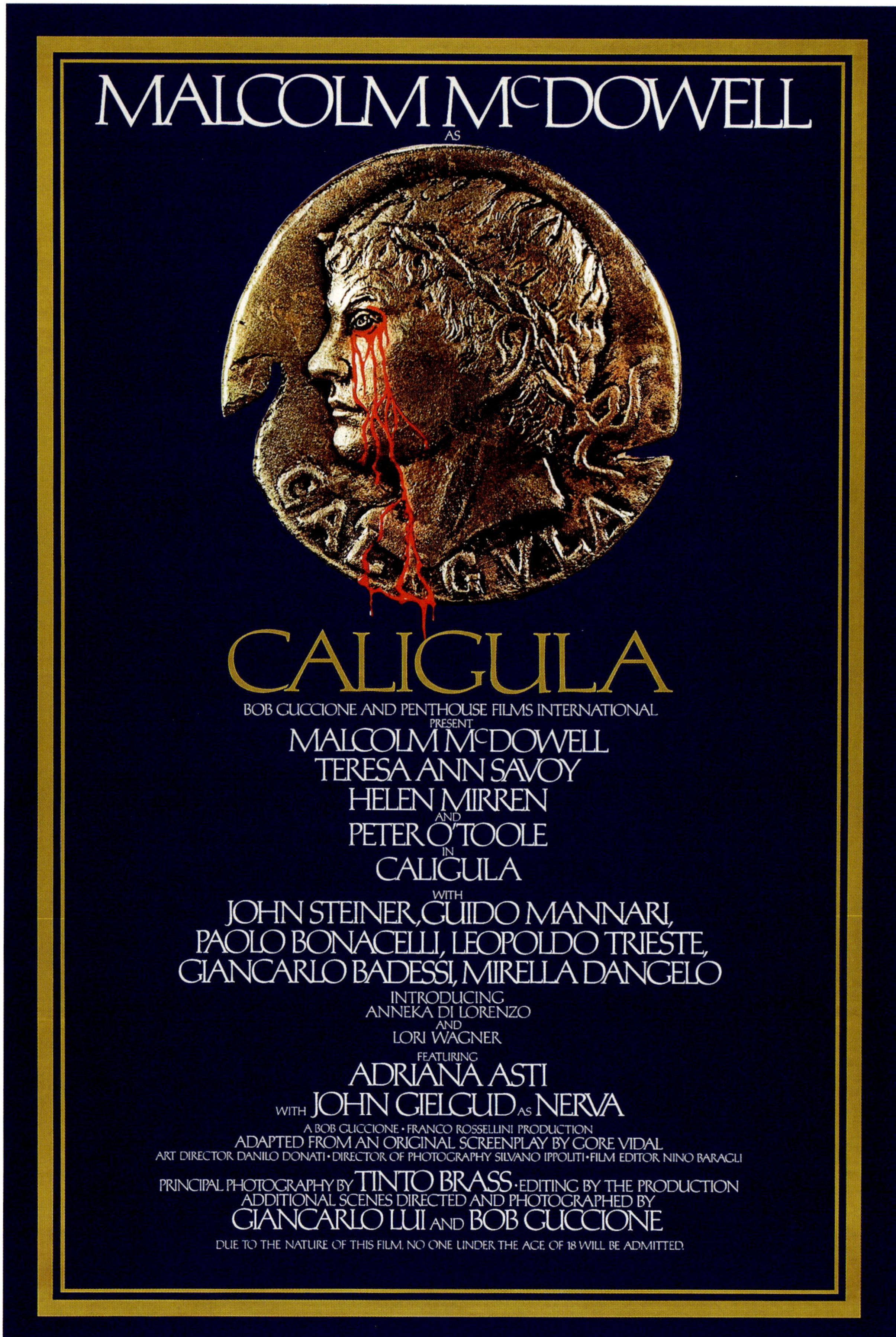

Left: U.S. One Sheet poster, 1980, Right: Italian 4-Fogli poster, 1979

L'ARTE È ANCHE FIGLIA DELLA STORIA.
E LA STORIA È FATTA DI
NEFANDEZZE E LUSSURIA.
(SVETONIO)
CALIGOLA
BOB GUCCIONE FELIX CINEMATOGRAFICA S.R.L. E PENTHOUSE FILMS INTERNATIONAL
PRESENTANO
MALCOLM Mc DOWELL TERESA ANN SAVOY
HELEN MIRREN E PETER O'TOOLE
IN
"CALIGOLA"
CON
JOHN STEINER, GUIDO MANNARI, PAOLO BONACELLI
LEOPOLDO TRIESTE, GIANCARLO BADESSI, MIRELLA DANGELO
CON LA PARTECIPAZIONE DI ADRIANA ASTI CON JOHN GIELGUD NEL RUOLO DI NERVA
TRATTO DAL SOGGETTO ORIGINALE DI GORE VIDAL SCENE E COSTUMI DI DANILO DONATI MUSICA ORIGINALE DI PAUL CLEMENTE
PRODOTTO DA BOB GUCCIONE FRANCO ROSSELLINI PER LA PENTHOUSE FILMS INTERNATIONAL E FELIX CINEMATOGRAFICA S.R.L.
RIPRESE DIRETTE DA TINTO BRASS EDIZIONE DELLA PRODUZIONE COLORE-SUONO: CINECITTA' UNA PRODUZIONE DI FRANCO ROSSELLINI
P.A.C.
CONSORZIATE
ROTOPRESS - ROMA ANNO DI EDIZIONE 1979

Left and Right: Italian Fotobusta posters, 1977

Left: Italian Fotobusta poster, 1977, Right: French Moyenne poster, 1980

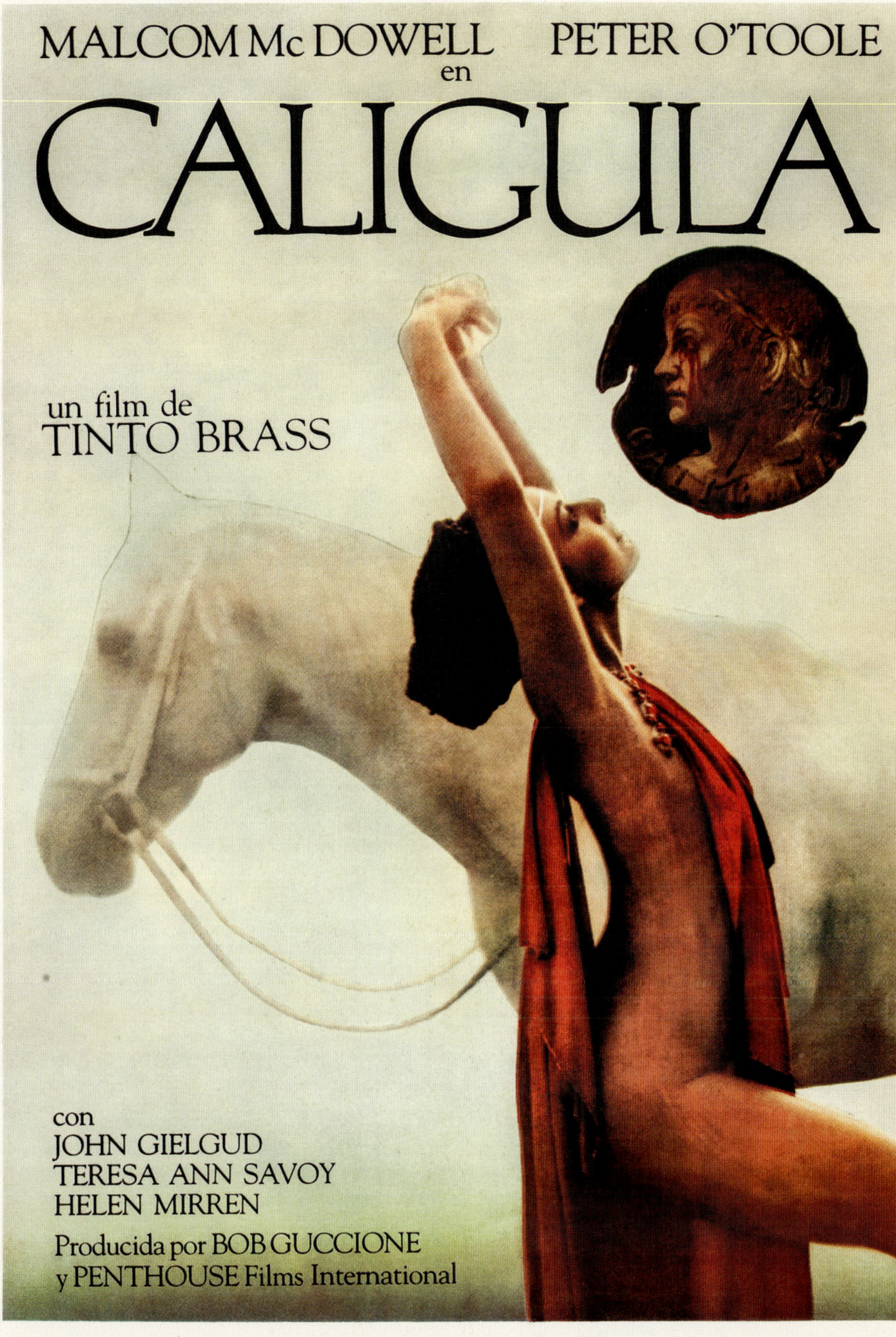
MALCOM Mc DOWELL
PETER O'TOOLE
en
CALIGULA
un film de
TINTO BRASS
con
JOHN GIELGUD
TERESA ANN SAVOY
HELEN MIRREN
Producida por BOB GUCCIONE
y PENTHOUSE Films International

Spanish One Sheet poster, 1982

Australian One Sheet poster, 1981

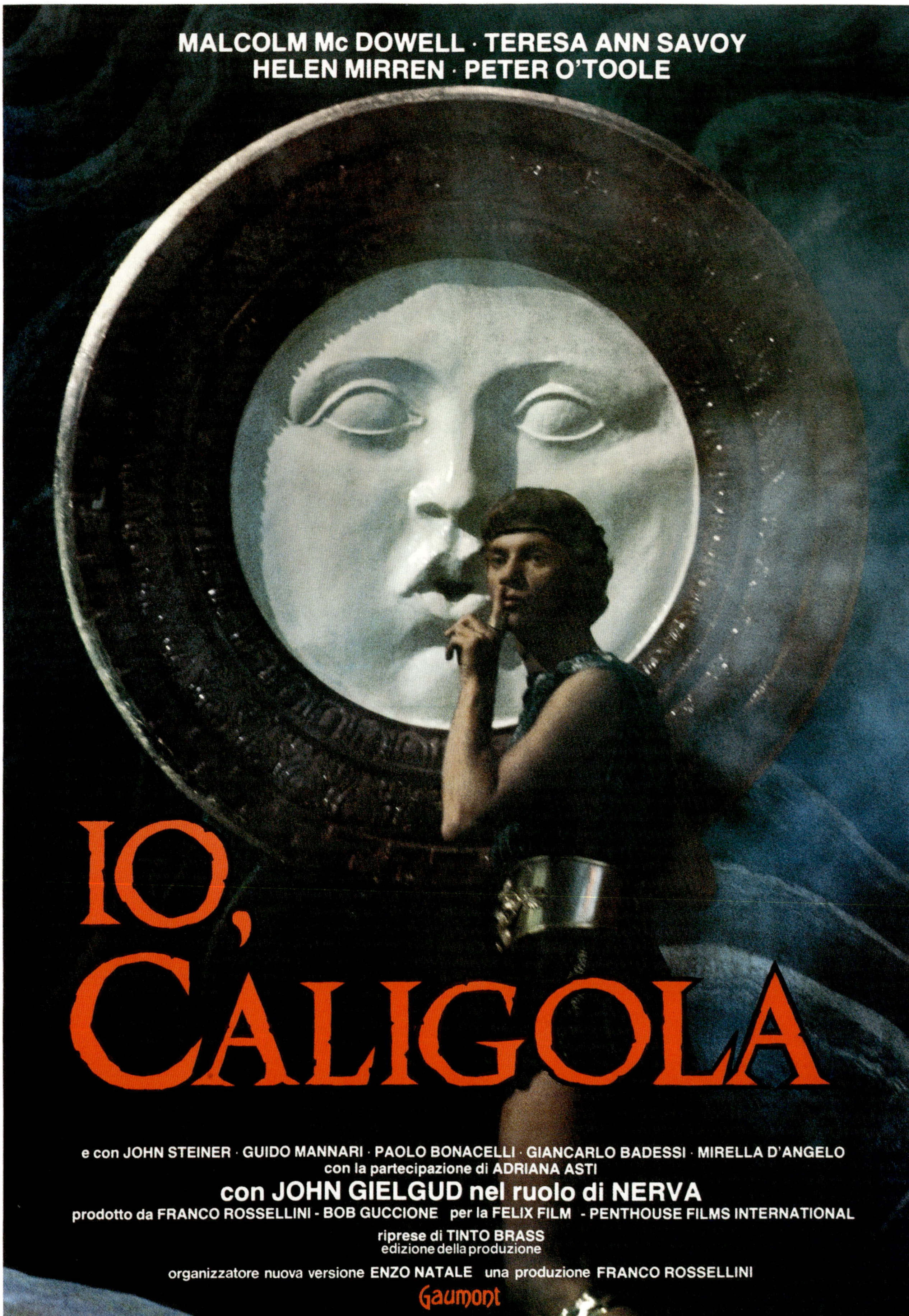

Left and Right: Italian 2-Fogli Reissue posters, 1984

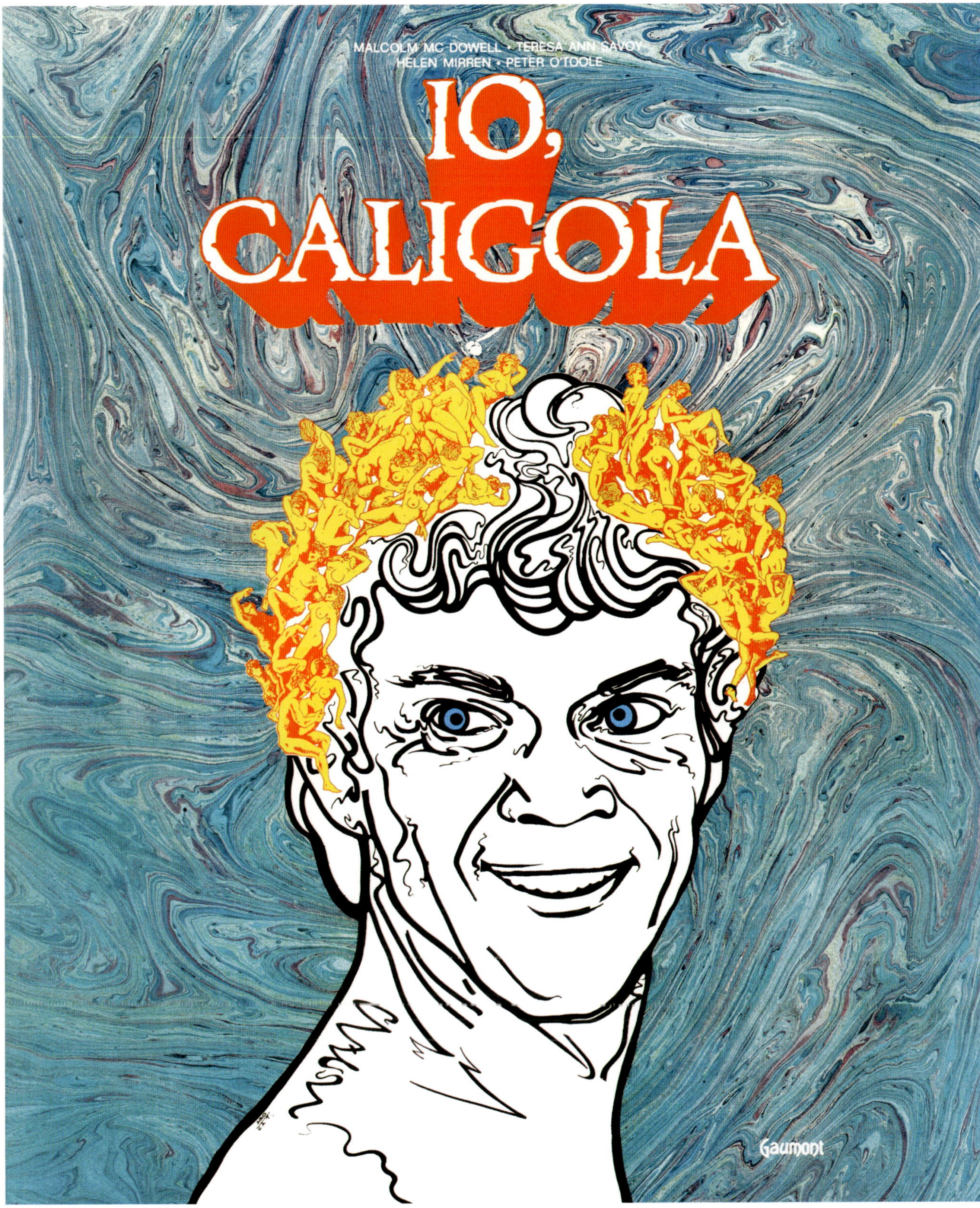

e con JOHN STEINER • GUIDO MANNARI • PAOLO BONACELLI • GIANCARLO BADESSI • MIRELLA D'ANGELO

con la partecipazione di ADRIANA ASTI con JOHN GIELGUD nel ruolo di NERVA

prodotto da FRANCO ROSSELLINI • BOB GUCCIONE

per la FELIX CINEMATOGRAFICA S.R.L. • PENTHOUSE FILMS INTERNATIONAL

riprese di TINTO BRASS

organizzatore seconda edizione ENZO NATALE una produzione FRANCO ROSSELLINI

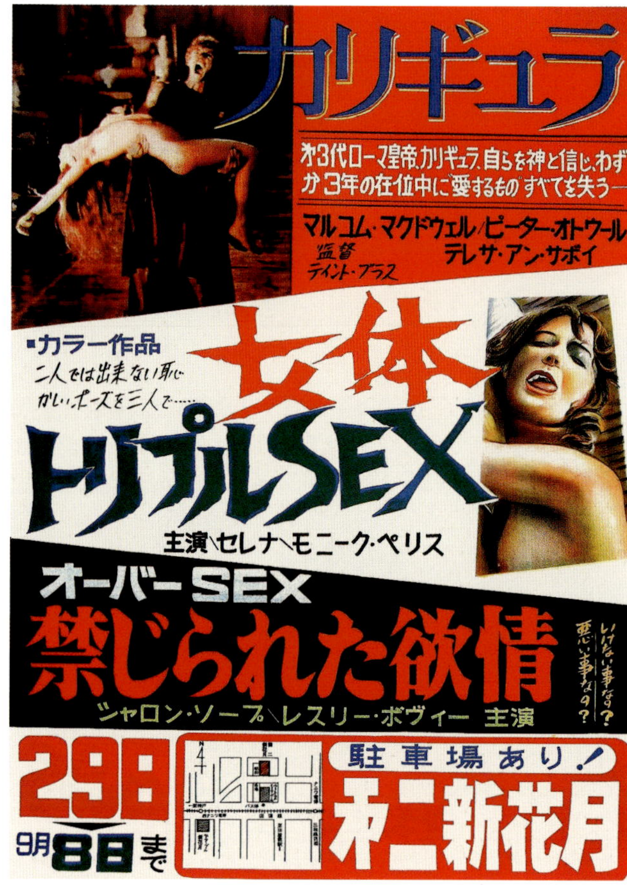

Top: Japanese B5 posters, 1980, Italian Fotobusta Reissue poster, 1984

Japanese B2 poster, 1980

Italian 4-Fogli poster, 1980

Top: Italian 1-Fogli posters, 1980

Bottom: Italian Fotobusta poster, 1980

un film di tinto brass
ACTION
LUC MERENDA
con ADRIANA ASTI
SUSANNA JAVICOLI
PAOLA SENATORE
e con ALBERTO SORRENTINO
JOHN STEINER
e con ALBERTO LUPO
e con la partecipazione di FRANCO FABRIZI
fotografia:
Silvano Ippoliti
musica:
Riccardo Giovannini
produzione:
Ars Cinematografica
COLORE TELECOLOR

Left: Italian 2-Fogli poster, Right: Italian 4-Fogli poster, 1980

Left: West German Lobby Cards, Right: West German A1 poster, 1980

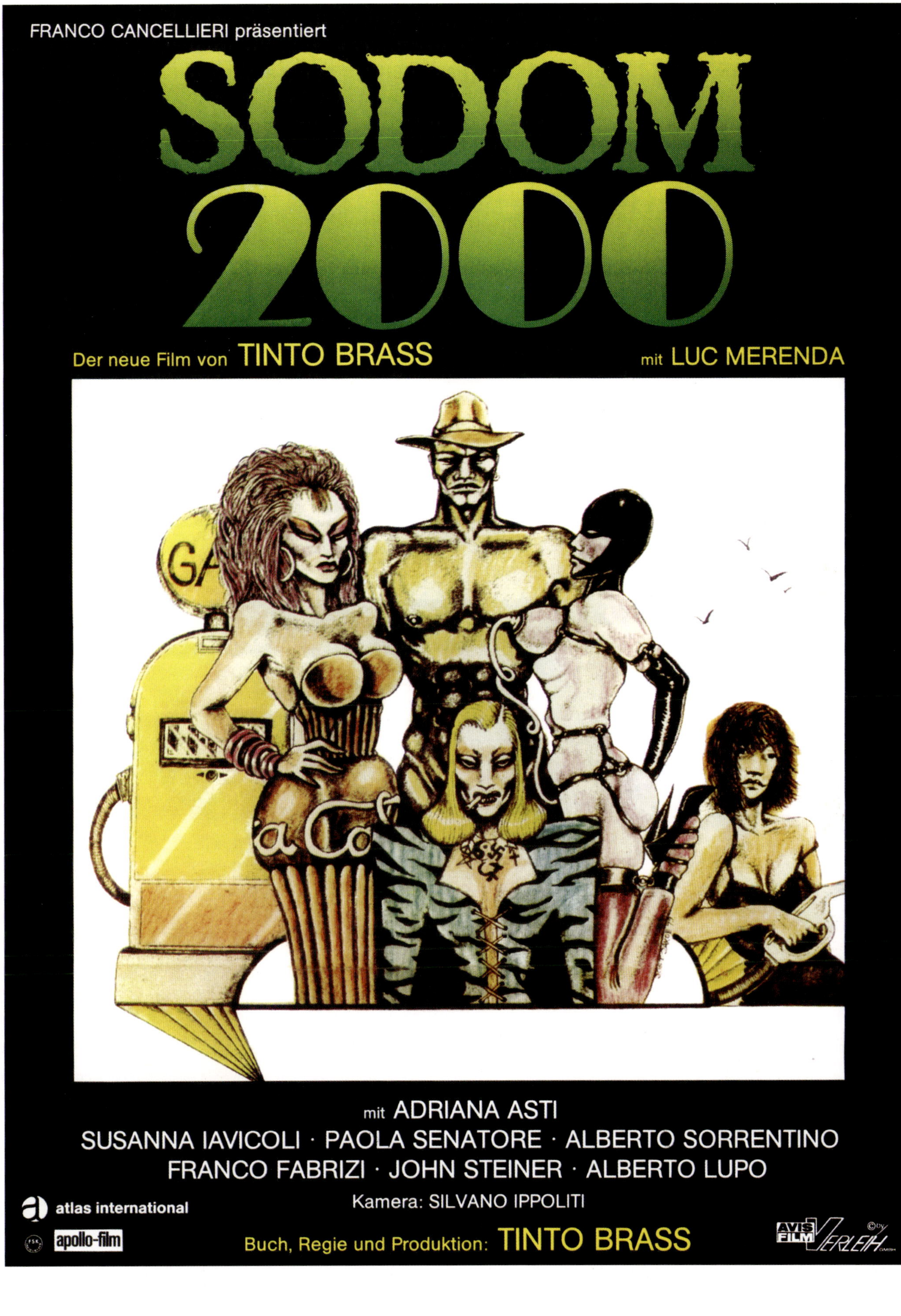
FRANCO CANCELLIERI präsentiert
SODOM 2000
Der neue Film von TINTO BRASS
mit LUC MERENDA
mit ADRIANA ASTI
SUSANNA IAVICOLI · PAOLA SENATORE · ALBERTO SORRENTINO
FRANCO FABRIZI · JOHN STEINER · ALBERTO LUPO
Kamera: SILVANO IPPOLITI
atlas international
apollo-film
Buch, Regie und Produktion: TINTO BRASS
AVIS FILM VERLEIH

TINTO THE FILMS OF BRASS

PART FOUR

EROTICA

Italian 2-Fogli poster, 1983

XVI
The Key
(La chiave)

WHEN *CALIGULA* was finally released and stayed in release for years, it surprisingly changed Tinto's life for the better. *Caligula* was a massive hit almost everywhere it played, and now, suddenly, producers wanted to hop onto the bandwagon. First was G.B. Milesi, who hired Tinto to make a movie of the Marquis De Sade's *Philosophy in the Bedroom*. Before the cameras rolled, Milesi dropped the project. Tinto would later direct it on stage.

Next was an offer from Harry Alan Towers for Tinto to write and direct a version of *Fanny Hill*. Tinto submitted several drafts of a screenplay, but then a rival production began and Towers decided to back that instead. The loss of *Fanny Hill* allowed Tinto to propose a film on Lord Byron, with Federico Aicardi as producer, but that fell by the wayside too. That opened the opportunity for another project that had been waiting in the wings. Producer Giovanni Bertolucci (cousin of Bernardo) was eager to produce Tinto's dream project, *The Key*.

Tinto had read Junichiro Tanizaki's 1956 novel, *The Key*, upon its 1965 Italian publication. He fell in love with it, though the novel is as cinematic as a multiplication table. It consists of parallel diary entries by a husband and wife, as the aging husband manipulates his wife and prospective son-in-law to have an affair. Tinto immediately licensed the rights from Tanizaki and spoke with him shortly before his death in July 1965. He would need to put his project in abeyance for several years, since the license for Kon Ichikawa's 1959 movie version had a while more to run before expiry of the film rights.

He wrote a script. The novel took place in the mid-1950s, when traditional society was beginning to break down with the influx of Western culture. By the mid-1950s, Italy was already well into Americanization and the sexual revolution, so to make the story realistic, Tinto needed to push the story back about 15 years. Tinto in his own words:

I had to make some changes from the novel, because Tanizaki's novel was written in the time of the '50s. But that was not believable in our world, in the West. Because it concerned the relationship between a husband and a wife who didn't talk to each other openly of their sexual problems, but they used the system of writing in a diary, and each one read the other's diary. That was absolutely unbelievable after the war in Europe; so I had to anticipate it to a time [1940] when there was a kind of formalism in a marriage between husband and wife, and certain things were not openly discussed. And then also for another reason, because I found it very exciting to make a contrast between a private, a very private story, the one of the husband and his wife, and a very public moment. And just juxtapose the supposed disorder of this private couple with the declared official order of fascism. The official order is responsible for the war; the couple is responsible for what, for having some fun, sexual fun, and that's all.[198]

He had attended a performance of *Amadeus* at Her Majesty's Theatre in London, sometime between late June and early October 1981, and he was quite taken by Frank Finlay, who portrayed Salieri. He proposed to Bertolucci that he hire Finlay, but his producer told him that the idea was useless, for Finlay was a devout Catholic who would never take part in such a story. Nonetheless, Tinto personally handed Finlay a copy of the script, and the next day his phone rang. It was Finlay excitedly telling him to stop looking for actors. He was desperate to play this part. Later, during the filming, when Tinto saw how modest, unassuming, and religious Finlay was, and saw that Finlay attended Mass at the Vatican every Sunday, he had to ask why he had wanted to play the rôle. Finlay replied that he was an actor, that his job was to portray all manner of characters. The rôle of John Brian "Nino" Rolfe was as different from his real self as could possibly be. He wanted the challenge of playing such a character convincingly. He did indeed play the character completely convincingly. When watching him in *The Key*, it is difficult not to imagine that he is simply portraying his own self, unfiltered.

In all of Tinto's previous films, the characters had been two-dimensional ciphers. For *The Key*, he needed to change that habit. He made all the characters, from the leads all the way down to the extras, well-formed, rounded, completely believable, completely human.

The Key opens unlike any other Tinto film, slowly and meditatively. The camera simply points at the ornate weathervane atop the Punta della Dogane as Ennio Morricone's Renaissance-style chamber music quietly accompanies. We know already that we are in for a different kind of experience. A New Year's Eve party celebrating 1940 opens the story which, surprisingly, is partly in English. Frank Finlay portrays an Englishman, a professor of art history and specifically Klimt, who remained in Venice upon marrying the much younger Theresa some 20 years before.

The New Year's Eve celebration begins with a hail to Il Duce. The polkas and waltzes are provided by a military band. When they get up to dance, Nino embarrasses his wife and creates a scandal by letting his hands wander over her body, and he sings praises to their prospective son-in-law. With such small gestures, we learn a great deal. Foreigner Nino is outgoing while his wife maintains traditional Italian modesty. The partygoers accept a military band and a salute to Mussolini as a normal part of life. We already know that Nino does not and cannot fit in. Inside the dining hall, all is propriety. The moment they step outside the dining hall, they are in a different world, with rowdy students who care not a fig for decorum, who spontaneously grab Nino, Theresa, and their daughter and add them to the photo they are taking. To get the right reaction, just as the shot is taken, they are all treated to a striptease. We see that every major character exhibits some rather strange behavior, and we soon realize also that Nino is terribly frustrated that a wife he deeply loves has never shared emotional or physical intimacy. He plays a game to change the situation. He takes every opportunity to bring Theresa and their prospective son-in-law, Laszlo, into ever greater contact, as he subtly makes suggestions about him to his wife. When Theresa passes out one evening, Nino, rather than worrying and calling a doctor as he normally would, decides to take advantage. He poses her in the nude and snaps photographs of her. When he realizes that she is partly awake, he continues, knowing that she would be too embarrassed to admit that she comprehends what is going on. Since nude photos are illegal, he needs a trusted friend to develop them for him. His trusted friend is Laszlo.

Their daughter Lisa discovers the photos and gets into a fury, assuming that her fiancé is having an affair with her mother. Theresa is caught entirely off-guard and doesn't even know how to make a convincing excuse. Father and daughter discover that they share a trait: Jealousy excites them, and so Lisa also arranges to have her mother spend time alone with Laszlo. During these bizarre developments, Theresa discovers a key to a desk drawer that contains a diary that she never knew her husband kept. She reads it in shock, as in it he details the lust he feels for her. Soon enough, she assimilates what she has learned and she joins the game as well. She purchases a diary book from a stationer and keeps her parallel diary, hiding it where she knows that Nino will discover it. They communicate through their diaries, revealing what they would never confess in conversation. By now she and Laszlo are lovers, and they understand that they are fulfilling the desires of Nino and Lisa.

Nino has quickly changed the entire family dynamic. As he looks out his window, he sees that the world is moving in an opposite direction. Laszlo and Lisa are utterly taken in by fascism. Young soldiers march double-time down the street. Theresa refuses even to think about politics. Nino's Jewish friends convert to Catholicism simply as a political precaution. Nino could never fit in to this new world, and when the family doctor explains that his drinking and active sex life will soon cause his death unless he stops, that only encourages Nino to double down. He muses to the doctor that at his stage of life, not to take risks is not to live, and he jokes about taking the risk of "leaving while coming." One night, Theresa surprises him by playing the rôle of a harlot, which she has learned is one of his dreams. Nino at last has the satisfaction of openness with his wife, even a heart-to-heart, which, touchingly, is not about anything distinctly personal. They talk about Giulio Romano and Marc Antonio Raimondi. It was a topic they would never have brought up before, as it was outside Theresa's limited interests. Those few words back and forth are, for them, the epitome of closeness. Nino is fulfilled, and, right at that moment of tenderness, he suffers a severe stroke. He passes away just in time not to witness the war.

How closely *The Key* captures the look and feel of the Venice of 1940 is hard to say, but it hardly matters. The Venice created in *The Key* is a different world, and, watching the film, we can feel it, we can almost smell it. There is an immediacy to the film. Even the smallest details, such as the spittle marks on the black robe worn by an elderly Catholic priest, the sounds made by raucous street urchins, the sights and sounds in a pub filled with despairing drunks, it all looks as though it were captured by hidden cameras. The passers-by outside, the artists painting on their easels, lovers seen momentarily, every last extra is entirely convincing. Each of these characters, glimpsed only for a second or two, has a story, a story that we shall never learn, but a story that may be as intricate as the story of Nino and Theresa. Even the added sounds of cats and of a student practicing the piano lend the story a realism that is rare in film. Nino makes an extra income by authenticating forgeries, and, without further explication, this demonstrates the widespread distress of the times. There is also a little throwaway, as a sign at the entrance to the Caffè Florian warns customers that it is a legal offense to speak any language other than Italian in the establishment. It's just a little flash, and perhaps not many in the audience would even notice, but it provides a sense of authenticity. It also serves as a good preface for the laughter elicited when pedestrians slip and fall on the slippery sidewalks in the rain. It's humor in the midst of an ominous threat.

The Key is the most emotionally complex film of Brass' career, and one of the most emotionally complex films he had made. *The Key* is a masterwork of erotica, and it is Brass' first love story. True, some of Brass' previous films contained romances, but those romances were elements in the general story lines. *The Key* is a love story from beginning to end, and it is a most effective one, as well as a most unconventional one. As Brass explained to Iain F. McAsh in Films on *Screen and Video 5* #2 (February 1988), "The story looks at adult relationships between a couple. Normally, in cinematic or TV terms, they fight and drama presents an ugly face but in *The Key* we look at the relationship of two people who enjoy themselves."

Almost every image in *The Key* is a work of art. The lighting and color design are splendid and evocative. The story is achingly moving. It is, beyond any question, the finest story in Tinto's career. *The Key* is the most technically accomplished of all of Tinto's films. It is the only one of his films that plays almost like a film from Visconti or Rossellini, and, as such, it was eminently suited for the "art houses." The film made a mint. The distributor, Bertolucci's San Francisco Film S.r.l., understood what most of Tinto's previous distributors failed to understand: Weak publicity would kill the film and result in a loss, but a strong publicity campaign would result in strong sales. That was a correct assessment, and it would have been equally correct for any of Tinto's earlier films.

Though the performers spoke mostly English on camera (except for Barbara Cupisti and Franco Branciaroli, who spoke Italian even in the English-language scenes), the Italian dub was prepared first, with Paolo Bonacelli's voice unexpectedly replacing Frank Finlay's, even though Finlay's Italian is fluent. After the Italian release, Brass collaborated with Gene Luotto on creating the English soundtrack. Stefania Sandrelli recorded her voice for both versions. The versatile Franco Branciaroli's voice is heard in neither. The actors who dubbed him in both versions were strangely unexpressive.

When the Italian dub was issued toward the end of 1983, it outgrossed all other films in Italy for that year.

Publicity photo: Stefania Sandrelli, 1983

The film was shipped to England, France, Germany, Australia, Japan, and to other countries as well. This film gave Tinto back his dignity, it gave him back his reputation, it gave him back his career. It gave him a new life and even a new identity.

The film was a sensation; the reason for its financial success seems to have been the nudity. This was the birth of the master of erotica, and producers desperately wanted his services to make other movies like *The Key*.

It was not only producers who wanted endless remakes of *The Key*. Tinto himself understood that he had finally created something that was both beautiful and financially successful. From now on, he would be determined to make films that were profitable. After all, *The Key* opened the door for a new entry in his career as the Maestro of Erotica, Tinto elaborates:

> **The Key is my first erotic film, I do not consider *Caligula* or *Salon Kitty* to be erotic films. At a certain moment I had this curiosity to try to talk, to express, to show eroticism. That is a matter that has been always avoided; a lot of people feel embarrassed when confronted with eroticism—mainly the critics.**[199]

Source Notes:

198 Nico B, "Tinto Brass: Maestro of Erotic Cinema," interview conducted 3 November 2001, Torcello (Los Angeles: Cult Epics, 2014)

199 Ibid.

XVII
Miranda

THIS IS SECOND entry in the Tinto Brass erotica canon. With the slimmest of story lines, Tinto concentrates on atmosphere and emotion rather than narrative. *Miranda* consists largely of set pieces and vignettes. Scenes of a country sunrise, singing at the inn, dancing at a picnic, dashing about town on a motorcycle—all evoke a wistfulness that is rare in movies. The most amusing scene occurs at the beach, where Miranda and her friend Leda fantasize about what the guys look like without their swimming trunks.

Having abandoned his plans to film an eighteenth-century British period piece (perhaps *Lord Byron?*), and not being able to find a producer for his proposed film of Mario Soldati's novel *Lettere da Capri*, Brass and his wife settled on freely adapting Carlo Goldoni's play *La locandiera*, creating a gentle follow-up to *The Key*. With most of his previous films, Brass had tried, in his small way, to change the world with his polemical messages of antiauthoritarianism and individualism. Seeing that changing the world was not possible so long as human nature remained the same, he began, with *Miranda*, a new quest: to change human nature. Fully aware now of his natural talent with erotica, he decided that the best way he could help transform humanity would be by making erotic films (his goal since his photonovel of *La contadina* in 1974).

Much of the resulting film is quite nice. The atmosphere is right. The countryside is lovely, and, as with *The Key*, the settings are completely convincing. The music by Riz Ortolani is gorgeous, the visuals are a delight.

The story is simple: Four men are rivals for the hand of Miranda, who is running her husband's inn in his absence. Though he was declared missing in action in the recent war, Miranda holds out hope that he will return. In the meantime, she is amused by the attentions she receives from others, and she plays each suitor off of the others. Apart from that basic premise, the movie has no plot. It is just a series of vignettes—villagers singing in the inn, people dancing at a picnic, select neighbors gathering in some sort of castle to have an orgy, relaxing at a beach, customers being swindled in a game of three-card monte.

There's a little joke at the end. Her husband confirmed killed in action, she marries not one of her three suitors, but her servant. She pays her final respects to her husband at a monument to those lost in the war. The names on the monument include variations on the names of three critics who had lambasted *The Key*: Cosulich, Rondi, and Kesich.

The lead was Serena Grandi, a bit actress who had appeared in several minor films. *Miranda* was her big break. Tinto explained:

> **My relationship with Serena Grandi during filming was very good. Really, maybe she is not a very great actress, but she has what I call "the charisma of the star": The moment she appears in a window of a little house in the valley where we shot, you felt that she was really Mother Earth... And it is a film that's very physical, very natural, with great sensuality, not only because of the nudity, but also the color. There are, how do you call, "papaveri," poppy in English, for the Day of the Dead. The color of the fields was dominated by this kind of flower. And they eat, there are all the senses involved, not only the sex. Serena Grandi was a kind of "archetipo" [archetype], perfect for that kind of sensuality. And the film is also structured in four—there are four lovers, and four seasons: There is the winter, the old fascist Interlenghi; there is the springtime, the young truck driver; there is summer, with the torrid story with the American forest; and there is the autumn, with the servant of the locando, the inn, whom she marries at the end, etc. I wanted really to make a film that has this sensual sentiment of nature, the full sentiment of nature.**[200]

Miranda has many virtues. One can easily view the film a second or third time just to look at the scenery, to pay attention to the extras, to revel in the music, to enjoy the warmth of the atmosphere and Serena Grandi.

When the film was released in Italy it caused quite a scandal on one of the Venetian islands. Tinto talks about Burano:

Publicity photo: Serena Grandi and Tinto Brass, 1985

Sometimes my films have been very violently disapproved of; they violently shocked the audience—just here, for instance, in Burano, an island next to Torcello: After I did *Miranda* I could not go to Burano anymore. They put up a poster of me and burned it in public, because they said that *Miranda* was a lady living there, and that I had taken my inspiration from her. I did say during a television interview, that, well, I put into the film something that I knew from living here in Burano. The wife of a fisherman wanted to know when her husband was supposed to come back, I said. Officially it seems it was because she had to prepare the soup; in reality she wanted to know so she could have the time free for her lover. That caused a revolution on the island. I could not go back there. I know that during the showing they shouted, people shouted at the screen.[201]

Brass' new mission cost him the admiration of many of his old intellectual supporters, who would write him off as a has-been. But his erotica won him legions of new fans. To an extent, Brass seems to have been successful in his goal of altering human nature. Films such as *The Key* and *Miranda,* which 40 years ago were considered scandalous by large sectors of society, are now considered mild and rather innocuous entertainment. That is surely why, with almost every succeeding film, Brass would push the envelope further and further.

Source Notes:

200 Nico B, "Tinto Brass: Maestro of Erotic Cinema," interview conducted 3 November 2001, Torcello (Los Angeles: Cult Epics, 2014)

201 Ibid.

XVIII
Capriccio

DINO DE LAURENTIIS had re-established himself in Italy by proxy. He put his older brother Luigi and his nephew Aurelio in charge of Famous Films Productions N.V., a limited-liability company registered in Curaçao, well-known as a tax haven. It was Dino De Laurentiis who proposed that Tinto Brass direct an adaption of Mario Soldati's famous novel *Le lettere da Capri* (The Capri Letters, Milan: Garzanti, April 1954), but the project was delayed for a few years. When Tinto wrote his script, he based it not on the novel per se, but only on a brief passage halfway through. It was that tale of a husband's and wife's parallel flings that captured his imagination. While Soldati viewed the story as a tragedy, Tinto could not agree. He turned it around so that the indiscretions would lead the husband and wife to rediscover one another. While the story, summarized on paper, can seem trite, its performance on camera is anything but that. It is insightful and we can feel everything the two main characters feel.

From its first frames, *Capriccio* exhibits a massive leap ahead of *Miranda* in a bigger production. The film is bursting with energy, the characters are intriguing, and the dialogue is spot-on perfect in its realism.

British Jennifer and American Fred, who had met during the war in Italy, have now married and return to Capri. Fred is with UNESCO to assess damage to art works during the war. Despite the sunny sky, the smiles, the upbeat music, we see right away that something is wrong. The greetings are just one degree too showy, ever so slightly exaggerated. Fred already regrets the marriage. Jennifer feels the same, and she has the servant hold and carry and care for their baby. Fred intends to leave his wife and baby alone at the hotel as he travels the land. Their elderly friend, Don Vincenzo, waits until he is alone with Jennifer for a moment to hand her a letter discreetly. "Oh. I'm sorry. I should have told you you'd be receiving mail for me." Don Vincenzo understands. "Always at your disposal. You can trust me." With those few lines, with those few visuals, with the dialogue delivered subtly off-key, we have the setup. No further explanations are necessary. Fred's plan is to combine work and pleasure by having his old flame Rosa by his side. Jennifer, too, has her own plan: Ciro. Hence the presence of the servant, who will care for baby Duccio while mommy and daddy are away at play.

The film maintains an intriguing mixture of joyful enthusiasm and ominousness. When Fred visits Rosa, her parents greet him at the door and remark about how he is a real gentleman. It by now seems that every Italian has learned fluent English during the recent war. (Hardly a word of Italian is spoken in the film.) Rosa is asleep in a gigantic bedroom, in the nude, fully made up, and we begin to wonder if her parents are pimping her. We gradually learn that they are not her parents.

As for Jennifer, she remembers first meeting Ciro, stunned by his beauty, as he freely wandered through a military hospital, unchecked, unescorted. What hold does he have over the military police that he can casually stroll through an emergency room without supervision? Why does she fall for him when he is clearly someone to be feared rather than loved? The most disturbing scene in the film, perhaps the most disturbing scene in any of Tinto's films, is when Jennifer, knowing full well that Ciro plans to assault her, leaves a party where she knows the crowd will keep her safe, and instead hides in a linen closet where she knows no one will witness anything. She is so desperately infatuated with the handsome Italian that she wants the rape to happen.

Curiously, the actress who portrayed Jennifer, Nicola Warren, understood exactly what this scene was about. It puzzled her then, and it continues to puzzle her today, why so many of the most intelligent women make themselves vulnerable to the most dangerous men. After this film, she entered a new career as a lawyer for female victims of domestic violence. She regards this rape scene as frighteningly true to life, which it is.

On his peregrinations with Rosa, we see another side to Fred, one too easy to anger. That is a trait that Rosa shares with him, and that is when we realize that nothing good can come of their courtship. They're not evil by any stretch of the imagination, but they're not thinking, and neither can understand the other. They pass through La Faggetta, a forest in Provincia di Viterbo, the location of the hunting scene in *Caligula*. For *Capriccio*, he re-imagined the scene and had Rosa in a see-through chiffon tunic prance through the woods as a nymph.

Jennifer is in the throes of agony. Ciro, who had promised to spend time with her, stands her up, day after day after day. There is no further word from him. She is lost in her memories, happy memories that are now poisoning her. She remembers her old rendezvous with her paramour, and we in the audience get to witness them. Their behavior is novel, and, to our surprise, we can understand why they had such hots for one another. The problem is that they simply could not understand one another. Ciro, for all his charm and enthusiasm, has something else on his mind, an ulterior motive, but it will be a while before we can figure him out. He is simply a pimp, and not even a successful one.

At the same moment, separated by many miles, both Jennifer and Fred have their epiphanies that their paramours were foolish mistakes. They are back together, and this time we know it will last, as they have both matured significantly.

Unlike Tinto's earlier films, *Capriccio* does not have infinite layers of meanings and references. It is a simple tale of a couple who rediscover one another. Yet it is beautifully done. Half the film is, again, so immediate and realistic that it almost seems as though it were showing real people caught by hidden cameras. Intermixed is the other half, extremely stylized and stylish, with a studio moon in a fake sky that radiates neon blue. One of the most striking sequences is of the outdoor dance at night, and the principal dancer, who calls himself Clark Gable, is played by none other than Pino Pennesi, who had begun working with Tinto on *Caligula*. His confident dancing, seen only for a minute or so, is a showstopper.

Another striking aspect of the film is the depiction of sexuality. Tinto had been forthright about sex since his first feature in 1963, but in *Capriccio* he went beyond anything he had done before. The sex scenes, few and brief, are almost unbelievably intimate. Probably few in the audience would be aroused, but the emotional impact is overwhelming. Tinto was exploring emotions much more than he was sensationalizing.

It was on *Capriccio* that renowned dubber Ted Rusoff first worked with Tinto, and he quickly decided that he preferred working with Tinto to working with anyone else. He once commented about "Tinto Brass, who loves to present a gruff, curmudgeonly exterior to the world, but whose pussy-cat interior is immediately apparent to most (but not all) people..."[202] He went on to tell an amusing story:

West German Lobby Card, 1987

Tinto is a great cinematographer. We were sitting in Cinecittà mixing the final version of *Capriccio* when these two guys let themselves into the recording studio. Tinto paid no attention to them. He was concentrating furiously. I could hear the two gentlemen whispering to each other, marveling at Tinto's color footage. One guy said, "Beautiful stuff! How did he get that effect? I've never been able to do that!" He was not saying this loudly for Tinto's benefit.At the end of the reel, the lights came on, and I saw that the gentleman in question was Federico Fellini!

Nicola Warren, many years later, had fond memories of the film and of the "hugely intelligent" Tinto, who affectionately bestowed upon her a nickname, Nicola Piccola. This was probably her only film. Prior to this, she had appeared only on the stage. It would be interesting to hear the opinions of others in the cast and crew. The aging Vittorio Caprioli as Don Vincenzo is marvelous in his few scenes. Andy J. Forest, who had appeared in *Miranda*, did a superlative job in *Capriccio*, and his two-week evolution from selfish to selfless is completely convincing. Francesca Dellera (who later became a star in Marco Ferreri's *La carne*, released by Cult Epics as *The Flesh*) as Rosa is also brilliant in her depiction of an immature but playful child who will never be able to grow up. Best of all, though, are the extras, who are absolutely true to life. One of the extras, glimpsed only for a few seconds, is Tinta, who exudes warmth.

Mario Soldati, upon viewing the film, refused to have his name appear in the credits, and he insisted that, to date, no film of his novel had ever been made. He was right to do that and he was right to say that, since *Capriccio* was freely adapted from only a few pages of his novel.

Capriccio is Brass' seventh and final film in English, and it was another great success in Europe. In the U.S., retitled *Love and Passion* and rated "R," it was shown only a few times on cable television. Despite the terrifying rape scene, it is a deeply affecting film that examines the lives of a couple who are a short step away from self-understanding. Its realistic yet lyrical Mediterranean atmosphere is almost tangible, and the eccentric little touches, such as wounded patients in a military hospital playing music and dancing, are unforgettable. Much of the acting and dialogue is so realistic that it seems almost documentary.

Capriccio, though far from one of Tinto's best films, is nonetheless something resembling a masterwork, and it is ripe for rediscovery.

Source Notes:

202 Harvey F. Chartrand, "Ted Rusoff: The High Priest of Dubbing," *The Film Journal: Dedicated to Serious Film Writing*, #10, 2005

West German Lobby Card, 1987

XIX
Snack Bar Budapest

TINTO'S CAREER had now taken a 90-degree turn. *The Key* had been loosely inspired by a novel. *Miranda* was adapted from a play. *Capriccio* was adapted from a small passage in another novel. He was now a recognized name and his films were profitable. His producer, Giovanni Bertolucci, now asked him to adapt another literary work for the screen, and Tinto happily agreed. It was a rather odd project to assign him, though. It was a crime thriller, from a novel jointly written by Marco Lodoli and Silvia Bre. The name Tinto Brass was by now firmly associated in the public's mind with erotica, not with gangster films. And that's unfortunate, for *Snack Bar Budapest* is a superior crime thriller, with its odd sense of morbid humor, its extremely moody, alienating look, and its effective music score by R&B composer Zucchero.

From the opening frame, the film is discomforting. The weather is dank, the sun is obscured, the people are cheerless, and the music is moody. Milena disembarks from a bus together with a disbarred lawyer for her abortion appointment. The lawyer is partners with Sapo, and both have been dating Milena. The lawyer checks into a hotel, the Snack Bar Budapest. Sapo instructs him by phone to see the local kingpin, a young pimp named Molecola (Molecule), who wants to offer a job. Wandering past a brutal beating and coked-up prostitutes in a pool hall, the lawyer makes his way to Molecola's office. The young gangster has a dream. He has been terrorizing local business owners to force them to sell their properties to him. With the real estate in hand, Molecola will build an Italian Las Vegas, but there is one property whose owners have yet to be approached: the owners of the Snack Bar Budapest. Can the lawyer persuade them? He is sure he can. With Sapo and a thug named Pappera, they attack the owners, and the lawyer is disheartened to see that the owners are his former clients. The lawyer murders Pappera, and from there the situation degrades into gunfights, mostly fought by Molecola's nightgowned hookers.

The story is surprisingly strong, the atmosphere of the film is intense. Tinto's old friend Osiride Pevarello lends some levity as a monk who parties with the hookers. Tinto and Tinta lend even more levity as judges. Producer Giovanni Bertolucci expressed a great deal of confidence in handing this project to Tinto. With three hits behind him, Tinto was again a viable director, and he did a powerhouse job. His frequent self-criticism that he is a rather poor director is not borne out by the performances on display here. The actors are all first-rate and frighteningly convincing.

With this film, Tinto went full speed ahead with style. Blue neon is omnipresent. The dark jazz score by Zucchero "Sugar" Fornaciari and David Sancious is overpowering. The story's assessment of human nature is quite grim.

Nobody would ever again ask Tinto to make such a film. By now he was typecast, pigeonholed. He was known as the director of warm erotica, not cold murder stories, and audiences were not interested in seeing him do something else. He later mused:

> ***Snack Bar Budapest*** **was misunderstood, thus it sank at the box office. Everybody thought I was going to launch a new starlet, while in fact it is the story of Giannini and this boy, Molecola. There was also Rafaella Baracchi, who played Giannini's lover, but she was not the central character. Anyway, there were lots of girls in the scene of the party by the sea; it's just that there wasn't a female lead. I remember that Giannini went mad while we were shooting. He told me, "Damn it, when you see an ass you forget all the rest!" I did not pay enough attention to the male actors! The real problem, anyway, is not that the film wasn't understood, it's just that nobody went to see it. The audience knew it was not the usual Brass film like *Miranda* or *Capriccio*, for instance, so they didn't even bother about it.**[203]

Source Notes:

203 Manlio Gomarasca and Davide Pulici, *99 donne: stelle e stelline del cinema italiano* (Milan: Media Word, 1999), p. 226

XX
Paprika

INSPIRED BY an anonymous story by Bernardino Zapponi, *Paprika* is Brass' most unabashedly sexual film, filled almost from beginning to end with countless naked women (and men) and loving close-ups of their various physical attributes. The film is an homage to the brothels of Brass' youth, where he would socialize after a day spent in the archives studying old films. In our interview he elaborated:

It happens that sometimes I've taken inspiration from books. Sometimes, as for *All Ladies Do It*, it was this article in the newspaper that gave me the idea to develop this scenario. And for *Paprika* it was an article of Bernardino Zapponi. He wrote it, but he didn't sign it. He wrote this story of a maitresse, of an owner of a brothel. I understood that it was not written by a maitresse, but by him, because I knew him. So I went to him. "It is you who wrote this?" "Yes," he said. "OK, let's make a film." And from that we developed a script and everything. I wanted to tell it my way, my memories, because I was a very keen brothel customer. When I grew up in Venice I would go to three brothels every day, because there were 30 brothels in Venice, in the '40s and '50s, and 30 cinemas.[204]

Giovanni Bertolucci had produced Tinto's previous four features, but he did not produce this one. Was that perhaps because their previous film together had not been profitable? Production honors for *Paprika* went to Augusto Caminito. There was definitely a change here, though, a change that was more than a mere swapping of producers. To explain what happened, the only evidence we have is the evidence on the screen, and the evidence on screen reveals that Tinto had learned his lesson. After a decade and a half, he was now identified as the maker of sophisticated erotica. When he deviated from that genre (*Action* and *Snack Bar Budapest*) it suffered financial failure. So, this time he now made a film that did not concern a love story and sensuous scenes, he made one that was strictly erotic, a film whose only value to arouse.

Tinto was obviously excited to try something new. First, though, he had to find the ideal actress to bring the story to life. Brass was unable to find the right face for the lead character—until he saw a photo of a tennis match in the newspaper. He called the photographer, who told him that the young lady watching the game was Klaus Kinski's ex-girlfriend, Debora Caprioglio. Brass then called Caprioglio's home and spoke with her mother.

I found her number and phoned her. It was her mother who answered. I told her my name and she replied, "But, are you really Tinto Brass? Oh, I'm going to run down my daughter for you at once! At once!" After a couple of hours Debora called me back and I asked her to do a film with me. She has a natural talent. I don't know if she trained afterwards, but she knew how to enter into her character's mind, learn her lines and so on.[205]

Obviously owing much to John Cleland's *Fanny Hill*, the book that Brass had once nearly made into a film, the resulting film is a work of simplicity. Eighteen-year-old Mimma Wassermann's fiancé Nino is a bit short on cash, and so she agrees to his plan to become a prostitute for a fortnight to boost the funds. She is accepted, learns the rules, promises not to orgasm with any client, is taught where to signal for help in an emergency, and the madam gives her a new name, Paprika. Just as Paprika launches her new career, she catches Nino two-timing her. That settles the matter. She takes ownership of her new career and decides it will last considerably longer than a fortnight. She tours the bordello circuit in Italy and France. Finally she marries a comical old count who soon dies. The new countess returns to see her friends at her first bordello as it's being closed by the government. Now a widow, she is free to pursue her romance with Franco, her first client.

In this film again, as with *Capriccio*, there are some genuinely extreme scenes. There is a scene on a train that is thoroughly ambiguous, as we are left wondering if what we just saw was a seduction or a rape.There are

Publicity photo: Debora Caprioglio and Tinto Brass, 1991

throwbacks to *Salon Kitty*, with the madam performin a cabaret number, and with a prostitute who inexplicably gets rabies. There are some quite amusing scenes as well. As Paprika begins her career, getting exhausted by the nonstop queue of clients, the musical accompaniment is "Ciribiribin" played at double speed, sounding like the Chipmunks. There is also a jewel of a scene with a count who orders two hookers. He is played by John Steiner, who gives one of the hammiest performances in movie history. On tour in France, Paprika's client of the moment is a comically dour French existentialist who takes her to a bar run by Tinta. As a crowning touch, a sex scene is scored with a song by Edith Piaf.

Tinto had enjoyed setting movies in the 1930s through the 1950s, as those were his youthful days. He knew how to incorporate his own memories into the stories to give the scenes immediacy. In *Paprika*, he does the same. This is 1950s Italy, but with a difference. It is not exactly Italy as it was, but Italy as Tinto wished it had been. What he put on screen were his fantasies of his preferred society, of his preferred leisure activities. To his fantasies he added endless images of mirrors and neon tubing. The movie is, for the most part, extremely light. Tinto was proud that he had a box-office sensation on his hands. He now knew the formula for his future films, and he would rarely deviate from it. Almost every subsequent film became lighter. He was now a genre filmmaker, making entertainment for the sake of entertainment, and the next one would become a classic.

Source Notes:

204 Nico B, "Tinto Brass: Maestro of Erotic Cinema," interview conducted 3 November 2001, Torcello (Los Angeles: Cult Epics, 2014)

205 Manlio Gomarasca and Davide Pulici, *99 donne: stelle e stelline del cinema italiano* (Milan: Media Word, 1999), p. 224

XXI

All Ladies Do It

(*Così fan tutte*)

GIOVANNI BERTOLUCCI must have been impressed by the ticket sales for *Paprika*, and so he hired Tinto once again, but this time he hedged his bets: he brought along a co-producer, Achille Manzotti, to share the risk.

The year was 1991, two hundred years after the death of Wolfgang Amadeus Mozart, and Tinto gave the composer something resembling an homage. He gave his new film the title of a Mozart opera, which was appropriate, considering a little item he had just read in a woman's newspaper. The basis of *Così fan tutte* was a series of letters to an advice columnist, all from happily married women who argued that they enjoyed having their little affairs on the side. Brass had always been in agreement with that idea, and now, with such an outpouring of similar sentiments from women throughout Italy, he decided it was time to make a film with that sole argument. The result was one of the least substantive but most popular films of his career.

There was a lady writing to the journalist, telling her that she had a very good relationship with her husband, she lived very well with him, but from time to time she had some adventures and she didn't feel absolutely guilty for that. The journalist, the one who owned the newspaper, instead of giving her own answer, asked all the women readers to give their opinion on that. She was submerged by tons of letters, all from women saying the same thing: We've the same situation, we like our husband, we live well, but from time to time we have some adventure and we don't feel guilty for that.

I understood that perfectly, because it is my opinion that fidelity is not a natural sentiment, it is something imposed by culture and not naturally; fidelity is for dogs but not for human beings. Fidelity is not a value, as transgression is something you do to make yourself feel free. The title came from the Mozart opera *Così fan tutte*, in which he said it; in his very merry cynicism, that was the point. You know that the libretto, the book of *Così fan tutte* for Mozart, was written by a Venetian, Lorenzo Da Ponte; he was my predecessor. I think that there are some things given to us as values that are not values: virginity, chastity, fidelity. But they are not values at all; they're something imposed by culture, history. I understand that in the époque, to be sure of the lineage of the sons, fidelity was important. But now, with contraception and everything like that, there is no more reason to consider it as a value; I mean it is not a value. And that was the main point of *Così fan tutte*.[206]

Tinto again worked with Bernardino Zapponi to write a light-hearted script. The story is about glamorous people who have no financial worries and who effortlessly live in luxury. They seem to have no interests outside their libidos. When Paolo discerns that Diana had a fling, he grows wild with rage and storms out. Diana, confused, goes on her own rampage as well. The two shortly reconcile when they discover that jealousy excites them and is a valuable ingredient in their marriage. There is no other complexity to the story. Yet there is something compelling about the picture. First of all, we have Diana, portrayed by Claudia Koll, a serious-minded actress who put her everything into playing the part of a trivial character of no other significance than being erotic.

The leading girl of *Così fan tutte*, Claudia Koll, came to test after I had already closed the cast of *Paprika*, the preceding film. But I liked her very much, I said "Well, I can give you a secondary role." "Oh no no; with you I only want to do the leading role." And I remembered her when I had to do *Così fan tutte*. I called her again and gave it to her...[207]

We have Franco Branciaroli, doing funny things with his voice, in the part of a Sadean character who is curiously named Alphonse Donatien. Jean René le Moine, who had appeared in *Miranda* as the three-card monte con artist, appears again as a not-so-innocent novice who decides to learn what sin is by joining an orgiastic party. He is a marvelously appealing actor.

Publicity photo: Claudia Koll and Tinto Brass, 1991

I very much like Franco Branciaroli, who's the best Italian actor in theatre, absolutely the best, number one, and he doesn't make films with anybody except with me. He likes me very much. He did one film with Jansko, many years ago and with Antonioni, but since then, he said "No, I don't want to work with other directors." He works only with me. He accepts the parts without reading the scripts; he trusts me. And yes, he is in a certain way my alter ego. He also imitates me; he tried to copy my way of speaking, my accent.[208]

Tinto himself gives another of his comical cameos, this time as the sleazy good-for-nothing Commendator Scarfatti. Tinto used every trick in the book to make the film look expensive and lush. He also used every trick in the book to turn an ecstasy rave into a work of art.

I always do it, like in *La chiave* I do the priest, in *Così fan tutte*, I am in it, I don't remember what I did[209]**—like Hitchcock used to do. I like to enjoy, just to say that I sign the films with my face. I want it to be clear that they are my films and I defend them, I don't consider them minor films because they are films on sex; no, not at all.**[210]

The camerawork and the editing are exhilarating, mesmerizing, and one wishes the scene would never end. Yet the scene does come to an end, revealing the desperate loneliness of those who had just spent the night partaking in the fun. *All Ladies Do It* was also the last film completed with cameraman Silvano Ippoliti, who started his career with *Deadly Sweet* and had worked with Tinto ever since.

My films, a big part of my filmography, has Silvano Ippoliti as lighting director, because I found myself to be very at ease with him. It started with *Col cuore in gola*, a film that I did in London. Before that I did three films with a Venetian cinematographer, Bruno Barcarol, then he died, so I had to choose another director of photography. And I met different directors of photography and I gave them a test: "Listen, I want to see the ash of a cigarette while somebody is smoking, to see the red." And there was one who said, "We put a resistor inside"—an electric thing, very complicated. Silvano Ippoliti said "We just do it, he smokes and I film"... And I decided that he was good for me, and in fact he was a very, very sensible man. He didn't use an exposure meter; he felt the light on his skin. He had a very sensual feeling for the light. And that was what I liked and what I needed. That was it. I always worked with him and it was a very good relationship until he died and then I changed again.

Brass fashioned another piece of erotic mastery, with more nudity and sex than anyone would expect to see outside of a porn cinema. Since Brass' previous films were all class-conscious, *Così fan tutte* comes as a genuine shock to the system with its approving focus entirely upon the bourgeoisie. The film's great success must have been food for serious thought for Brass. Sadly, not everyone would see the original version that he created, as it was released cut in many countries. Tinto elaborated in our interview:

Sometimes my films in the English version, I know later on that they've been cut. I don't give any authorization to cut them, but they do it, because I have been told, people told me, "But we saw the Italian version; they say our version has been cut, yours is much better." Of course it is much better. They cut it because, I don't know the reason, really don't understand, I don't know why, they are prudes, I cannot understand.[211]

After *Così fan tutte*, Brass was finally green-lighted a film he had had on the back burner for several years.

Source Notes:

206 Nico B, "Tinto Brass: Maestro of Erotic Cinema," interview conducted 3 November 2001, Torcello (Los Angeles: Cult Epics, 2014)

207 Ibid.

208 Ibid.

209 Client of the erotic shop

210 Nico B, "Tinto Brass: Maestro of Erotic Cinema"

211 Ibid.

XXII
The Voyeur
(*L'uomo che guarda*)

FAMOUS AUTHOR Alberto Moravia had long been friendly with Tinto Brass, whose films he greatly admired. Brass had wanted to convert Moravia's *L'uomo che guarda* (The Man Who Watches) into a film, and the author was enthusiastic about the project. But production was delayed seven years, and by the time the cameras started rolling, the novelist had died.

Moravia's book detailed the romance of Valerio and his fiancée Lavinia, concentrating on Valerio's obsession with finding a reason to be jealous. Brass' screenplay owes only its theme to the novel, as both the characters and the story are entirely different. The examination of the terminally lovesick Dodò is beautifully detailed, and his mysterious, aloof, almost cold wife is unfathomable, not at all in keeping with Brass' previous oeuvre. Silvia is reminiscent of Hitchcock's icy-blonde protagonists, and indeed the film does contain homages to Hitchcock, even in the poster which reveals the silhouette of a most Hitchcockian Brass with a cigar in his mouth.

We see new names in the production credits. Principally we see Angelo Rizzoli, who distributed through his company DARC, and who co-produced along with Marco Poccioni and Marco Valsania. We may conjecture that prior producers had not shown an interest in this project. If that is correct, those producers missed a golden opportunity.

The Man Who Watches, published in the U.S. as *The Voyeur*, was an inner dialogue of a husband in a personal crisis, worried to distraction about nuclear annihilation and worried even more that his wife has vanished from his life, except for the occasional surprise reappearance of a few minutes, upon which she vanishes yet again. It was a perfect vehicle for Tinto, but Tinto simplified the characters quite drastically, and he eliminated any existential worries about the bomb. While keeping fairly true to the general story and to Moravia's dialogue, he twisted every situation to find a constant stream of excuses to have the characters lose all their clothes. He also made a change.

Yes, there is an image from my childhood that is indelibly imprinted on my imagination. As a child I happened to see my mother through her half-closed bedroom door. Her robe was unstitched at the back, which allowed the superb "slit" to be seen, the cross of symmetrical orifice lips formed by the intersection of the midline with the horizontal line of her thighs.[212]

That childhood memory was replicated in *The Voyeur*, but dramatically, as little Dodò sees not only his mother, but his father as well, and they see him. Mother is horrified. Father is furious. That is how Tinto introduced an element into the story that Moravia had not even pondered. In Tinto's iteration, Dodò's wife looks strikingly like his deceased mother. Dodò's father is as attracted to Dodò's wife as Dodò is, and Mrs. Dodò's feelings are reciprocal.

This is one of the few movies that Tinto wrote the script entirely on his own, and, in keeping with the lesson he had learned, he introduced his audience to some new starlets. There was Cristina Garavaglia as Fausta, the father's personal nurse who provides more than medical care. She also knows how to manipulate Dodò into a fuming rage by offering him well-placed hints about little things she sees. Then there was Silvia, Dodò's ever-disappearing wife, portrayed by Polish actress Katarzyna Kozaczyk, who adopted the screen name Katarina Vasillissa, a striking Hitchcockian blonde. Her character is cold, remote, manipulative, ambiguous. One can never know what's really on Silvia's mind. Dodò's mother, who lives on only in his memories, is portrayed by Gabri Crea, and she is regrettably relegated to only a few seconds of the running time.

The story is of secondary importance to the feel of the film. Tinto made the movie as an exercise in style. Every moment is an experiment with lighting, texture, camera movement, décor. Images are inspired by great Italian paintings of centuries past. The music by Riz Ortolani is hypnotizing. Tinto from the very first had been a master of sound, but in *The Voyeur* he expanded upon his techniques, creating an unreal audio world of reverberations, silences, vague and almost imperceptible noises in the distance. Then, unexpectedly, a strum of a distant mandolin entirely overpowers everything else. Not a moment of the film conveys realism. Everything is stylized and modified. The acting is intentionally over-rehearsed, so perfected that it loses all spontaneity, and that was another aspect of the artificiality that Tinto was after. Though he had long ago abandoned his rapid cut-up manner of editing, he introduced some new editing ideas that would take anyone by surprise.

The technical credits are all first-rate, as Brass, with the collaboration of designer Maria Luigia Battani, costume designer Millina Deodato and cinematographer Massimo Di Venanzo, the camera operator on *Paprika*, as well prior on Antonioni's *Identification of a Woman*, who became the replacement when Tinto's first cameraman Silvano Ippoliti passed away during the shoot of *All Ladies Do It*. The compositions, lighting, filtering, and languorous camera movements are nothing less than mesmerizing. These, combined with Riz Ortolani's hypnotic jazz score, produce an overpowering visual and aural experience, one that is not easily forgotten. Haunting and luscious, *L'uomo che guarda* is one of Brass's finest erotic films. We can easily say that visually, *The Voyeur* is Tinto's most stunning work, and in that respect it is glorious.

Also, it is clear that by the time this movie was being made in 1993, Italy's censorship laws had been weakened quite significantly. A few of the sexual images on display here, notably an erection, would have gotten the cast and crew in trouble in years past.

Alberto Moravia had been looking forward to the film, but now that he had passed away, with the executors of his estate (his wives) were not happy with Tinto's result and would not permit Moravia's name to appear in the credits. Fortunately, though, Moravia's novel is seen twice on screen, and the executors either did not notice or did not object after all.

Source Notes:

212 Mario Gagliardotto, *Obiettivo Brass: Il cinema secondo Tinto Brass* (Modena: Edizioni Il Fiorino, January 2005), pp. 8–9

Publicity photo: Katarina Vasillissa, 1994

XXIII
P.O. Box Tinto Brass
(*Fermo posta Tinto Brass*)

A MOST AMUSING WORK, with parts that are laugh-out-loud funny. The film had a rather unexpected origin. Tinto had begun to receive fan mail from female admirers who regaled him with stories of their own sexual adventures. Tinto used some of those ideas to fashion a series of brief sketches. Inexplicably, he did not hire women to help him write the script. He hired two men, Aurelio Grimaldi and Claudio Lizza.

The story was filmed in Tinto's office, with cans of his previous films on the shelves and with posters of his previous movies and photographs of his family adorning the walls. He has hired a secretary who performs no useful function except to look cute, which she does, wearing frames without lenses. The story goes as follows: Tinto Brass and his secretary (Cinzia Roccaforte) spend their work hours reading mail from female fans who confess their sexual adventures.

"Glances": We open with a simple sketch about a young woman making out with her boyfriend on the beach. He is certain they are alone and unseen. She is quite aware that someone is looking at them. The idea is so thin that it does not seem worth committing to paper. Yet it is done in an ironic way, with such exaggeration and with over-the-top jazz scoring. The music is so unaccountably bouncy that the result is hilarious. This

Publicity photo: Tinto Brass and Gabriella Barbuti, 1995

is Tinto's sense of humor, treating a trivial, irrelevant moment in an overpowering way, almost as though it is of epic proportions.

"The Condom": Husband Guido doesn't understand why wife Elena has a condom in her purse. She explains it away, but the truth is that she has a secret day job in a brothel, to increase the household's income, where she works under the pseudonym Michelle. At her job, all the ladies are called to the lobby to be looked over by the new client, who is, of course, Guido, who gives his name as Carlo. Which lady does he prefer? Michelle, of course!

Elena/Michelle is played by a marvelous actress named Erika Saffo Savastani, who has a natural-born comic sensibility and who can make an audience laugh by her mere presence. Riz Ortolani's hyperbolic music is another highlight, as he does more than complement or underscore the action and emotion; he boosts it all to comical heights.

"Panties": The next letter is from Betta, who noticed a Japanese tourist gazing at her from across a ruin. While her boyfriend was away to get a snack for lunch, Betta removed her panties and put on a one-woman show for the tourist.

"Home Videos": Tinto and Lucia open a package with a VHS tape and photos, in which restaurant owner Renata and her husband make out. Tinto remarks "everyone is a director these days," looking at his own work. Then in another more amateuristic video, they meet another couple, aroused by a pee scene; they end up swapping partners in the country.

"The Phone Call": Rossella argues on the phone with her husband, who has called to say he will be late, despite promising earlier to be on time to spend a nice evening with her. After hanging up with her husband, the phone rings again. It's a wrong number, as the caller was hoping for a session of phone sex. Rossella decides to oblige him, delightfully surprising her husband with her antics when he shows up on time after all.

"Meetings": Francesca objects to her husband Paolo's liberal ideas, but she allows him to talk her into going to a swingers' party. Though repulsed at first, she finds that she enjoys herself at least as much as Paolo does. This nearly XXX episode was censored in many countries.

"I Lost You": This one is a minor gem. Ivana is furious when her husband Filippo returns home drunk again late one night. He is a compulsive gambler who never fails to lose his bets. Tonight, not only has he lost all his money, he also lost a bet in which he gambled his wife away. After thinking things over the next day, Ivana wonders what it is about her that Filippo's two gambling partners find so attractive. So she agrees to pay off her husband's debt.

"The Secretary": Tinto and Lucia are briefly interrupted by an intrusion from a fellow who is trying to sell Tinto on the idea of hiring his secretary/girlfriend Gabry. Tinto gives her an audition in which he tosses a coin on the ground to see how much Gabry reveals to him when she bends over to pick it up. This was something Tinto would repeatedly use for auditioning his actresses in his later films.

"Red Tango Boots": The best is saved for last, and in this sketch, Tinto insists that it's Lucia's turn to tell her own story. Lucia would never dream of fooling around with anyone except her fiancé, but she did have a sexual dream, which Tinto asks to hear. In the dream, Lucia and her fiancé entered a shoe shop filled with mannequins, each one a character from a previous letter. The proprietor turns out to be Tinto himself, who fits her and transforms into an elephant in heat when he sees that she's not wearing any panties.

No analysis is needed. Nothing needs to be explained. This is pure candy, constant amusement, frequent laughs, with wall-to-wall female nudity pushing the envelope to XXX, as the release was censored in many countries. Nothing else can be said. Yet Tinto said something else:

> ***Fermo posta*** **is an omnibus movie representing a map of women's erotic universe; I wanted to explore sex through various Italian dialects (Torinese, Venetian, Neapolitan, and so on), each corresponding to a peculiar way for Italian women to deal with their own sexuality; therefore I needed different actresses, each representing a single regional type. I think I made good choices, as I was satisfied with all of them...**[213]

Source Notes:

213 Manlio Gomarasca and Davide Pulici, *99 donne: stelle e stelline del cinema italiano* (Milan: Media Word, 1999), p. 226

XXIV
Frivolous Lola
(*Monella*)

THIS FILM IS A PURE delight and quite ingenious. It has something to say, but it says more than Tinto realized it said.

Monella, has a double meaning, either *Rascal* or *Kid*, and indeed the title is an homage to Charlie Chaplin's *The Kid*, known in Italy as *Il monello*. The title *Frivolous Lola* was put on later by the distributor.

Giovanni Bertolucci was back as producer. He must have made a good offer for Tinto's services, which were now in high demand.

Monella is wish fulfillment. This is 1950s Italy the way Tinto wishes it had been. This is the youth he wishes he had had. It portrays people he wishes he had known. He decided to film this story in the same general region he had used for *Miranda*, and his point here was to show the love of life that the locals freely exhibited.

The story was inspired by niece Lulù, whom he had put in all his films beginning with *The Key*, when she was just a toddler. She was now in her mid-teens and was discovering the wonders of young adulthood. Tinto was enchanted and wrote a script together with his wife, who contributed her own youthful memories, and with a writer friend named Barbara Alberti.

The story needed to start with a young woman riding a bicycle, and Tinto found the perfect actress when he nearly ran over her.

> **For *Monella*, for instance, the lead was chosen in a very strange way. I needed a girl who knew how to ride a bicycle. I can't drive; my wife drives for me. One day at a "semaforo" [traffic light] in the streets, she just lightly touched a girl on a bicycle. It was Anna Ammirati. She fell to the ground and then she recognized me. She made a joke, "Now I denounce you.[214] You hurt me." "Well, instead of denouncing, come and do a test." It happened like that. I didn't know her before at all.[215]**

Anna Ammirati had done some acting on television. She was marvelous, a true find, a natural performer, quite versatile, boisterous, and bursting with energy.

The rural story is beautifully photographed and it is, once again, remarkably basic. The story line was as follows:

Lola, an irrepressibly enthusiastic youngster, is irritated that her fiancé Tomasetto refuses to have sex with her until they're married. Lola has grown up in a most liberal family, with mother Zaira (*Miranda*'s Serena Grandi, once again) happy to give birth to her out of wedlock, despite living in a conservative country village, and with stepfather (possibly father?) André who makes a living taking erotic photos, openly dallying with his models. Despite its conservatism, the country village exudes sexuality, with voyeurs and sunbathers relaxing in their secret hideouts by the river, and with many locals secretly and not-so-secretly admiring and envying Lola's habit of going about town dressed somewhat more scantily than a proper girl of the 1950s should.

Trying everything she possibly can to break Masetto out of his mold, with her increasingly aggressive attempts at seduction, she finally tries to arouse his jealousy by flirting with some soldiers in his presence. When Masetto attacks all three soldiers at once, Lola calls off the wedding and makes a dash for it. With an injured Masetto in hot pursuit, she hops into a passing car whose driver attempts to assault her. But feisty Lola turns the tables and beats him to a bloody pulp. Wandering back home in the rain, she chats with André, and finally confesses her secret desire: She is and always has been in love with him. Though a most excited André sensibly rebuffs her advances, it appears otherwise to Zaira who bursts in upon them.

Having created a domestic ruckus, Lola tries one last strategy with a now turbulent Masetto. Claiming that the driver in the car had indeed succeeded in assaulting her, she puts all the blame for the circumstances on Masetto, who had embarrassed her with his violent jealousy. An enraged Masetto takes out his revenge on her obvious lies by finally doing what she had always wanted.

At the wedding party, Lola and André excuse themselves for a private conversation in the house, where

André proclaims her an honorary member of his exclusive *Joie de Vivre* club, and where Lola openly offers herself to him. Back at the party, Lola hints to Masetto that she has every intention of dallying with others, but warns him that he must never pry. Zaira wonders which of the two will cheat on the other first, and André insists that it doesn't matter, as fidelity has nothing to do with love.

As in some of Tinto's other films, the characters rarely restrain themselves. They are loud, demanding, quick to anger, eager to party. Eventually, the increasing rage between Lola and Masetto resolves itself in fits of jealousy that bring them together just in time for their scheduled wedding.

Lola and Masetto are hopelessly immature, and we in the audience would probably not place high bets on their long-lasting wedded bliss. Yet Tinto is of another mind. He is convinced that they are perfect for each other, provided they can learn to be accepting of the occasional extramarital fling.

By this time, Tinto had abandoned multicam filming. Actors felt too intimidated with three to five camera crews following them around. For *Monella*, Tinto used only one camera, but mimicked the multicam look by grabbing close-ups and inserts right and left. In common with some of Tinto's other films, *Monella* breaks all the rules about lighting and sound mixing. Brights and darks share the same frame, and natural lighting is often used regardless of how much it mismatches from one shot to the next. Darker scenes are not cheated with extra light sources.The dialogue is not tempered, but is almost all exaggerated and relentless. The camerawork is highly creative, filled with unexpected angles, even shooting down from the ceiling and up from the floor, and slow-motion shots mixed in with regular motion. The actors once again, without exception, give brilliant performances. Even extras glanced only for the briefest second are entirely convincing.

It is the warmth that makes this film special. True, the characters are frequently undressed, but audiences may be concentrating so much on the characters' personal appeal that the nudity might go unnoticed. Tinto's affection for his cast shines through, and the cast members' affections for one another are also quite real. That is what makes *Monella* the most easily accessible of Tinto's erotic oeuvre.

Publicity photo: Anna Ammirati, 1998

Source Notes:

214 Meaning, "Now I'll press charges against you."

215 Nico B, "Tinto Brass: Maestro of Erotic Cinema," interview conducted 3 November 2001, Torcello (Los Angeles: Cult Epics, 2014)

XXV
Cheeky!
(*TRAsgreDIRE*)

AFTER PLAYING a caricature of himself in Massimo Ceccherini's wild comedy *Lucignolo*, and after introducing a series of 12 erotic short videos, in most of which he played more caricatures of himself, and after doing a joke interview on Britain's *EuroTrash* in which he played the most outrageous caricature of himself yet, Brass decided to do a caricature of his career.

This time it was Massimo Ferrero who managed to become producer of a Tinto Brass film. This film transcends the limits of sexual adventures, and there is something endearing about it.

Cheeky! is a title added by a foreign distributor, and it has stuck. A previous attempt at an English title, used in England, was *Transgressing*. Neither matches the clever word play of the Italian original, which consists of two words rolled into one: *tradire* (to betray) and *trasgredire* (to transgress). Those two words pretty much sum up the entire plot.

He wrote a script together with Tinta. Also invited to toss in their ideas were three young directors he had met through another production: Nicolaj Pennestri, Silvia Rossi, and Massimiliano Zanin. What the fivesome concocted was more light, even lighter than usual, with

Publicity photo: Yuliya Mayarchuk, 2000

the by-now standard and simple message that men had just better get used to the idea that their girlfriends will occasionally have a romp with somebody else.

The opening scene is a reminder of the park scene in *Nerosubianco*, and it may well have been shot on the same location, though this time Tinto and his crew definitely had permits. The parkgoers who are walking the dog, jogging, soaking in the sun, and playing are all doing so in overtly sexual ways. Through the park walks an unaccountably bubbly Carla, who was Tinto's latest find, a Ukrainian who was working in a pizza parlor in Naples. Tinto was enchanted by her sweet disposition and by her looks, he recalls:

Yuliya Mayarchuk was working as a hostess in a pizzeria in Naples. She was serving pizza at the table and she bent over, next to me. Bending over she showed me a wonderful bottom; so I asked her if she would like to make films. She was already doing some modeling, and then she came, she did a test, she was very good. Surely that happens when they are absolute beginners. When they are known actresses, well then there is a test, a real test, with some scenes, and I see the way they, not as much interpret, but just what is the reaction between me and the actress. I have to know. Otherwise, with the beginner, I do the coin test. I ask them to come wearing a short miniskirt and no pants. I throw a coin on the floor and I ask them to bend over and collect it. The way in which they bend to collect it and how much they show me of their bottom, gives me an idea of how good, or not good, they are for the rôle. [*Laughs*][216]

Carla continues her bobble-headed walk and is eventually confronted with a flasher. She frightens him off by flashing him back. She is in London to soak in the language, but the real estate agent who tries to find her lodging recognizes that it is not so much linguistic immersion that Carla is after, but sexual immersion. The agent is Moira, played by Francesca Nunzi, who had briefly appeared in *Monella*. In *TRAsgreDIRE* she displays her considerable talents. Every line she delivers, every motion she makes, every facial expression, is done with a comical physicality that would have made her a headliner in vaudeville. It is truly a pity that her career never took off.

Nearly every scene is a contrivance to allow us to see pretty young nude women at a gym, to see more pretty young nude women at a party, to watch the real estate agent get her way with Carla, to watch Carla and her previous boyfriend cavort nude at a secluded beach, and to watch, over and over and over, Carla get undressed. The effect, at least on some people, will not be the expected one of arousal, but the unexpected one of uncontrollable laughter.

When her boyfriend back in Venice discovers old love letters in her closet, he follows her to London to confront her. There then follow the usual rages and fights and upsets, which dissipate in an instant when she is invited to an orgiastic party. That, in essence, is the narrative. The rest is just a series of excuses to have an hour and a half of cheerful music by Pino Donaggio and cheerful people dressing glamorously and just as cheerfully dropping all their clothes, along with cheerful flashbacks to a cheerful beach romp, and, at the end, a cheerful reconciliation.

Interestingly, *TRAsgreDIRE* cribs images not only from *Nerosubianco*, but also from *Who Works is Lost*. There was probably no reason for that apart from the sheer joy of reliving a few happy memories. Just as interestingly, Tinto himself plays the lecherous owner of a photography shop which has walls apparently decorated with photographs of Ernest Hemingway, Roberto Rossellini, Ingrid Bergman. Those were photos on display at the Locanda Cipriani.

Brass dared, and he was fiercely proud of his new work. He had intended to follow it up with a film to be shot in Ukraine (his ancestral homeland, as well as Yuliya Mayarchuk's birthplace), and he also worked on some projects called *Invisible Lovers* (proposed Italian title: *Una coppia senza volto*) and *Una donna al giorno* (A Woman by Day), but these never came to pass. And then, unexpectedly, his next film would be a serious production.

Source Notes:

216 Nico B, "Tinto Brass: Maestro of Erotic Cinema," interview conducted 3 November 2001, Torcello (Los Angeles: Cult Epics, 2014)

XXVI
Black Angel
(*Senso '45*)

TINTO ONCE AGAIN had a new producer. This time it was Giuseppe Colombo on behalf of a firm called Cine 2000. This was not intended to be a typical Tinto Brass entry, and it was not. It was adapted from a novella by Camillo Boito, *Senso*, which had been adapted for the cinema once before, by Luchino Visconti. While admiring the earlier film, Tinto was somewhat dissatisfied with it and wondered if Visconti had even read Boito's original. He wanted to make a version more faithful to Boito's story and ideas, though he would update the story from 1866 to 1945. He explained his intention:

> **_Black Angel_ is the latest film that I've done. It is a little different from the most recent production, because it is a film based on a novel by Camillo Boito, the same novel from which Visconti did a film called _Senso_. That's why in Italian I call it _Senso '45_, just to make it clear that the novel takes place in 1865. Visconti's film was in 1865, but I transported the situation to 1945—that's the end of the war.**[217]

One of the most visually lush and beautiful of Brass' films, *Senso '45* is a return to such works as *Salon Kitty* and *The Key* and even *Caligula* on a production scale. Again, Brass concentrates on emotional complexity and confusion. The clearly stated theme is betrayal—the title of the film-within-a-film over which Helmut presides. The betrayals in this film are multifaceted: betrayals against loved ones, against country, against state, against humanity, against one's own people, against one's own ideals, against one's own self, against one's own conscience. Moral ambiguity is the stance of every main character in the story. While Helmut callously takes advantage of others, he does so partly to escape from Hitler, Mussolini, and the war, for which he has no sympathy. Carlo and Ugo manipulate their positions in society not as a rebellion against the prevailing order, but simply out of self-interest, and play both sides against each other. The Partisans, in defending their country against the Nazi-fascists, terrorize their own people at least as much as the Nazis do. Livia's moderate politics, and her resentment against the rebellious "fanatics," come to haunt her and allow her to collaborate with the Nazi occupiers. Those who profit by the war and those who suffer seem almost unaware of each other's existence.

Those expecting another Brassian experience in erotica will probably be surprised, as *Senso '45* deals more with confused emotions. The sex scenes between the two leads are far more romantic than arousing, and the stylized orgy scene is surprisingly unsensational. *Senso '45* consists in large part of echoes of previous films, which are here summed up in a gentle symphony of homages.

Synopsis: Leaving with Ugo on a rainy night, a most agitated Livia encourages him to reach their destination more quickly. They have made a pact, a pact that will be honored upon their arrival in Venice.

The story is told in flashback. At a performance of a play at the Goldini Theatre in occupied Italy, a young Lieutenant Helmut Schultz makes a spectacle of himself, as he declines the opportunity to take action against Partisan guerrillas who interrupt the show, and instead shows off to the audience the prostitute who has accompanied him. On his way out of the auditorium, he makes eye contact with the middle-aged Livia, correctly judging that she will be attracted to him.

Livia's husband Carlo and their mutual friend Ugo explain to her that Helmut is able to carry on his scandalous behavior with impunity in return for supplying a bedmate for Goebbels. Livia refuses to believe their stories of Helmut's unscrupulousness, corruption, and numerous lovers. The next day, after Livia has witnessed some Partisans humiliate a fascist civilian, she notices that Helmut is also in view. He follows her home and seduces her. Livia does not resist; instead, she begins an affair. Despite the clear evidence of his taking money in return for contraband medications and outlawed "decadent" art works, Livia continues on with him, supporting his extravagant gambling debts. Helmut, who is secretly

Publicity photo: Tinto Brass and Anna Galiena, 2002

opposed to the war, convinces Livia to finance his fraudulent discharge from the military. Later, in return for a promise to convey her to Helmut, who is now living in Venice, Livia promises to leave Carlo and become Ugo's mistress. But upon their arrival, Livia discovers Helmut in bed with a younger woman. The unrepentant Helmut scornfully introduces his new lover to Livia, explaining what lengths he had to go through to get her to fall for his scheme. The mortified Livia informs on Helmut, whom the Nazis then execute in view of his young girlfriend. Livia and Ugo head off for their new life.

It is not surprising that Tinto moved the story to 1945. The 1940s were the years of Tinto's youth and he enjoyed re-creating those years for the cameras. He was also fascinated by the immense changes wrought upon Italy because of the war. He further stated that he did not wish to compete with Visconti's re-creation of the 1860s, but there is another reality. To have the film take place in 1866 would have cost a fortune, and investors would have demanded that Tinto's every move be supervised. Such a situation would be intolerable, and so Tinto saved money by making the story more modern. As lush as the visuals are, the production was more expensive than his erotic productions. The sets looked stunning; the rest was shot on natural locations.

Tinto explained some of his ideas:

...It is the story, the passionate story, of an older woman who loses her head for a young officer. In the novel by Camillo Boito, and in Visconti's film, it was about an Austrian officer. In my film he is a young German SS officer. As beautiful and as damned as a god, very beautiful, he has a very strong physical attraction. That means she forgets everything; she commits adultery with him. But what I liked, it is strange, I mean I'm curious to see what it gives the film, as I'm still editing now. It is a strange story, because he is a coward and she an adulteress; but in that historical moment, being a coward means that he doesn't want to fight, he doesn't believe in Hitler, in Mussolini, etc. I mean, there are two people who choose an ideology of life, eroticism, and sexuality, instead of this context of death that was the Nazi-fascism of the period. So it is a strange mixture; there is sex, a lot of sex, surely, but the sex is more at the service of the tale, of the story, rather than the story at the service of the sex, like it was in other films. I don't know if it can be considered an erotic film, though for sure there is a lot of eroticism. The difference between my film and Visconti's film is that in his film, because it was in 1865, this relationship was more sentimental. In '45 and in my film the attraction is just based on the senses—"senses" was the title of the original novel—and in sex.[218]

This was by all means Tinto's biggest production since *The Key*, with once again Ennio Morricone on board for the score. It cost roughly $5 million total, of which the Italian Ministry of Culture deemed the production cultural enough to donate 1.6 million euros of the budget. It was rated 14 in Italy and that may have been the reason his audience stayed home; the total box office was no more than $350,000, and Tinto went back to the erotic productions he was so successful with.

Source Notes:

217 Nico B, "Tinto Brass: Maestro of Erotic Cinema," interview conducted 3 November 2001, Torcello (Los Angeles: Cult Epics, 2014)

218 Ibid.

XXVII
Private
(*Fallo!*)

WITH *BLACK ANGEL* not having the success that he had hoped, Tinto went back to his standard formula. Giovanni Bertolucci agreed to produce, again sharing the risk with two co-producers, Roberto Girolamo and Ugo Tucci. Yes, it was Tinto's formula, a follow-up to *P.O. Box Tinto Brass*, an omnibus of six comical episodes, none of them deep but all of them rather amusing. Tinto and his crew inexplicably traveled to Cap d'Agde, Málaga, Casablanca, London, Côte d'Azur, and South Tyrol (a.k.a. Alto Adige) in order to film the scenes in the proper locales, but the locales were not used. Nearly everything was shot on studio sets. Two scenes resemble others from *Paprika* and *Black Angel*. Censorship laws had obviously been relaxed even further, and so Tinto had screen-filling close-ups of female genitalia. He seems to have done this not for aesthetic reasons, but just to test the law.

As with its predecessors, *Paprika*, *Così fan tutte*, and *TRAsgreDIRE*, this new film has no intellectual pretensions whatsoever. It is sheer brain candy—and eye candy, a 90-minute series of nonstop silly excuses to show lots of naked young women, sometimes with intrusive vaginal close-ups that fill the entire screen. The title means both "Do It!" and "Phallus!". As Tinto Brass said of the film:

> **"Fallo" is the imperative of the verb "to do"; at the same time it is also the infringement of a rule, the name with which Lady Chatterley evoked and invoked the sexual sceptre of the housekeeper Mellors. My film is all this, and therefore it's undoubtedly phallocentric, even if, despite the exclamation point in the title, it's more phallocritical than phallocratic!**[219]

Yet if we travel back in time a bit, we learn that Brass' original intention was radically different from the film that ultimately emerged. As he explained to Stefano Iori, "I had already thought of a film, which I then never made, that should have been entitled *Fallo*, and it was more or less similar to my first, *Chi lavora è perduto*, but a feminine interpretation. Instead of being the story of *him*, it ought to be the story of *her*, a jump to the feminine universe. The title was inspired by the heading of an insert in an alternative newspaper that I read years ago: *Do It*" (Stefano Iori, *Tinto Brass*, Rome: Gremese Editori, 2000, p. 82). Incidentally, Maruska Albertazzi won her rôle as Anna when she came to Brass' notice for her dissertation on *The Key*.

Though the crew traveled to the actual locations to shoot the film, it is puzzling that no real use was made of those locations, as most of the film was shot on studio sets, and the few exteriors were shot outside of Rome at a mansion. The innumerable erections are again hyperbolic prosthetics, though there were undoubtedly some real ones thrown in (for example, the oral sex scene between Silvia Rossi and Max Parodi).

"Alibi": On their seventh wedding anniversary vacation in Casablanca, a husband grants his wife an alibi for a fling to cure the inevitable seven-year itch: Gianni notices that his wife Cinzia is attracted to the young Moroccan bartender. Cinzia is too shy to admit to such a thing, but that doesn't stop Gianni from getting her an anniversary present: a one-time-only threesome with the Moroccan.

"Double Trouble": The double meaning of the original title *Montaggio Alternato* will be lost on non-Italian speakers, as "montaggio" literally means "assembly" or "editing," but it has a slang meaning as well: "making love." Stefania and Bruno play a game of tennis, but this time without their spouses, who are busy that day. Piecing things together, they easily discern that their spouses, Erika and TV producer Luigi, are spending time together, "auditioning" for a new series. As their spouses enjoy a rendezvous in Luigi's Roman office, Stefania and Bruno decide to enjoy themselves in the shower room.

"Two Hearts and a Hut": This is the funniest of the sketches. In "Alto Adige" (South Tyrol), scantily clad hotel maid Katarina understands that she is to provide more than room service to guests Frau Bertha and Herr Otto, who want her for fetish games on a regular basis. Katarina's

Publicity photo: **Private**, *"Double Trouble" episode, 2003*

fiancé, the Neapolitan cook Ciro, is all in favor of the arrangement, as the guests pay well, and he and Katarina need the money to purchase the hotel for themselves.

"Jolly Bangs": At a beach in Malaga, Raffaella and Ugo have a row, as he is having one of his bouts of jealousy, remembering Raffaella's brief affairs. They recall the time, when they were still engaged, that Raffaella played around with Pablo during a treasure hunt. Then there was the fling at a party with a railway guard. Seeing that his jealousy arouses him, Ugo demands that Raffaella continue with her affairs and stories as she has always done.

"Evil to Him Who Thinks Evil": Visiting Cap d'Agde, Franco takes rolls of nude photos of his fiancée Anna, who refuses to have sexual intercourse with him prior to marriage. The photographer who develops their pictures is impressed enough with their quality to recommend that the couple pay a visit to his British photographer friends, Noel and Helen Merritt. To everyone's surprise, Helen and then Noel seduce Anna, and Franco and Helen have sex in full view of their significant others. Despite this, Anna still refuses to have sex with Franco prior to marriage.

"Call me Pig... I Like It": In London, newlyweds Rosy and Oskar visit a lingerie shop, where Rosy is surprised to see that the female salesclerk is attracted to her. Back at the hotel, Oskar prefers to close the curtains, but Rosy insists that they be left open, for she knows that a voyeur is watching them from across the street.

This time Tinto pushed the envelope even further to XXX than the shorts on *P.O. Box Tinto Brass*. In what is essentially a porno flick, the only evidence that the filmmaker is one of the most progressive on the planet is the technical virtuosity, the breathtaking set design and costume design, and the vibrant energy that is simply nowhere in evidence in the materials found in "adult" shops. Anecdote: in a rare uncut DVD version we can see a blowjob scene, which was later pulled from the market by Cult Epics distributor Ryko, owned by Warner, when they came under fire in an article about them distributing pornography. The sales agent later delivered to Cult Epics the producer's cut version (instead of the uncut version) of the film in HD for Blu-ray release, reasons unknown.

Source Notes:

219 Tinto Epigram, 2004

XXVIII
Monamour

TINTO MADE a change. He shot this movie on digital video. That reduced costs drastically, and so he decided he needed a new producer: Tinta! She produced under a one-time imprimatur, Monamour S.r.l. By now, Tinta was ill and she was not on set, but she did contribute to the script and her presence was felt.

This was based on a 1998 novel by Alina Rizzi, *Amare Leon*, which utilized Tinto's favorite theme of jealousy as an aphrodisiac. Dario is required to attend the Festivaletteratura in Mantua, a five-day affair. He brings along his wife, Marta, but by now he has come to take her for granted. He leaves her behind at the hotel while he attends to business. Marta wanders about town and has an affair with a young Frenchman, Léon. When Dario learns of this, he bursts into fury but will no longer take his wife for granted.

There is nothing more to the story, but there are nice images and nice visual jokes. Marta visits an art gallery, a scene that almost exactly duplicates a moment from Roberto Rossellini's *Journey to Italy*. In a park, she is eyed by some black men, in images that closely remind us of images from *Nerosubianco*. The actress who portrays Marta, Anna Jimskaya, looks startlingly like Anita Sanders in that earlier film. She was originally from Uzbekistan and grew up in a circus family. Performing is second nature to her, and she was entirely nonchalant about acting in the nude.

Léon's camera is named Tinta. A catatonic elderly hotel proprietor stares blankly at a TV set that is showing *Tempo libero*. Mario Gagliardotto, who had just published a lovely book-length interview with Tinto, appears as an extra.

Monamour is the last feature entry in Tinto's canon and it was enormously popular, selling as many video copies as other erotic Tinto films. So, though this is not his best film, Tinto knew and understood exactly what his audience wanted, and he delivered once more.

Looking back, many of his erotic films were censored, something Tinto did not understand:

The worst censorship is not by the public, because these kinds of films are very successful. I have become famous, very well known, because of these kinds of films, because people recognize themselves in the way in which I express sexuality and eroticism. Censorship comes always from the state, from finance, from the church and from culture, because when culture is confronted with eroticism it has a very hypocritical attitude; they do not feel at ease. It is something that has not been discussed by the culture.[220]

He defended this further in a philosophical way in a later interview, which sets him aside from the usual pornographer a.k.a. smut peddler. His later work that made him the Maestro of Erotic Cinema, after being an avant-garde filmmaker first, is highly regarded by his fans and admirers.

Sex, the subject of sex, has no less cultural worth than any other subject: politics, philosophy, history, mathematics, science, it's culture. Because sex in itself is nothing, it has no meaning. It's just the most splendid source of pleasure bestowed on human beings. Culture, then, has intervened to change, to deform this source of pleasure into a monstrous machine of madness, creator of taboos, anguish, fear and frustrations. How? Through laws, commandments, edicts...[221]

Source Notes:

220 Nico B, "Tinto Brass: Maestro of Erotic Cinema," interview conducted 3 November 2001, Torcello (Los Angeles: Cult Epics, 2014)

221 Interviewed by Massimiliano Zanin, *Istintobrass* documentary (2013)

XXIX
Kick the Cock

2008 WAS A BUSY YEAR for Tinto Brass and Cult Epics. On the release of *The Voyeur* Special Edition DVD it was announced in an interview with Tinto on the disc, with the appearance of Angelita Franco, Nico B's girlfriend at the time, that a new short film would be produced.

The short story *The New Maid* was written by Angelita Franco, who had just starred in *SIN*, a sort of vintage erotica series of three short films which Nico B directed. *The New Maid* was a simple but amusing sketch featuring Angelita as an irresponsible cook dressed in almost nothing, or fetish costuming, based on her real-life experiences, with Tinto in the movie as the boss who leers at her. As Angelita's story was short, Tinto added the kitchen dream sequences where Angelita appears in his fantasies and masturbates with vegetables. When he delivered his edit of the short, he retitled it *Kick the Cock*. It seems at first glance a vulgar title for a movie, but it had a double meaning, which in Dutch is a saying translated as "A Peek in the Kitchen."

The short was shot outside of Rome, where some of the scenes of *Private* (Fallo!) also were shot in a mansion —a huge part of the $80K budget, but perfectly suitable for the two-day shoot. In an interview shot on the set by Nico B, which became "The Making of *Kick the Cock*," Tinto explains his intention together with Angelita Franco.

Publicity photo: Angelita Franco, 2008

Tinto: She wrote the script that corresponds with her life. She's a very messy girl, in terms of the better, it was nice, nice images, she's a very graphic model and everybody enjoys her.

Angelita: The idea for the movie came from three things: My dislike for washing dishes. One big thing is like my life, I actually have a history of creating messes and making disasters on so many things that I set out to do but ultimately end up with a masterpiece. And the third thing, Nico said, you have to write a script and get to pick your own rôle.[222]

The film was originally part of a series of erotic short films Cult Epics was producing at the time starring and penned by Angelita, which were planned also with director Radley Metzger, Anna Biller and Nico B himself, but before going into production for his film Radley passed away, and the others were put on hold.

Kick the Cock premiered at the Venice Film Festival in 2008, where Tinto appeared with Caterina Verzi, the actress of his next film, and said in an TV interview about the format:

I think shorts are a great exercise to experiment with film language. The conventional 1hr-45min rule doesn't apply. This was also Roberto Rossellini's obsession. He'd say, "Why should I have inspirations that only last an hour and 45 minutes? If it's for one hour or 40 minutes, should I still have to make a 1hr-45min movie?" The conventional length of a movie is a big limitation. It doesn't exist in literature. You can write a 50-page book or a 500-page book. That's more pertinent with what your message is. Shorts can have different run times. It's a very interesting exercise of expression.[223]

Source Notes:

222 "The Making of *Kick the Cock*" bonus feature by Nico B, *Kick the Cock* Blu-ray/DVD (Cult Epics, 2010)

223 "Venice Film Festival" bonus feature, *Kick the Cock* Blu-ray/DVD

Publicity photo: Angelita Franco and Tinto Brass, 2008

XXX
Hotel Courbet

IN 2009, TINTO DIRECTED his final work, *Hotel Courbet*, a short film featuring his current wife Caterina Varzi. *Hotel Courbet* tells the story of a woman who lets herself go so she can assuage her erotic affliction. The provocative intimacy, violated unseen, is worth more for the burglar (Alberto Petrolini) than any of the things he has stolen.

A brief synopsis of the scenes: a woman undresses, dresses, undresses, and in front of a mirror touches her breasts, in the bedroom. The music accompanying a striptease is "Baby Doll" by Laurie Anderson. She puts on a top hat, and dresses again. Meanwhile a man breaks into the villa (outside of Rome) to steal her valuable belongings. When we hear the sound of children laughing, the song "Come un Pierrot" by Patty Pravo starts, and the woman sits in an outfit in front of a mirror. After the phone rings (a wrong number?) she takes off her earrings, and then her makeup. Her face is sad, remembering a man, a memory of the past. She lays in a bed naked, her legs posed similar to the painting of Courbet's *Origine Del Mondo* above the bed; instead, with sperm on her vagina, a little spider appears above her crotch. A man we see first with his lip bleeding says farewell to her, the spider goes inside of her; out of anger she throws a book, *La Chamber Bleue* by George Simon, across the room. We are back in time to the woman in front of the mirror: her makeup is the same as Gigi Proietti in *L'urlo*. The makeup fades, and she starts drinking a bottle of alcohol, undresses to lay in bed, and cries. The burglar is in the room where she now sleeps, stealing her valuables and looking at her, when the noise he makes wakes her up. Aldo Carotenuto's book *Attraversare la vita* shows as reference. Next she is touching herself accompanied by the song Gianna Nannini's "Amandoti." The burglar who has been watching her leaves and looks at a nude photo of her, puts it back in the bag, then closes the door and rings the doorbell. They both look at each other, he cites Shakespeare: "Beauty tempts the thief more than gold," then gives her photo back. We hear Edith Piaf singing "Non je ne regrette," and Tinto appears and says in Italian: "Art, says Picasso, is never castrated... if it is, it's not art."

Although the story is credited to Caterina Varzi, Piero Fontana, and Tinto, he was surely unaware that this story had already been produced, almost exactly, in "The Intruder," a short sketch in a cable TV series called *Electric Blue*, episode 13, from 1983. Tinto did, though, give it a new twist at the end.

The 18-minute *Hotel Courbet* was presented as part of three short films by Tinto at the Venice Film Festival in 2009. After this Tinto retired from filmmaking; a few films were announced, but did not result in any new work to be produced by him. In our interview, when asked what was his favorite film he had made, he answered:

I very much like those that have less success. For instance *L'urlo*, which didn't get released, *Action*, which wasn't successful. I have a concept of work in progress. My films are all together one film. Each time I do something that maybe I forgot, or didn't think to do, in the previous film. I think that the best definition of myself was by Andy Warhol. Once he did an interview for his paper *Interview*, and the journalist asked him: "Who is the worst Italian director?" And he said, "Tinto Brass." "And who is the best?" "Always Tinto Brass." [*Laughs*][224]

Source Notes:

224 Nico B, "Tinto Brass: Maestro of Erotic Cinema," interview conducted 3 November 2001, Torcello (Los Angeles: Cult Epics, 2014)

The Remaining Works and the Unmade Films

THE PRECEDING HIGHLY abbreviated and simplified account of Tinto's career leaves much out, as it is difficult to work it into the narrative. Prior to leaving for the Cinémathèque Française, Tinto made a 16mm silent movie with his Paillard-Bolex starring his American friends Wolf and Emily Kahn, the well-known painters. He shot it on reversal film but never finished editing it. He submitted it to the Cinémathèque where his *Nouvelle Vague* friends promised to complete it for him. The film's title is unknown, and whether it survives is unknown.

He had a momentary cameo in a Moris Ergas production called *La donna è una cosa meravigliosa* (Woman Is a Wonderful Thing). There were also the projects that never got off the ground. *A Clockwork Orange* was mentioned, but *Imago* was not. When *Barbarella* became a hit, Dino De Laurentiis asked Tinto to direct a sequel, *Barbarella Goes Down*, but if the script was ever written remains unknown. With leftover funds from *Dropout*, Tinto and Vanessa Redgrave and Luigi Proietti made a follow-up called *DNA*. It was nearly finished when the money ran out completely, and so the film was abandoned, of which footage still exists.

Daniele Senatore offered Tinto the job of directing *The Evasion*, to have starred Gianni Morandi, but the project never came to be, and so instead Tinto made *Vacation*. When *Vacation* was finished, Tinto was scheduled to make a commercial thriller of some sort, to recover his losses from his previous films. What that thriller was to have been, who was to have produced it, and why it was forever shelved remain mysteries. During Tinto's exile from the movie industry, he co-authored a script called *Order and Sex Discipline*, to have starred Macha Méril, who planned to co-produce. What happened? The most likely explanation is that no distributor or exhibitor would invest, since Tinto had just suffered a series of non-profitable films. At the same time, Tinto had another script, *History of Italy*, presumably a comedy, but that too never came to be and nothing is known about it.

Mentioned in passing was Tinto's TV commercial for Vespa motor scooters. It was called *Le sardomobili* (The Sardine-Mobiles), and it occasionally pops up on the Internet, only to have RAI TV force it to be taken down again. If you keep looking, you will find it sooner or later, and it is a delight, a ballad performed by youngsters aboard a train, who bring a moment of joy to the weary passengers.

Together with Roberto Lerici, Tinto wrote an epic script on *The Borgias*, and plans were scuttled during a meeting with the investors. Wolf Mankowitz, who was involved, tried to dissuade Tinto from mentioning the outrageous scenes of sex and violence that he planned to shoot. Tinto would not be put off. He wanted to be honest, and so he told this consortium of strait-laced businessmen his plans for *outré* sensationalism in relentless detail, and they unanimously withdrew their offers. Nonetheless, he tried to revive the project in 1975 and nearly succeeded. He tried again in later years, but to no avail.

A dream project was *Punch*, to have starred Gigi Proietti. Tinto explained the plot:

> **It had a double meaning of *Punch* and *punk*. It was the time of punk. The title originated from the English satirical newspaper that began publication in the eighteenth century, the satirical newspaper par excellence, and the freest. Oddly enough, instead of starting from figures belonging to their own world, the English editors had been inspired by that of Punchinello. What stands out about this script is the almost nonexistent depth of the characters who were, however, extraordinarily funny.**[225]

The project was almost ready to go when, yet again, the funding vanished.

In 1974, Coralta Cinematografica hired Tinto to direct a satire called *Stormtroopers*, but for reasons undisclosed gave him the boot.

After *Caligula*, when he again was an unemployable pariah, he tried to revive *The Borgias* and he had written another script as well, *The Pig Advantage*, about which nothing is known.

Publicity photo for the unmade film **Tender is the Flesh**, *1993*

As it was *Caligula* that made Tinto unemployable from 1977 through 1980, apparently in an act of mercy and solidarity in 1981 Giglio Faenza hired Tinto Brass to be an actor in a film called *Champagne*, and assigned him to be film editor as well. Almost nothing is known about this project, as it was never made. Tinto also appeared on camera in a four-part TV series called *La felicità*, which seems no longer to be available anywhere.

After *The Key*, when Tinto's reputation was at its height, RAI-2 and a production company called Hera hired Tinto to direct a TV miniseries called *3-13-33*, of which a variant version would be released to cinemas. Again, nothing more is known. Tinto was also trying to get up a British project, something along the lines of a *Tom Jones* or a *Fanny Hill*, but nothing came of it.

At some time or another, Tinto toyed with the idea of making a movie about Rasputin. He found the monk's ideas amusing. Since penitence is mandatory, so Rasputin reasoned, the penitents must have a reason for their penance. Since most people do not have any reason, he would supply one: sex orgies, which he encouraged so that believers would have something for which to ask forgiveness.

In 1990, Tinto was hired to direct a TV commercial for Calze Levante underwear. In 1993, Tinto began production on the film called *Tender is the Flesh*, from the novel *The Butcher* by Alina Reyes. Filming ground to a halt when the producer died. Then, in 1996, after *The Voyeur*, he was hired to appear in a TV commercial for Reggiseni Infiore, in a hilarious sketch Brass appears as Monica Bellucci's most curious floor manager and gropes her breasts, with consequences. Three years later, he was interviewed for a documentary about a documentary: *Quando l'Italia non era un Paese povero*. In 1999, Massimo Ceccherini hired him to portray a spoof of himself in *Lucignolo*. At the same time, Tinto hoped to make a movie in Ukraine, but what it was supposed to have been, we do not know.

In 1999, Tinto was paid for the use of his name for a series of 12 erotic video stories, collectively called "*Corti circuiti erotici*" (Erotic Short Circuits). The official story is that this series began as a competition, judged by Brass, for short erotic scripts which elicited over six hundred entries. The unofficial story is that there was no competition, that Brass was simply paid for the use of his name and image. Tinto Brass had the job of introducing, Hitchcock-like, the 12 shorts, and he made a cameo appearance in all but one. One of the shorts, *Giulia*, was apparently a separate independent video production that had already begun production, and so it is the only one with a different crew and without a cameo. This was supposedly done in the style of the Maestro himself. The makers of those videos did not learn the principal lesson about inventing interesting characters who are bursting with life and enthusiasm.

These video makers began with the sex and then tried to make excuses for it with uninteresting stories. The sole worthy entry was *Giulia*, by Roy Stuart. *Giulia* in no way resembles Tinto's works. Yet it was a beautiful video.

There was another feature-length video from 2003 called *Unchained Melanie*, performed in English but shot seemingly in Turkey. Tinto is credited as executive producer, but surely he was just paid for the use of his name on this entirely unremarkable story.

There were also the plays that Tinto directed when he was not busy in the movies. He directed Roberto Lerici's *Family Lunch*, and the few published stills indicate that it was wildly unreal and borderline nightmarish, as members of a family begin eating one another. That was in 1973, and it was revived in 1976 and in 1983. In 1976, Tinto also directed a Riccardo Reim play called *The Man of Sand*. After plans for a film called *Boudoir*, based on de Sade's *Philosophy in the Bedroom*, were abandoned, Tinto adapted the script for the stage in 1985. Finally, he directed an adaptation of the recently recovered authentic script of Frank Wedekind's *Lulù*, starring Debora Caprioglio in the lead rôle.

Tinto also did uncredited work somewhere. He once mentioned that he had done some sound mixing for another film, as a favor. His name appears as sound engineer on a vinyl album by eastwest called *The Big Strip!* but when asked he claimed to know nothing about it.

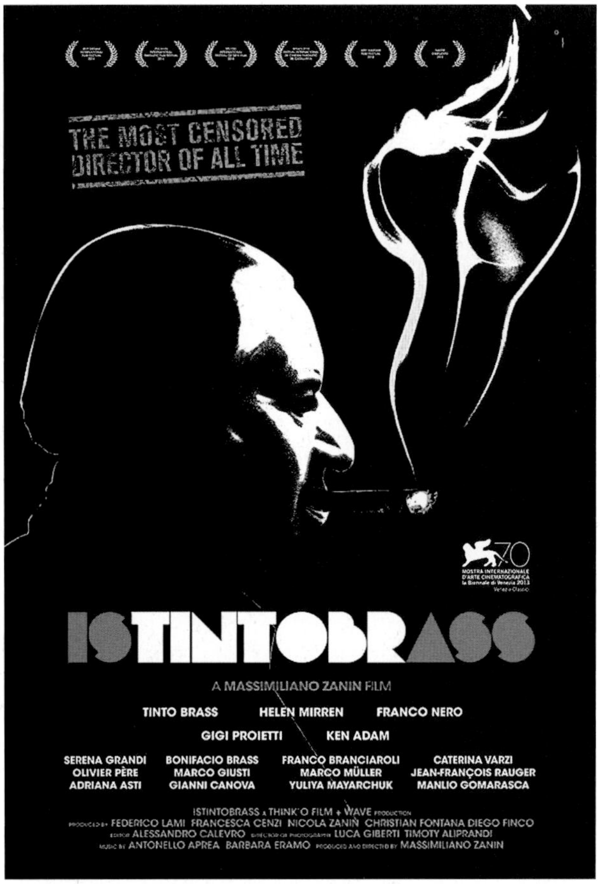

Top: Promotional poster, 2010, Bottom: Italian promo poster, 2013

After a life time marriage, Tinta passed away in August 2006. Tinto eventually remarried in 2017. After a lengthy bereavement time, he rallied enough to continue working in the movies again, but he made only short subjects or appeared in cameos.

Around the same time, Louis Nero, Franco's son, hired Tinto to portray a porn director in *La rabbia*, and Tinto also appeared in a cameo in *Our Messiah*.

In 2009 he appeared in *Existential Impotence*. In 2010 he had planned, with Filmexport and Cult Epics on board as co-producer, to make *Caligula 3D* a.k.a. *Who Killed Caligula?* The plot synopsis was published ahead of time. Before he could begin shooting, he was in the hospital, presumably with a stroke. When he emerged, he wanted to return to his roots with a serious story about an elderly man who urges his grown daughter to assist with his suicide. That was never made.

Then, in 2012, Tinto had a cameo in *Crazy Dog*. In 2013 he was featured in the documentary *IsTintoBrass*, directed by his former assistant and co-writer Massimiliano Zanin, and was interviewed and filmed along with Franco Nero, Helen Mirren, Serena Grandi, and Sir Ken Adam, among others. When the documentary premiered at the Venice Film Festival, Tinto announced he wanted to make a film about ex-premier Silvia Berlusconi's escorts. "I want to make a film about Berlusconi. I had in mind the title *Thank You, Daddy*," Brass said, referring to the nickname given to Berlusconi by the girls who attended the famously bawdy parties in his villa. It was never made either. And finally, in 2015, he appeared in another short called *Eve in the Nude*, made by an otherwise all-female cast and crew.

He hoped to make a new film, *Ziva: Never-Never Land*, a World War II story about lost MIA soldiers taking refuge in a lighthouse operated by a lady named Ziva. There was more: For years he was a regular on TV, reducing his audiences to laughter with his wild stories. He twice appeared on a British show called *EuroTrash*; he has written introductions to several books, and he put out a few erotic pamphlets. In his 1993 appearance on *EuroTrash*, made while he was in the midst of working on *The Voyeur*, he summed up his career: "I put two balls and a big cock between the legs of the Italian cinema!"

Source Notes:

225 Lorenzo Codelli, *Nerosubrass* (Udina and Rome: Dino Audino Editore, 1996), pp. 76–77

Spanish One Sheet poster, 1984

Left and Right: Spanish Lobby Cards, 1984

Giovanni Bertolucci PRESENTA
STEFANIA SANDRELLI
FRANK FINLAY
LA LLAVE SECRETA
MUSICA: ENNIO MORRICONE
Un film de TINTO BRASS
VENUS

Giovanni Bertolucci
PRESENTA
STEFANIA SANDRELLI
FRANK FINLAY
LA LLAVE SECRETA
MUSICA ENNIO MORRICONE
Un film de TINTO BRASS

Giovanni Bertolucci PRESENTA
STEFANIA SANDRELLI
FRANK FINLAY
LA LLAVE SECRETA
MUSICA ENNIO MORRICONE
Un film de TINTO BRASS

Giovanni Bertolucci PRESENTA
STEFANIA SANDRELLI
FRANK FINLAY
LA LLAVE SECRETA
MUSICA ENNIO MORRICONE
Un film de TINTO BRASS

ERWIN C. DIETRICH
zeigt
DER GRÖSSTE PUBLIKUMSERFOLG
AN DEN FILMFESTSPIELEN VON
SAN SEBASTIAN UND VENEDIG
ASCOT
THE
KEY
DER
SCHLÜSSEL
EIN FILM VON
TINTO BRASS
MIT
FRANK FINLAY
STEFANIA SANDRELLI
NACH DEM ROMAN «THE KEY»
DES LITERATUR-NOBELPREIS-
TRÄGERS
JUNICHERO TANIZAKI
MUSIK
ENNIO MORRICONE
EINE PRODUKTION VON GIOVANNI
BERTOLUCCI IM VERLEIH DER ASCOT

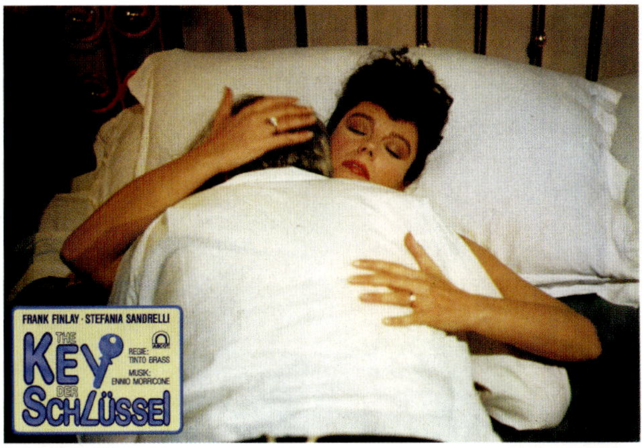

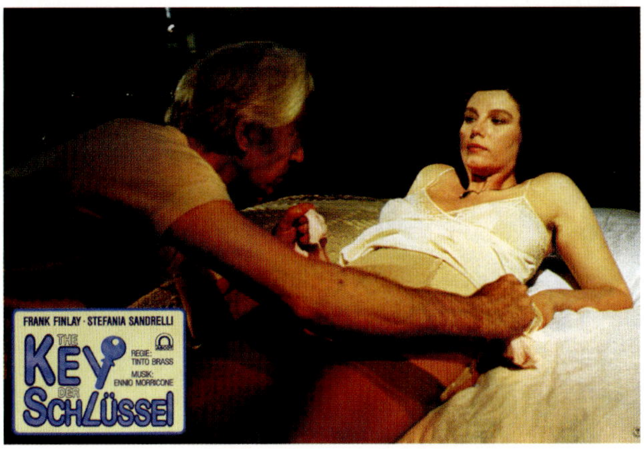

Left: West German A1 poster, Right: West German Lobby Cards, 1984

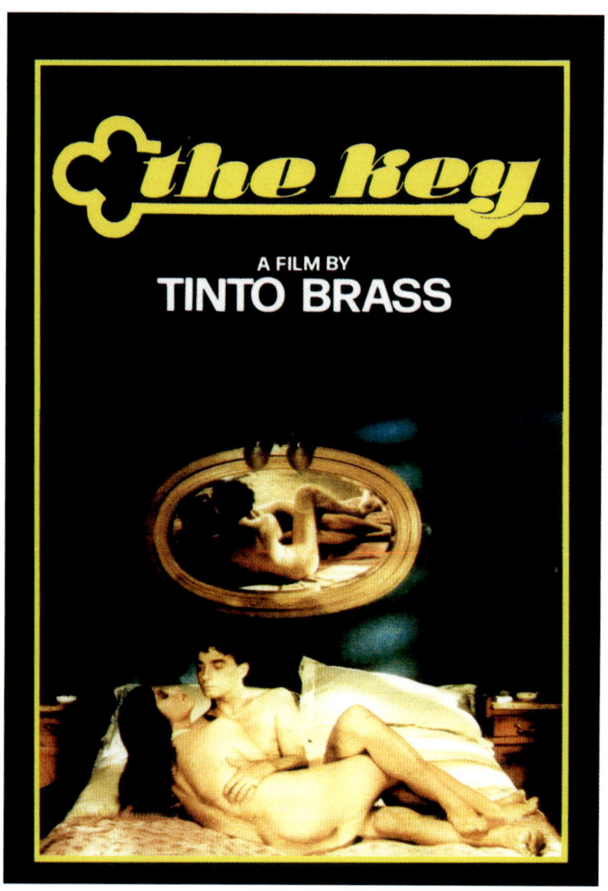

International Brochure, 1984

Top: Mexican Lobby Card, 1988, Bottom: Japanese B5 poster, 1984

French Grande poster, 1984

GIOVANNI BERTOLUCCI
presenta
un film di
TINTO BRASS
con
SERENA GRANDI
MIRANDA
L. CROVATO
con ANDREA OCCHIPINTI
FRANCO INTERLENGHI
ANDY J. FOREST
e con FRANCO BRANCIAROLI
nel ruolo di Toni
soggetto CARLA CIPRIANI sceneggiatura TINTO BRASS fotografia SILVANO IPPOLITI · ERICO MENCZER
COLORE CINECITTÀ
scenografia PAOLO BIAGETTI costumi su disegni di JOST JAKOB musiche RIZ ORTOLANI
montaggio TINTO BRASS · FIORENZA MULLER prodotto dalla SAN FRANCISCO FILM s.r.l.
IDIF
PRIMA EDIZIONE ITALIANA 1985
IT 96

Left: Italian 2-Fogli poster, 1985

West German Lobby Cards, 1986

Left: West German Lobby Cards, Right: West German A1 poster, 1986

ERWIN C. DIETRICH
ZEIGT:
EIN FILM VON
TINTO BRASS
ASCOT
MIT:
SERENA GRANDI
MIRANDA
EINE GIOVANNI BERTOLUCCI/SAN FRANCISCO FILM-PRODUKTION IN EASTMANCOLOR IM VERLEIH DER ASCOT · MUSIK: RIZ ORTOLANI

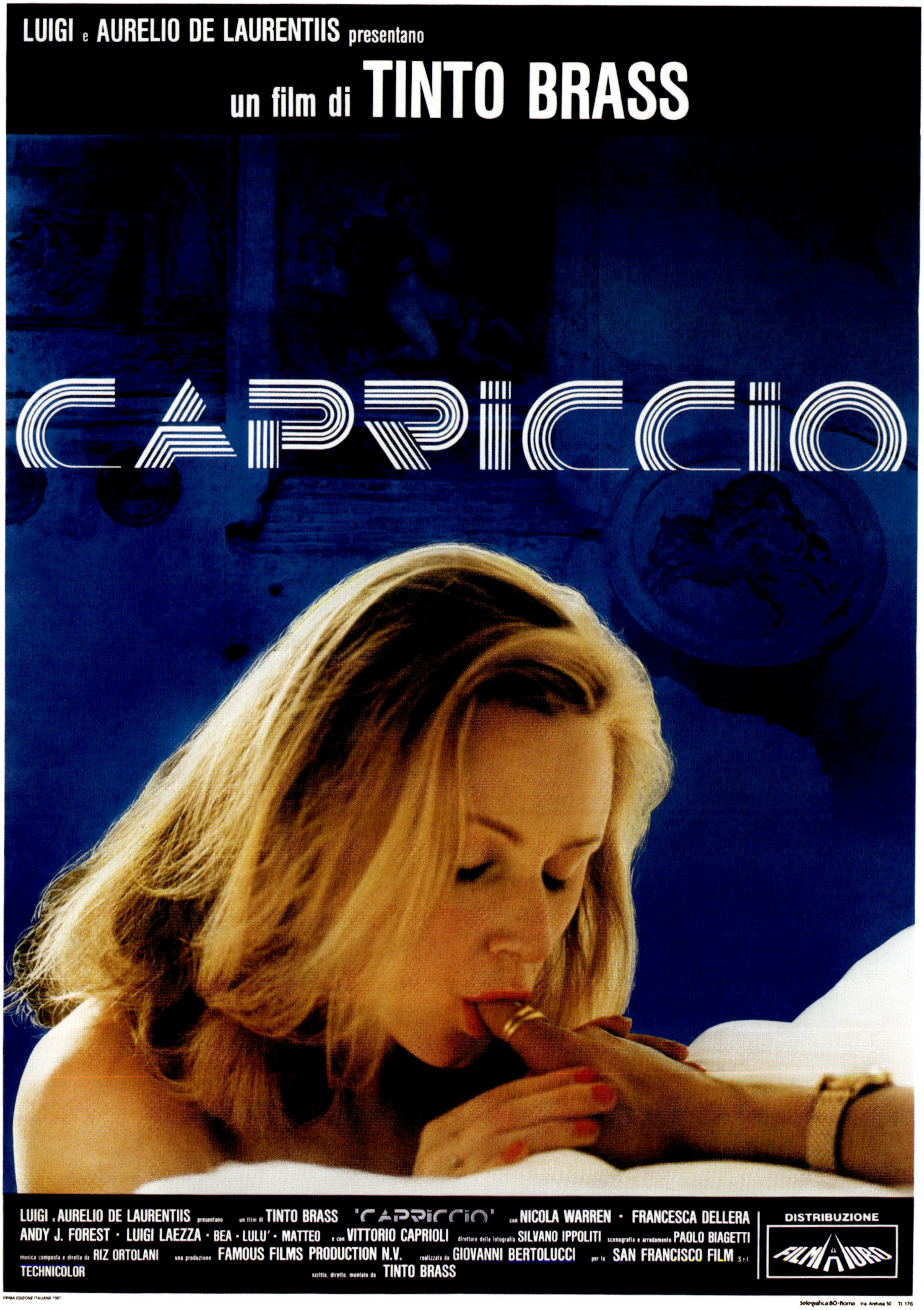
LUIGI e AURELIO DE LAURENTIIS presentano
un film di TINTO BRASS
CAPRICCIO
LUIGI . AURELIO DE LAURENTIIS presentano un film di TINTO BRASS "CAPRICCIO" con NICOLA WARREN · FRANCESCA DELLERA
ANDY J. FOREST · LUIGI LAEZZA · BEA · LULU' · MATTEO e con VITTORIO CAPRIOLI direttore della fotografia SILVANO IPPOLITI scenografia e arredamento PAOLO BIAGETTI
musica composta e diretta da RIZ ORTOLANI una produzione FAMOUS FILMS PRODUCTION N.V. realizzata da GIOVANNI BERTOLUCCI per la SAN FRANCISCO FILM S.r.l.
TECHNICOLOR
scritto, diretto, montato da TINTO BRASS
DISTRIBUZIONE
FILMAURO
PRIMA EDIZIONE ITALIANA 1987
Selegrafica 80-Roma Via Antusa 50 TI 176

Left: Italian 2-Fogli poster, 1987, Right: West German Lobby Cards, 1988

GIOVANNI BERTOLUCCI · GALLIANO JUSO · RETE ITALIA presentano
un film di TINTO BRASS
con GIANCARLO GIANNINI
SNACK BAR
BUDAPEST
ZUCCHERO SUGAR FORNACIARI
DOLBY STEREO IN SELECTED THEATRES
GIOVANNI BERTOLUCCI · GALLIANO JUSO · RETE ITALIA presentano
un film di TINTO BRASS con GIANCARLO GIANNINI 'SNACK BAR BUDAPEST'
con FRANCOIS NEGRET · RAFFAELLA BARACCHI · PHILIPPE LEOTARD · SILVIE ORCIER · GIORGIO TIRABASSI
KATALIN MURANY · e con CARLO MONNI
sceneggiatura di TINTO BRASS liberamente tratto dall'omonimo romanzo di MARCO LODOLI e SILVIA BRE edito da BOMPIANI
production designer PAOLO BIAGETTI · direttore della fotografia ALESSIO GELSINI
music by ZUCCHERO additional music by DAVID SANCIOUS
MEDUSA DISTRIBUZIONE
una coproduzione RETEITALIA S.p.A. · SAN FRANCISCO FILM s.r.l. · METRO FILM s.r.l. · scritto, diretto, montato da TINTO BRASS · colore della TELECOLOR

Left: Italian 4-Fogli poster, 1988, Right: Japanese B5, 1990

TINTO BRASS
RIAPRE LE CASE CHIUSE
AUGUSTO CAMINITO presenta un film di TINTO BRASS
PAPRIKA
DEBORA CAPRIOGLIO
STEPHANE FERRARA • MARTINE BROCHARD • STEPHANE BONNET
RENZO RINALDI • ROSSANA GAVINEL • NINA SOLDANO e con ELIZABETH KAZA
costumi JOST JAKOB • scenografia PAOLO BIAGETTI • direttore della fotografia SILVANO IPPOLITI
soggetto e sceneggiatura di TINTO BRASS e BERNARDINO ZAPPONI
produttore esecutivo GIUSEPPE AURIEMMA
prodotto da AUGUSTO CAMINITO per la SCENA GROUP
regia di TINTO BRASS
CHANCE FILM
DISTRIBUZIONE
PRIMA EDIZIONE ITALIANA 1991
Selegrafica 80-Roma | Via Aretusa 50

Left: Italian Locandina poster, Right: Italian Fotobusta posters, 1991

Italian Fotobusta posters, 1991

German Lobby Cards, 1991

Left: Italian 2-Fogli poster, Right: Italian Fotobusta posters, 1992

GIOVANNI BERTOLUCCI presenta un film di
TINTO BRASS
COSI' FAN TUTTE
GIOVANNI BERTOLUCCI presenta un film di TINTO BRASS con CLAUDIA KOLL "COSI FAN TUTTE" con PAOLO LANZA, ORNELLA MARCUCCI, RENZO RINALDI con la partecipazione di LUCIA LUCCHESINO e PIERANGELA VALLERINO e con FRANCO BRANCIAROLI
Sceneggiatura TINTO BRASS, BERNARDINO ZAPPONI, FRANCESCO COSTA Scenografia PAOLO BIAGETTI Costumi JOST JAKOB Musiche di PINO DONAGGIO
Fotografia SILVANO IPPOLITI, MASSIMO DI VENANZO Prodotto da GIOVANNI BERTOLUCCI per la SAN FRANCISCO FILM S.r.l. e FASO FILM S.r.l. Diretto e Montato da TINTO BRASS
© 1992 S. Francisco Film - Faso Film
AA 65

GIOVANNI BERTOLUCCI presenta un film di
TINTO BRASS
COSI' FAN TUTTE
© 1992 S. Francisco Film - Faso Film

GIOVANNI BERTOLUCCI presenta un film di
TINTO BRASS
COSI' FAN TUTTE

GIOVANNI BERTOLUCCI presenta un film di
TINTO BRASS
COSI' FAN TUTTE

International Brochure, 1992

Top and Bottom: German Lobby Cards, 1993

Top and Bottom: German Lobby Cards, 1993

Japanese B1 poster, 1995

MARCO POCCIONI, MARCO VALSANIA e ANGELO RIZZOLI
presentano
un film di
TINTO BRASS
L' UOMO CHE GUARDA
Foto G. SALIS
con KATARINA VASILISSA FRANCESCO CASALE CRISTINA GARAVAGLIA
RAFFAELLA OFFIDANI e con FRANCO BRANCIAROLI
Direttore della Fotografia MASSIMO DI VENANZO Scenografia e Arredamento MARIA LUIGIA BATTANI Costumi MILLINA DEODATO
Musiche RIZ ORTOLANI Organizzatore Generale CLAUDIO GRASSETTI Sceneggiatura, Regia, Montaggio TINTO BRASS Teatri di Posa e Laboratorio
Produzione RODEO DRIVE Srl - ERRE CINEMATOGRAFICA srl - Distribuzionc
DC 18

Left: Italian 2-Fogli poster, Right: Italian Fotobusta posters, 1993

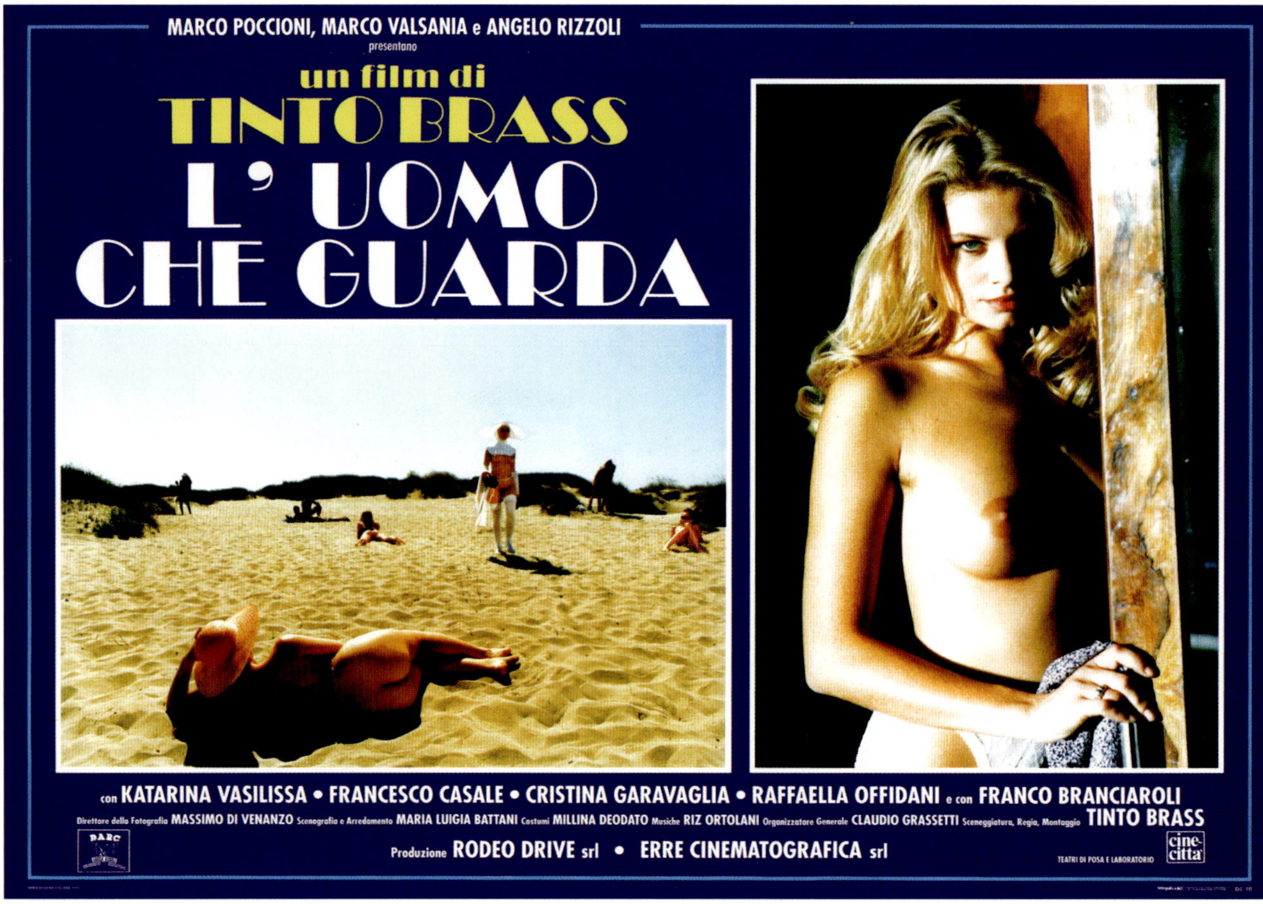

Top: Italian Fotobusta poster, 1993, Bottom: Italian 1-Fogli poster, 1994, Japanese B5 poster, 1995

Italian 2-Fogli poster, 1995

Italian Fotobusta posters, 1995

Japanese B5 poster, 2001

Italian 2-Fogli poster, 1998

Top: Italian 2-Fogli poster, Bottom: Italian Fotobusta poster, 1998

Top: German A1 poster, 1998

Left and Right: Italian Fotobusta posters, 1998

un film di TINTO BRASS
MONELLA
Artisti Associati
NEW MEDIA

un film di TINTO BRASS
MONELLA
Artisti Associati
NEW MEDIA

Left and Right: Italian 2-Fogli posters, 1999

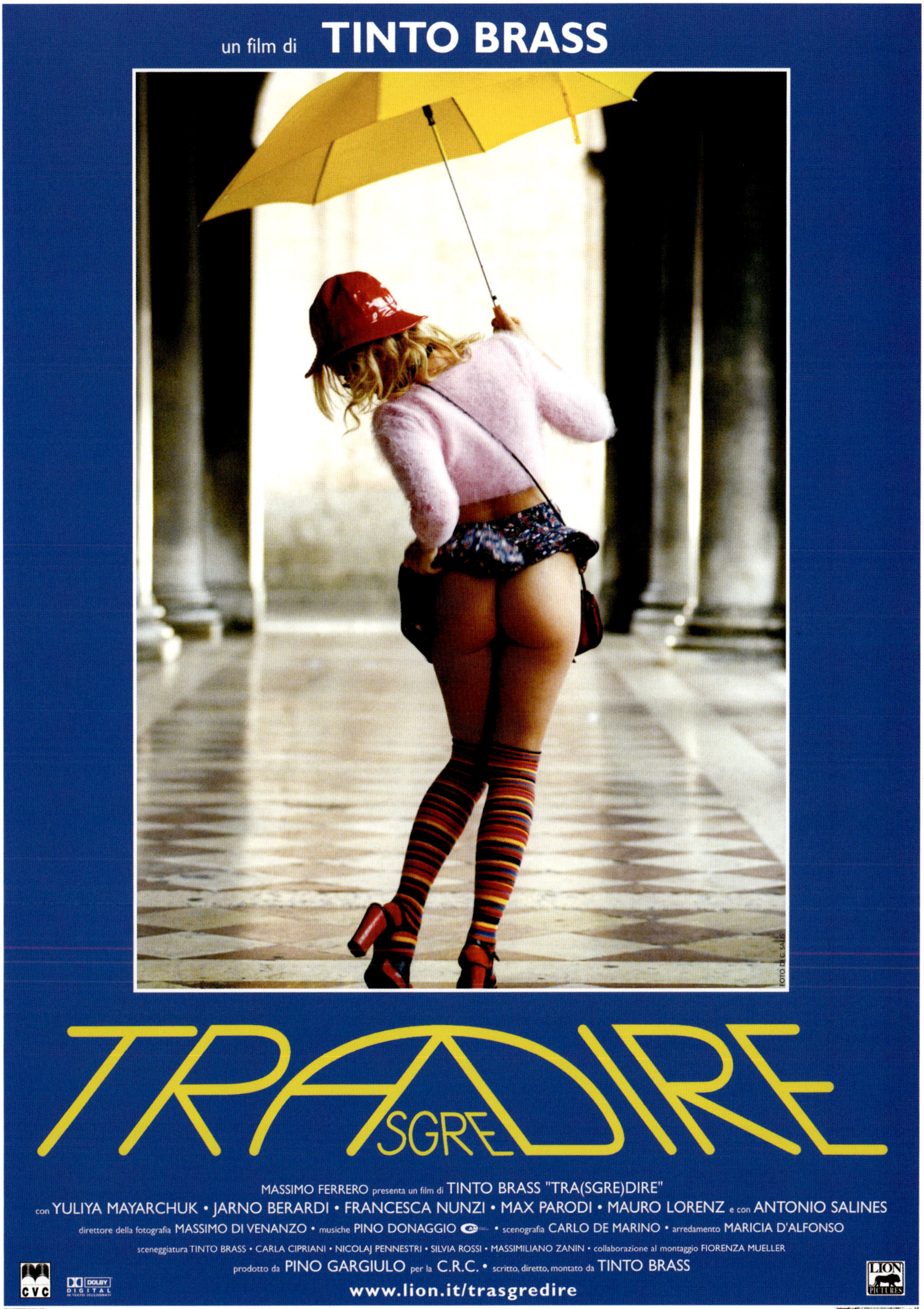
un film di TINTO BRASS
TRA SGRE DIRE
MASSIMO FERRERO presenta un film di TINTO BRASS "TRA(SGRE)DIRE"
con YULIYA MAYARCHUK • JARNO BERARDI • FRANCESCA NUNZI • MAX PARODI • MAURO LORENZ e con ANTONIO SALINES
direttore della fotografia MASSIMO DI VENANZO • musiche PINO DONAGGIO • scenografia CARLO DE MARINO • arredamento MARICIA D'ALFONSO
sceneggiatura TINTO BRASS • CARLA CIPRIANI • NICOLAJ PENNESTRI • SILVIA ROSSI • MASSIMILIANO ZANIN • collaborazione al montaggio FIORENZA MUELLER
prodotto da PINO GARGIULO per la C.R.C. • scritto, diretto, montato da TINTO BRASS
www.lion.it/trasgredire

Italian Fotobusta posters, 1999

un film di TINTO BRASS
TRA SGRE DIRE
MASSIMO FERRERO presenta un film di TINTO BRASS "TRA(SGRE)DIRE"
con YULIYA MAYARCHUK • JARNO BERARDI • FRANCESCA NUNZI • MAX PARODI • MAURO LORENZ e con ANTONIO SALINES
direttore della fotografia MASSIMO DI VENANZO • musiche PINO DONAGGIO • scenografia CARLO DE MARINO • arredamento MARICIA D'ALFONSO
sceneggiatura TINTO BRASS • CARLA CIPRIANI • NICOLAJ PENNESTRI • SILVIA ROSSI • MASSIMILIANO ZANIN • collaborazione al montaggio FIORENZA MUELLER
prodotto da PINO GARGIULO per la C.R.C. • scritto, diretto, montato da TINTO BRASS
www.lionpictures.it/trasgredire

un film di TINTO BRASS
TRA SGRE DIRE
MASSIMO FERRERO presenta un film di TINTO BRASS "TRA(SGRE)DIRE"
con YULIYA MAYARCHUK • JARNO BERARDI • FRANCESCA NUNZI • MAX PARODI • MAURO LORENZ e con ANTONIO SALINES
direttore della fotografia MASSIMO DI VENANZO • musiche PINO DONAGGIO • scenografia CARLO DE MARINO • arredamento MARICIA D'ALFONSO
sceneggiatura TINTO BRASS • CARLA CIPRIANI • NICOLAJ PENNESTRI • SILVIA ROSSI • MASSIMILIANO ZANIN • collaborazione al montaggio FIORENZA MUELLER
prodotto da PINO GARGIULO per la C.R.C. • scritto, diretto, montato da TINTO BRASS
www.lionpictures.it/trasgredire

un film di TIN
TRASGREDIR
MASSIMO FERRERO presenta un film di T
con YULIYA MAYARCHUK • JARNO BERARDI • FRANCESCA NU
direttore della fotografia MASSIMO DI VENANZO • musiche PINO DONAGGIO
sceneggiatura TINTO BRASS • CARLA CIPRIANI • NICOLAJ PENNESTRI • SILVIA
prodotto da PINO GARGIULO per la C.
CVC
DOLBY DIGITAL
www.lionpictu

Italian Fotobusta poster, 1999

Dopo "Salon Kitty" e "La Chiave" il nuovo film di uno straordinario TINTO BRASS
Giuseppe Colombo presenta
Un film di TINTO BRASS
con
ANNA GALIENA
GABRIEL GARKO
SENSO '45
"Forte, bello, perverso, vile: mi piacque"
e con FRANCO BRANCIAROLI ANTONIO SALINES
SIMONA BORIONI LOREDANA CANNATA ERIKA SAVASTANI
TINTO BRASS ANNA GALIENA GABRIEL GARKO "SENSO '45" FRANCO BRANCIAROLI ANTONIO SALINES SIMONA BORIONI LOREDANA CANNATA ERIKA SAVASTANI
MUSICHE DI ENNIO MORRICONE DIRETTORE DELLA FOTOGRAFIA DANIELE NANNUZZI SCENOGRAFIA DI CARLO DE MARINO ETTORE GUERRIERI ALBERTO MORETTI ALESSANDRO LAI TINTO BRASS
LIBERAMENTE ISPIRATO AL RACCONTO "SENSO" DI CAMILLO BOITO EDIZIONE · POSTPRODUZIONE CARLA CIPRIANI FIORENZA MUELLER AIUTO REGISTA CLAUDIO BERNABEI ASSISTENTE OPERATORE ANDREA DORIA
PIETRO SANTARELLI FOTOGRAFO DI SCENA GIANFRANCO SALIS PROMOZIONE SAVERIO FERRAGINA MARIO DI BIASE PRODOTTO DA GIUSEPPE COLOMBO PER CINE 2000 TINTO BRASS
EAGLE PICTURES
CINE CITTÀ STUDIOS
DOLBY DIGITAL SURROUND-EX
www.eaglepictures.com
Kodak MOTION PICTURE FILM
TELE+

Left: Italian 2-Fogli poster, 1999, Right: Spanish One Sheet poster, 2002

Italian 2-Fogli poster, 2003

Top: South Korean poster, Bottom: Italian 2-Fogli poster, 2006

Top: Japanese B5 poster, 2004, Bottom: Italian 2-Fogli poster, 2006

에로틱 무비의 세계적 거장
틴토 브라스의 논란과 화제의 최신작!
5일간의 섹스 페스티벌
틴토 브라스의
아모르
A FILM BY TINTO BRASS 〈MONAMOUR〉
amour

Left: South Korean poster, 2007, Right: International One Sheet poster, 2008

CULT EPICS

Tinto Brass Video Releases

VHS • DVD • BLU-RAY • 4KUHD

DVD (2002)
CAT# CE009 *Out of Print*

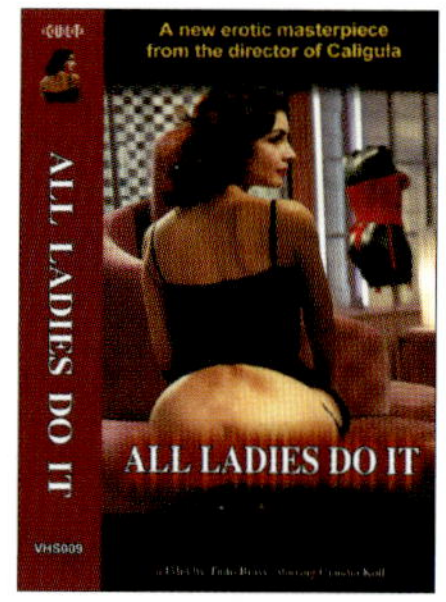

VHS (2002)
CAT# VHS009 *Out of Print*

DVD (2002)
CAT# CE011 *Out of Print*

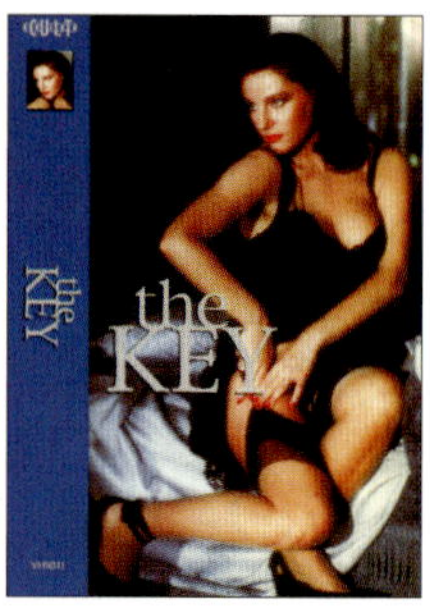

DVD (2002)
CAT# CE012 *Out of Print*

VHS (2002)
CAT# VHS011 *Out of Print*

VHS (2002)
CAT# VHS012 *Out of Print*

Special Edition DVD (2002)
CAT# CE015 *Out of Print*

3xDVD Box Set (2002)
CAT# CE016 *Out of Print*

Special Edition DVD (2004)
CAT# CE025 *Out of Print*

Director's Cut DVD (2006)
CAT# CE040 *Out of Print*

Producer's Cut DVD (2006)
CAT# CE041 *Out of Print*

Director's Cut DVD (2006)
CAT# CE044 *Out of Print*

Producer's Cut DVD (2006)
CAT# CE045 *Out of Print*

Director's Cut DVD (2006)
CAT# CE046 *Out of Print*

Producer's Cut DVD (2006)
CAT# CE047 *Out of Print*

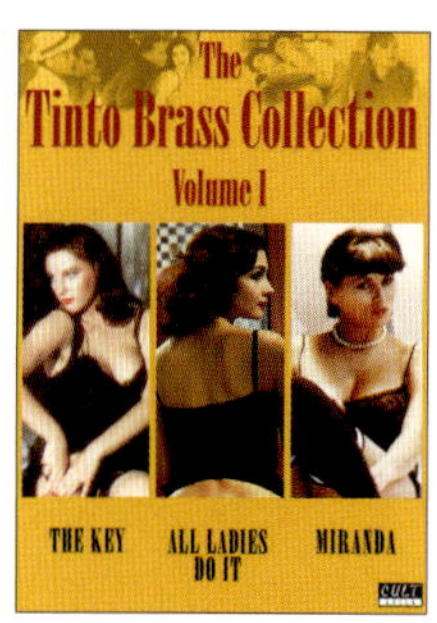

3-Disc DVD Box Set (2002)
CAT# CE048 *Out of Print*

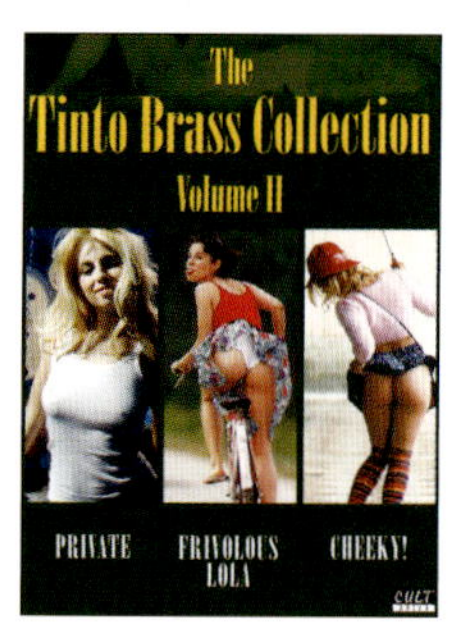

3-Disc DVD Box Set (2006)
CAT# CE049 *Out of Print*

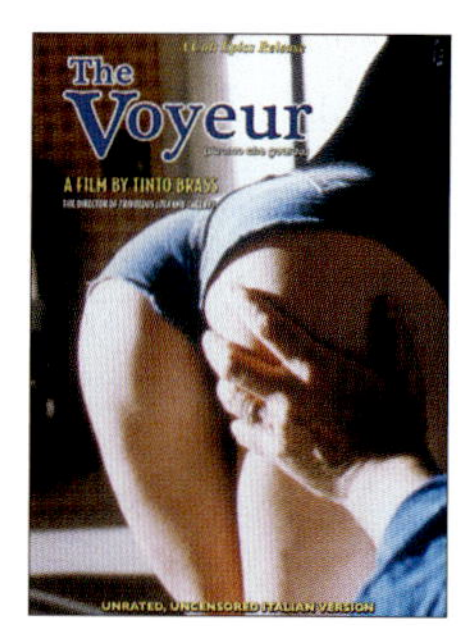

Director's Cut DVD (2007)
CAT# CE060 *Out of Print*

Producers's Cut DVD (2007)
CAT# CE061 *Out of Print*

DVD (2009)
CAT# CE072

DVD (2009)
CAT# CE073

DVD (2009)
CAT# CE074

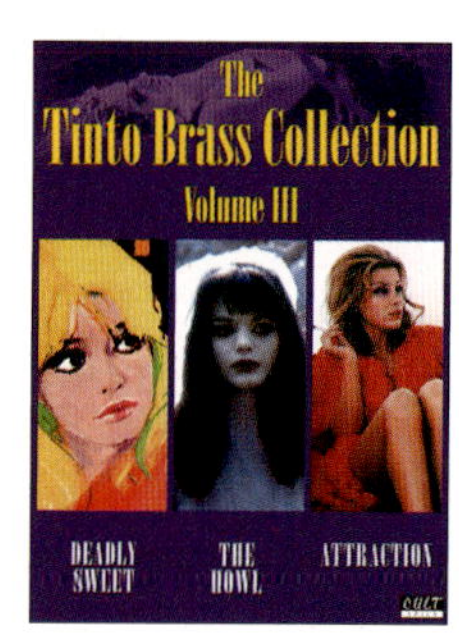

3-Disc DVD Box Set (2009)
CAT# CE075 *Out of Print*

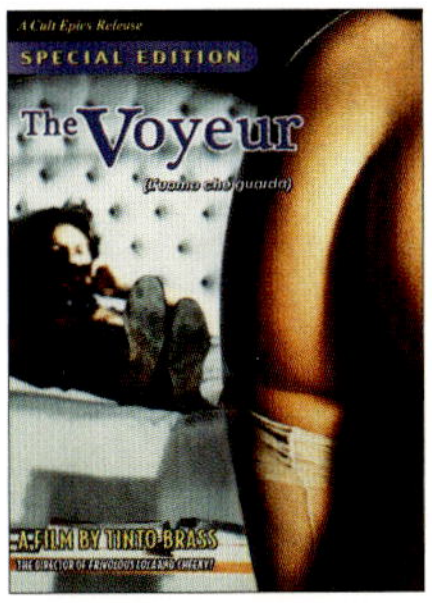

Special Edition DVD (2010)
CAT# CE088 *Out of Print*

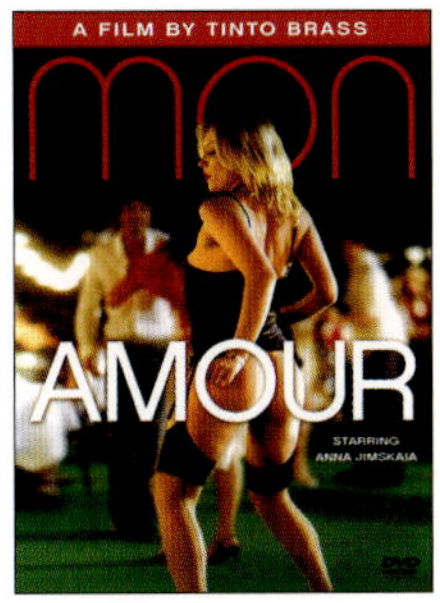

DVD (2010)
CAT# CE091 *Out of Print*

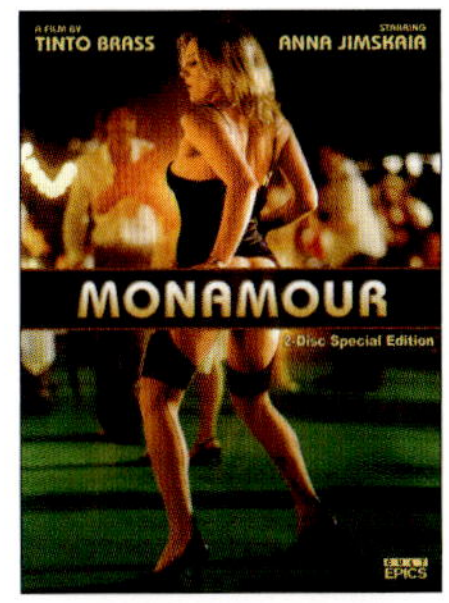

Special Edition 2-Disc DVD (2011)
CAT# CE098 *Out of Print*

Special Edition 2-Disc BD (2011)
CAT# CE099 *Out of Print*

DVD/BD (2011)
CAT# CE098/CE099 *Out of Print*

Special Edition DVD (2012)
CAT# CE116 *Out of Print*

Special Edition BD (2012)
CAT# CE117 *Out of Print*

Special Edition DVD (2014)
CAT# CE120 *Out of Print*

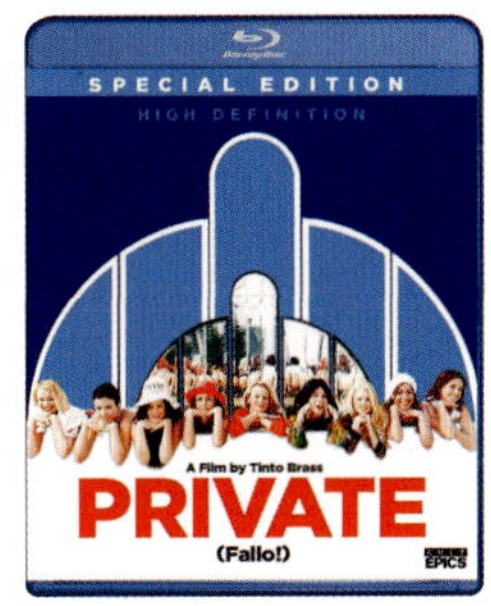

Special Edition BD (2014)
CAT# CE121 *Out of Print*

DVD (2013)
CAT# CE123 *Out of Print*

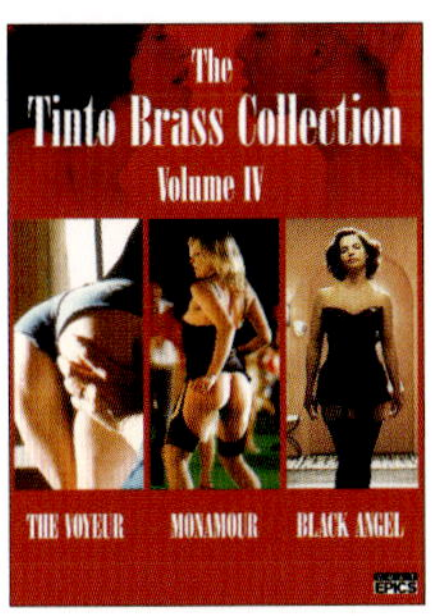

3-Disc DVD Box Set (2013)
CAT# CE124 *Out of Print*

BD (2014)
CAT# CE126 *Out of Print*

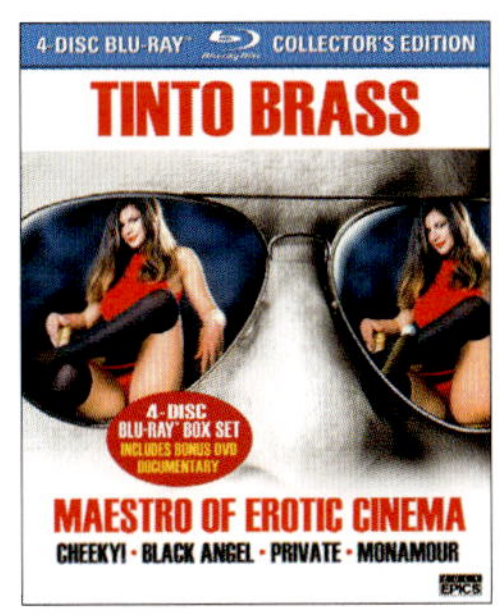

4-Disc BD + DVD Box Set (2014)
CAT# CE128 *Out of Print*

Director's Cut BD (2015)
CAT# CE139 *Out of Print*

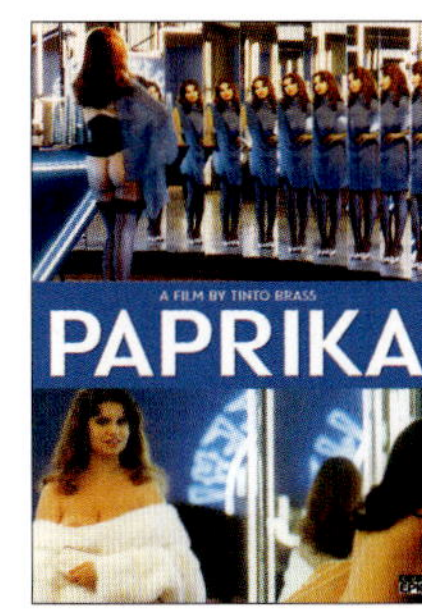

DVD (2016)
CAT# CE142

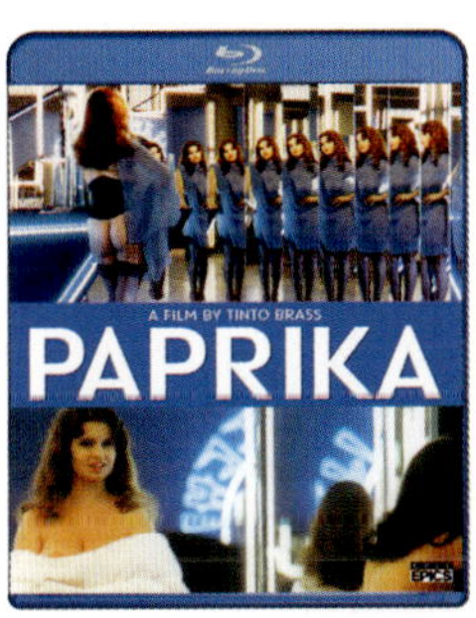

BD (2016)
CAT# CE143

Limited Edition 2-Disc BD (2020)
CAT# CE166 *Out of Print*

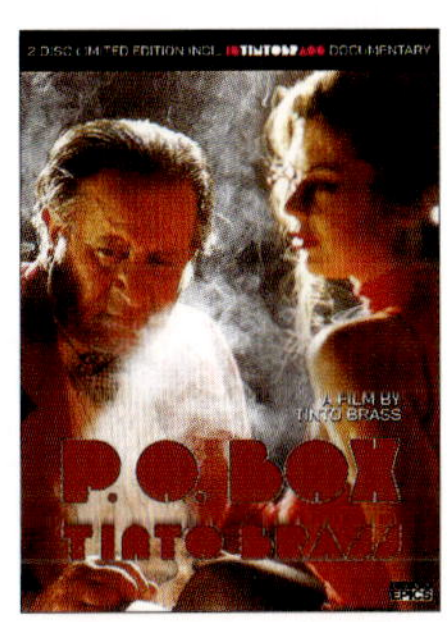

Limited Edition 2-Disc DVD (2020)
CAT# CE167 *Out of Print*

4KUHD + BD (2024)
CAT# CE214

BD (2024)
CAT# CE215

4KUHD + BD (2024)
CAT# CE216

BD (2024)
CAT# CE217

4-Disc BD + DVD Box Set (2024)
CAT# CE218

?

P.O. Box Tinto Brass, 1995

THIS BOOK WAS MADE POSSIBLE THANKS TO THE CONTRIBUTIONS FROM:

Abby Braunsdorf
Adam Kearney
Adam P Savje
Adam Raifsnider
Adam Schoon
Adam Wright
Adrian Jones
Akira Yamamoto
Alain St Pierre
Alan Cartwright
Alan Smithee
Albert Jin
Alex Braunstein
Alex Valero (Danda)
Alex Ward
Alfonso Carrillo
Alfredo Arcila
Alistair Helfer
Andreas Riis Paulsen
Andrew Featherstone
Andrew Nguyen
Andrew Thomas
Andy Wright
Anthony Di Mieri
Anthony Marra
Anthony Michael Cuiffo Jr
Anthony Testani
Anthony Wynne
Antonio Lopez
Antony Elia
Arjen van der Lely
Arnold Bachman
Art Vereecke
Arthur Crabtree
Arthur Ruple
Artin Aghanian
Ashley N Spicer
Astthor Gudfinnsson
Barry Meikle
Barton Young
Bas van der Schoot
Bechara Helal
Benoit Farvet
Bernd Robel
Big Carlos White
Bill Bryant
Blake Krippendorf
Brad Katz
Bradford Harris
Brandon Brock
Brandon M Williams
Brandon McKenna
Brandon Upson
Brian Kelleher
Brian Laude
Brian Long
Brian Matherly
Brian Thompson
Bruce Douglas
Bryan Robert Connolly
Bryan S Jackson
CandyGirl Video
Carl Ellis
Carlo Barbieri III
Carlos Osegueda
Charles Beaumont
Charles Bourque
Charles Jenes
Charles Nuckols
Charles Patroske
Charles Wilkins
Charles Zigman
Chris Carlucci
Chris Groves
Chris Gurley
Chris Jones
Chris Lucas
Chris Mendoza
Chris Sienko
Christian Bütikofer
Christian Genzel
Christian Ostermeier
Christian Rademaker
Christina and Josh Greer
Christoph Marek
Christopher Ceder
Christopher Devlin
Christopher Norton
Christopher Vick
Chuck Aliaga
Chun Hei Cheung
Clint Eisinger
Clyde Gentry III
Corbin Phillips
Corey Cochran
Cory Bevilacqua
Craig Howarth
Dale White
Daniel Daley
Daniel Gonzalez
Daniel Kegler
Daniel Schubert
Daniel Williams
Darrel Griffin
Darren Tan
Dave Curtis
Dave Kelly
Dave Rudin
David Barraclough
David Bray
David Jacobs
David Libby
David Osborne
David Paul Wyatt Perko
David Rains
David Smith
David Tischer
David Vick
Denis Zubakhin
Derek Smith
Desmond Reddick
Dillon Curtner
Don Sjoerdsma
Drew Huntley
Dr Manuel Ebert
Dustin Fine
Dylan Cheung
Dylan Connelly
Edward Deveney
Edward Smith
Eerik Dickinson
Epe Tenhunen
Eric D Garrett
Éric Peretti
Erik Leeming
Erik Nelson
Ethan Miller
Evgueni Mlodik
Fabien Perissinotto
Fedi Bruni
Fjodor Vinokurov
Flici Arnaud
Florian Schiffmann
Francesco De Belvis
Francesco Domaneschi
Frank Coveleski
Frank Hewlett
Frankie Dees
Gabriele Regini
Gareth Park
Gary Beauvais
Gary Rhodes
Geeki VonHalogen
Geoffrey F Toole
Gerald McCarthy
Glenn Forbes
Gregory Kam
Gordon Sullivan
Greg Barber
Hans van Duivenboden
Harold R Smith Jr
Hiromasa Fukumoto
Holden Oliver
Ian Courtney
Irene Micheli
Jake Schelbauer
J Anthony Hernandez
James Bell
James Lunan
James H Mahoney
James O'Neal
James Robinson
James Ropp
James Schrader
Jared Nagel
Jason Clark
Jason Coffman
Jean-Roch Parichet
Jeff Kline
Jeff Price
Jeff Wilhelm
Jeff Wolman
Jeffrey Tom
Jeremy Chang Hoe Yuen
Jeremy Handley
Jeremy Riegel
Jesse Calderon
Jesse Card
Jia Zhang
Joe Price
Joel Ray
John Alo
John Dagostino
John Edwards-Younger
John Enger
John Gruber
John Melligh
John Nelka
John Scoleri
John Taylor Jr
Johnny Ryan
Jon Cott
Jon Nelson
Jon Wong
Jonathan Adey
Jonathan Milakovic
Jonathan Mullen
Jonathan Riley
Jonathon Doyle
Jonathon Ponce
Joost van den Ossenblok
Jordan Johnson
Jose Castanon
Joseph V Sarmento
Joshua Bossie
Joshua Palace
Jürgen De Waele
Justin LaLiberty
Justin M Johnson
Justin W Dekker
Karl Wasmuth
Kenny Neal
Kevin Graper
Kevin Porter
Kevin R Johnson
Kevin Smith
Kier-La Janisse
Kifah Foutah
Kirk Lund
Kristof van Langenhove
Kroz Rodriguez
Kurt Jensen
Larry Phillips
Lawrence Deckelbaum
Lee Vile
Llewellyn McGee
Logan Smith-Marston
Lou Jacobs
Luke Safely
Marc Rouleau
Marc Wade
Marcin Rybowski
Marco Provenzali
Mariusz Nowak
Mark A Spieckerman
Mark Donoho
Mark Murray
Mark Sturdy
Mark Turner
Mark Weddington
Marta Soria Torres
Matt Dorbin
Matthew Grim
Matthew Rabinowitz
Matthew Tilt
Melissa Kusia
Michael de Wee
Michael Italiano
Michael J Monson
Michael Jaynes
Michael John Simmons
Michael Kimmins
Michael Koutouzakis
Michael Logan
Michael Mariano
Michael Mohnach
Michael Pearson
Michael S Corfield
Michael T Johnson
Mikayel Abazyan
Mike Haushalter
Murray Lothian
Nate Liquor
Nathan Baran
Neal Laubach
Neetzan Zimmerman
Neil D Vokes
Neil Devlin
Nicholas Diak
Nicholas Lockwood
Nicholas Petrecca
Nicolas Liscic
Nikolai Adams
Nils Pommerenke
Olena Kukhtareva
Oliver Meinved
Panagiotis Athanasiou
Patrick Kennelly
Patrick Lujan
Patrick Strawderman
Patrick Wilson
Paul B Davis Jr
Paul Kazee
PaulinhoDJ
Perry Glorioso
Peter Han
Philip Egerhazy
Philipp Sokolean
Phillip Qin
Quentin Turnbull
Ralf Marczinczik
Randall R Ronne
Raul Svarc
Ray Gregory
Raymond Lacken
Remedial Dan
René Pedersen
Rich Wojcik
Richard Dulik
Richard Fowler
Richard Hershal Cunningham
Richard Longmore
Richard Lumley
Rikard Lundstrom
Rob Vaughan
Robert Boichot
Robert Dunkelberger
Rob Perron
Robert V Musilli
Rocco Giordano
Rodolfo Urrea
Roger Quillman
Roland Wessel
Ronald Hannes Tuschl
Roy Pascarella
Ryan Cheek
Ryan Heffernan
Ryan Verrill
Ryan Williams
Sam Cohen
Sam Ly
Saul Moreno Serrano
Scott Fulmar
Sean Baker
Sean Corrigan
Sean Greenwood
Sean Pham
Sean Ryall
Sebastian Gauvey
Sebastian Mueller
Sebastian Veronesi
Shane Pavlo
Shane Tucker
Stanley Robert Wilkes
Stephen Kent
Stephen Lentz
Stephen Moreau
Stephen Taylor
Steven Crockett
Steven Lewis
Steven M Harris
Suman Chatterjee
Tanden Hovey
Tarek Elsokari
Terry Nixon
Terry Osterhout
Teruhiko Nishino
The Cube Cinema
Thomas Alsup
Thomas Avallone
Thomas Counts
Thomas L Watts III
Thomas N Witherspoon
Thomas Nelson
Thomas Neumeier
Thomas Reed
Tim Anderson
Tim Greaves
Tim Hicks
Timothy Houser
Tobias Zurfluh
Todd Slawsby
Tomek Gibaszek
Tommy Murphy
Tony Fleming
Tony Strauss
Travis Kostell
Travis Linthicum
Travis Stevens
Travis Woodliff
Travis Youmans
Troy Weets
Turi Dell'Amore
Vaughn Kuhlmeier
Vere Chappell
Vincent Dailor
Vincent Myles
Vy Lenza
Wassim Oueida
Wayne Engebretson
Wesley Austin
Will Dodson
William Berry
William Bryant
William Hudson Jr
William King
William Moitoza
William Ramirez
Wolfgang Roesch
Yu Seungyoung
Yves Van Den Eynde
Zachary Perez